Junete Texas

Essays in African-American Folklore

Publications of the Texas Folklore Society LIV

▼ Other Publications of the Texas Folklore Society

Extra Books:

Juneteenth
✦ Texas ✦

Essays in African-American Folklore

Publications of the Texas Folklore Society LIV

FRANCIS EDWARD ABERNETHY, Senior Editor
CAROLYN FIEDLER SATTERWHITE, Assistant Editor

COEDITORS

PATRICK B. MULLEN, Director
Center for Folklore Studies
Ohio State University
Columbus, Ohio

ALAN B. GOVENAR, President
Documentary Arts, Inc.
Dallas, Texas

University of North Texas Press
Denton, Texas

3114300910388
398.0899 Juneteenth
Juneteenth Texas : essays
in African-American
folklore

© 1996 Texas Folklore Society

First Edition 1996
Second Printing 2010

10 9 8 7 6 5 4 3 2 1

Requests for permission to reproduce materials from this book
should be directed to:

Permissions
University of North Texas Press
PO Box 13856
Denton TX 76203

The paper used in this book meets the minimum requirements of the American
National Standard for Permanence of Paper for Printed Library Materials,
z39.48.1984. Binding materials have been chosen for durability.

Library of Congress Cataloging-in-Publication Data

Juneteenth Texas : essays in African-American folklore / Francis Edward Abernethy,
    senior editor ; Carolyn Fiedler Satterwhite, assistant editor ; coeditors, Patrick B.
    Mullen, Alan B. Govenar.
        p.   cm. —— (Publications of the Texas Folklore Society ; 54)
    Includes bibliographical references.
    ISBN 1-57441-018-0
1. Afro-Americans—Texas—Folklore. 2. Folklore—Texas. 3. Afro-Americans—Texas—
Social life and customs. I. Abernethy, Francis Edward. II. Series: Publications of the
Texas Folklore Society ; no. 54.
        GR1.T4   no. 54
        [GR111.A47]
        390 s——dc20
        [398'.089960764]   96-21854
                                                                        CIP
    ISBN 13: 978-1-57441-283-3
    ISBN 10: 1-57441-283-3
                        Design by Amy Layton

Cover art: John Biggers, *Shotguns, Fourth Ward*, 1987
Hampton University Museum, Hampton, Virginia

▼ Table of Contents

▼ Appendices

▼ Contributors

▼ Index

▼ Preface

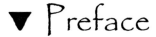

by Patrick B. Mullen and Alan Govenar

Juneteenth Texas represents a wide variety of viewpoints on African-American folklore in Texas. The essays range from personal memoirs to scholarly treatises and are written by both white and black writers. Given the volatile nature of writing about race in the 1990s, it is important to state the obvious at the outset: European-American and African-American perspectives on black folklore will differ; any culture will be viewed differently from the outside and from the inside. Black writers will bring certain assumptions to presentations of their own cultures that white writers will not have in writing about the same subject. It is a commonplace now in the sciences, social sciences, and humanities that all viewpoints are subjective. This does not mean that all viewpoints are equally valid but that different views are constantly being negotiated. This negotiation process is going on right now in publications about African-American culture in folklore and other fields.

We do not write about race and culture in a vacuum but within the context of the larger American society in which race is a controversial issue. A large group of scholars across disciplinary lines now considers race as a social invention and not a biological fact. This idea has been around long enough to be the subject of a cover story in *Newsweek* magazine in 1995, but there are still some scholars who do not agree with this perspective. To state the case for the "social construction"in a somewhat over-simplified way: genetic evidence indicates that all humans are the same and that physical differences are superficial and meaningless as demarcations of separate races. If race is to be a scientific classification system, then there should be some point where we can say one race ends and another begins, but if we look at the spectrum of color in human skin, it becomes clear that there is no clear dividing point as there is in such scientific categories as genus and species. Even if one does not accept the idea of race as a social construct, it should be evident that culturally learned attitudes toward racial difference are the main ways in which the social reality of race is created.

What does this have to do with folklore? Everything. If race is culturally created rather than natural, then all cultural expressions—including folklore and writing about folklore—are influenced by prevailing social attitudes about race and are thus part of the process of creating race as a concept. When folklorists collect and write about African-American folklore, the final product—filtered through their own ideas about race—in turn influences social attitudes about race among their readers. Every essay in this volume—in fact, every essay ever written about African-American culture—is a part of the social construction of race in America.

An important factor in how we construct images of other cultures is the way speech is represented. Some of the authors in this collection use dialect spellings in quoting the speech of black informants; others do not. This is an ongoing controversy in folklore scholarship because many scholars feel that the use of dialect spellings stereotypes the speaker. Also, there is no accurate way of rendering oral speech on the printed page other than phonetic symbols which, of course, hinder the reading of the text. Some writers use dialect spellings in order to capture the quality of spoken language and to personalize the speaker. The editors left this decision up to the discretion of individual authors.

Francis Edward Abernethy as editor of the Publications of the Texas Folklore Society had the original idea of a collection of essays on African-American folklore in Texas, and he asked Pat Mullen and Alan Govenar to help him co-edit the book. Pat was a student of Ab's back in the early 1960s, and Alan was a student of Pat's in the 1970s; thus the three editors represent three academic generations of folklorists. The fact that they grew up in different places at different times influenced the way each perceives the study of African-American folklore. Ab's childhood was spent in segregated East Texas, but he questioned Jim Crow as an adolescent and became a desegregationist in college in the 1940s. During the 1940s, Pat was spending his childhood in the segregated city of Beaumont and did not think about racial issues much until college in the early 1960s, when he became a supporter of the civil rights movement. Alan's experience was quite different since he grew up at a later time in the racially integrated environs of Boston, Massachusetts. Two Texans and a New Englander transplanted to Texas did not always see the contents of this book in the same way, but we thought that it was important to represent a wide variety of points of view whether we agreed with them or not. This book reflects many dimensions of race relations in Texas history; there are indications of both racial harmony and of ongoing racial divisions in the state. Since *Juneteenth Texas* is itself a cultural product, it has the same limitations which characterize any new book written by numerous authors from different cultural backgrounds.

The editors and writers of *Juneteenth Texas* do not agree among ourselves about everything regarding the presentation and analysis of African-American culture, but we are all in agreement about the value of studying cultural differences as well as cultural similarities.

The present collection begins with some essays based on personal experiences. These reminiscences about the past are written from both black and white perspectives, and all of them contain some of that romantic glow with which we all tend to view our formative years. As memoirs, they also project attitudes toward race more directly than some of the later analytic essays which have a built-in scholarly distance from the subject matter, although these too have their subjective side. The personal papers are followed by essays which describe and classify various aspects of African-American folk culture in Texas. Then there are studies of specific genres of folklore, such as songs and stories; of specific performers, such as Lightnin' Hopkins and Bongo Joe; and of particular folklorists who were important in the collecting of African-American folklore in Texas, such as J. Mason Brewer. Finally, there are theoretical studies of African-American folklore as a scholarly concept, the kinds of study that step back from the material to examine the processes whereby scholarly and historical concepts are created. In some ways, then, the organization of the book moves from the personal and immediate to the analytic and distant. There is an additional section at the end which gives some resources for the further study of African-Americans in Texas.

We won't mention every essay in this preface, but we shall consider several representative ones in order to give some idea of the various points of view and approaches. Donald Ross recalls his experiences as a white person hearing black Sacred Harp singing in East Texas, and Jesse Truvillion reminisces about growing up as a black person in the Big Thicket. Both pieces vividly evoke an earlier time filtered through memory and the experiences of intervening years. Ross's is clearly the perspective of a visitor from another culture, a welcome visitor but still an outsider who is aware of the division of race. Truvillion's is the insider's perspective of someone who learned at an early age the social consequences of racial difference. These are two very different points of view, but both men mention instances of interracial communication, and both have an underlying idealism about the possibilities of racial healing in Texas and America.

Like Truvillion, Clyde Daniels provides a personal perspective on growing up in East Texas. Interspersed in his narrative are a series of poems, which are not folklore *per se*, but are nonetheless a distinctive African-American expression. Among African-Americans in Texas, there is a relatively undocumented tradition of folk poetry. In part, poems of this nature are inspired by the oral tradition, but they are ostensibly written texts. Regardless of their origin, however, they have an important role in the families and communities in which they are performed and transmitted. Aside from their obvious role in preserving oral history, they validate a culturally-specific experience.

Lorenzo Thomas, who is himself an accomplished poet, has been an insightful commentator on African-American literature and music. Using a methodology that combines journalism, first-person observation, and scholarly research, Thomas's essays are a complex mix of the impressionistic, the evocative, and the historical.

Among the scholarly essays, John Minton's utilizes first-person narratives collected from slaves as a means to better understand fiddle styles in the nineteenth century. Alan Govenar presents an overview of the musical traditions of African-American cowboys in the twentieth century through an examination of the repertory of songs remembered and currently performed by ranch hands. Govenar's essay is based upon recent fieldwork and thus is more descriptive than analytical.

Alvia J. Wardlaw explores the importance of African-American folklore in the visual imagery of John Biggers. In addition to illustrating the work of J. Mason Brewer, Biggers is himself a collector of folklore, who over the course of his career has drawn attention to the significance of the oral tradition in his prints and paintings through a kind of metaphorical representation. Wardlaw indicates how Biggers's view of African-American folk culture is a blending of his own experience as a member of the community with ideas from elite European artistic tradition. Several incidents in his life show how his representations of black folklife were contested and negotiated even within the black community.

Two of the essays illustrate the subjective difference between insider and outsider perspectives in the supposedly objective scholarly approach. Trudier Harris writes about a legendary black woman in nineteenth century Texas history from the perspective of a black woman scholar of the 1990s, and Patrick Mullen writes about a black street performer from the perspective of a white folklorist reexamining fieldwork in the 1960s. Harris takes a postmodern stance in which she plays with the categories of folklore which most of us take for granted, calling into question our assumptions about legend, history, fact, and fiction so that we can finally see that there is some truth in all of these cultural expressions. Her point seems to be that an imaginative account of "The Yellow Rose of Texas" can in some ways make a more truthful statement about black experience in Texas than a conventional historical account. Mullen tries to take his own 1960s romantic concepts about African-American performers into account as he rewrites a paper originally published in 1970, but, of course, he cannot remove himself from the 1990s context of racial assumptions, and neither can any other writer, black or white, who contributed to this volume.

Those assumptions will vary among individuals depending on race, age, class, and other cultural factors, but every writer here shares a conviction that whatever the conflicts of the past, the ongoing cultural and racial dialog in which we are engaged will produce a greater understanding in the future.

James W. Byrd, professor of English at East Texas State University, J. Mason Brewer's friend and biographer, student of African-American folklore and literature.

Martha Emmons (1895-1990), professor of English, Baylor University, teller of tales and collector of African-American folklore, author of "Tone the Bell Easy" and *Deep Like the Rivers*.

African-American Folklore in Texas and in the Texas Folklore Society

by Francis E. Abernethy

Black people were a long time into Texas before the Anglos came to claim that territory as their own. Blacks of all hues and mixtures landed on the Carribean islands with Columbus's expeditions, and they landed on the American mainland with Cortez, Pineda, and Narvaéz in the early 1500s. Black culture had been part of Spanish culture for over five hundred years of Moorish occupation, and black culture remained a part of Spanish culture in the New World.

And black people became a part of Texas folklore and legendry in these earliest of historical times.

Esteban (or Estevanico) the Moor was the first black man to set foot on Texas soil, as far as we know. He certainly became the most memorable of early black explorers. He was with Cabeza de Vaca when four survivors of the Narvaéz expedition walked for eight years (1528–1536) through Texas and Mexico, from Galveston to Culiacán. Esteban was not only a survivor; he was an adapter. He was a natural linguist, quickly learning Indian dialects as the small band of Europeans passed through one tribal territory after another.

As a consequence of his linguistic and social skills among the Indians, Esteban was chosen to accompany Friar Marcos de Niza's vanguard

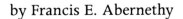

of Coronado's expedition in search of El Dorado in 1539. Esteban was a wily rascal, as keen after great wealth and fame as any Spanish grandee. On the journey north the Moor collected gifts and a large following of beautiful women and tribesmen who followed him in remembrance of times past with Cabeza de Vaca. It was Esteban who was the first European to discover Hawikah, the first of the fabulous Seven Cities of Cibolo. He found no City of Gold, only a large village of adobe buildings which glowed golden in the light of the rising and setting sun. And it was at Hawikah, in present New Mexico, that the Moor's luck ran out.

Esteban, with his retinue of women and loyal followers and baskets of goods to trade for things of gold and silver, found no wealth in Hawikah. The City of Gold was made out of mud. The Moor was quickly and unceremoniously seized and flung into a cell. The elders of the village deliberated three days about the meaning of this intrusion. Then, fearful of such another invasion, they killed him. Friar Marcos, the appointed leader of this vanguard who was miles behind Esteban literally and figuratively, retreated and spread tall tales of the fabulous but well protected cities of gold. It is unfortunate that Esteban was not able to return with the truth. He would have saved Coronado a long wandering through the wilderness (Abernethy 1984, 6–10).

In 1791 nearly a quarter of the Spanish population in Texas was classified as Negro of some degree. Although free blacks could not hold government jobs, they were able to pursue any profession, marry whom they wished, and enjoy the freedoms of any Spanish citizen. The frontier allowed more racial latitude than did the city. Even so, slavery existed in Spanish Texas, and Indians and other unfortunates shared that condition with blacks (Campbell 10–12).

Bureacratic Spain did recognize rank, and the Spanish conquistadors and nobility held social precedence over all others. Spain also recognized gradients of ethnicity—that is, of Spanish (Caucasian)-Negro-Indian-etcetera miscegenation—and filed its citizens under distinct categories. A catalog of those individuals who were drafted to accompany the Marques de Aguayo on his 1721 expedition to settle East Texas listed seventeen *mestizos* (Spanish father and Indian mother), twenty-one *coyotes* (unidentifiable Spanish-Indian mix), thirty-one *mulattoes*

(Spanish-Negro mix), two *castizos* (Spanish mother and mestizo father), one *lobo* (Asiatic-Negro father and mulatto mother), one free Negro, one Indian, and forty-four Spaniards (Buckley 24).

Spanish rule ended with the Mexican revolution of 1821, and for the next fifteen years Mexico determined racial policy in Texas. Blacks had considerable social, occupational, and political latitude when Texas was under the Mexican flag. Blacks could hold political office under Mexican law, and slavery was legally banned. Mexico, however, realizing that prohibiting slavery absolutely would inhibit both the coming of Anglo settlers and the economic growth of Texas, failed to enforce the ban. Also, incoming Anglos from the slave-holding Southern states circumvented the anti-slavery law by freeing their slaves on the east bank of the Sabine and "indenturing" them on the west bank (Campbell 23).

Three centuries and many black explorers and settlers after Esteban—during this Mexican period of racial ambivalence—an Afro-Texian of legendary proportions appeared on the East Texas scene. This man was William Goyens, whose life was not quite as dramatic as Esteban's but who has a large 1936 Texas Centennial marker on Goyens Hill near Nacogdoches to prove his historical worth. Goyens came to Texas around 1820 and established himself as one of Nacogdoches county's most successful (richest!) businessmen.

William Goyens' father had gained his freedom by serving in the North Carolina Militia during the Revolutionary War, so Goyens came to Texas as a freedman. Because of his high black profile, legends grew up about him, some erroneously describing him as a runaway slave. One tale tells how a white man walked into Goyens' blacksmith shop during the 1840s and identified himself as Goyens' previous owner. Goyens recognized his former master and asked him how much he was worth as a slave. The man told him $5,000. Goyens then went to the back of his shop, scraped some rubbish off an old box, and pulled out $5,000 in gold coins. The man took the money, gave Goyens a bill of sale for himself, and left.

That story is folklore. By 1840 Goyens had long ago quit working as a blacksmith. The real story is that some con man did come to

Nacogdoches in 1826 with spurious evidence of Goyens' servitude and blackmailed him for 1,000 pesos—a bitter pill, no doubt.

William Goyens must have been a man of tremendous energy. He began his business life in Texas as a blacksmith and then became the gunsmith and armorer for the Mexicans stationed in Nacogdoches, which brings up another legend in Goyens' life. When Colonel Piedras was about to make his exit from Nacogdoches in 1832 he came to Goyens one evening for some secret blacksmithing. Piedras had two metal containers—each about the size a man could carry in his arms—and he wanted Goyens to weld a lid on them. He kept the contents covered, but Goyens got a glimpse of gold coins and other valuables before he sealed them up. According to reports Piedras buried this treasure in Ysleta Creek. Piedras lost the Battle of Nacogdoches and was killed in a later battle before he could return and retrieve his treasure. Goyens passed the story on but nobody ever found those two cans—unless Goyens himself did. He was a wealthy man.

Goyens was wealthy but he worked for it. In addition to being a blacksmith and gunsmith, he built and sold wagons and ran a freight line from Nacogdoches to Natchitoches—and was fined once when he was caught trying to smuggle goods past customs. He also had a sawmill and a gristmill, and operated a rooming-boarding house. He made most of his money, however, buying and selling land.

Goyens was a close friend of Sam Houston's, and during the Texas Revolution he spent much of his time as an intermediary between Houston and the East Texas Cherokees. He spoke Cherokee and Spanish and is considered to be responsible for holding off the Indians while the Anglos fought the Mexicans.

William Goyens had the respect and friendship of Nacogdoches. After the Republic of Texas disallowed the citizenship of freed blacks, Thomas J. Rusk, Adolphus Sterne, Elisha Roberts, and fifty other Nacogdocheans signed and sent a petition to the Legislature asking for special consideration for Goyens in light of his service to the Republic. It was granted, of course.

William Goyens died in 1856 leaving money, goods, five slaves, and 12,423 acres, none of which he had received in grants (Prince passim; *Handbook* I, 713–14).

During the Texas Revolution freedmen and slaves fought alongside their fellow Texians for independence. The first blood shed in the final series of battles was by a free Negro named Samuel McCullough, who was wounded in the capture of Goliad in October of 1835. Of the two soldiers cited for conspicuous bravery in Ben Milam's storming of San Antonio in December of 1835, one was Hendrick Arnold, a freedman and one of the two scouts, along with Deaf Smith. Arnold later married Deaf Smith's daughter. William Barrett Travis' slave Joe Travis endured the thirteen days of the Alamo and survived to tell the tale. Dick the Drummer set the march step that carried the Texians to victory at San Jacinto, and the black Maxlin Smith shared in the violence and the victory of that April 21st day in 1836.

The situation for blacks changed drastically under the Anglo government of the Texas Republic. The Constitution of the Republic of Texas ("General Provisions," Section 9) recognized the legality of slavery and prohibited freedmen from remaining in the country without congressional approval. Although most free blacks who had settled in Texas before the revolution were allowed to stay on, the spirit of this Draconic legislation became the same spirit that rushed the state into secession and the Civil War in 1861.

Many Texas slaves went with their masters to fight in the War Between the States. They suffered the same hunger and cold and disease that the rest of the southerners suffered. There were many instances of sacrifice and devotion and heroism among the blacks with the Confederate armies, but the most famous black Texan fought for the other side. Milton Holland had left Carthage, Texas, and moved to Ohio, and in 1861 he joined the Quartermaster Corp of the Union Army. As a sergeant-major he was wounded in the 1864 Battle of Richmond, where he led his troops in a gallant charge that won him a Congressional Medal of Honor.

The Emancipation Proclamation was delivered to Texas by General Gordon Granger on June 19, 1865—"Juneteenth"—and an already traumatized South changed for blacks and whites alike. After the initial shock, disbelief, and then jubilation, came the black experience of wandering loose in an antagonistic country with no means of support. This time of readjustment and reconstruction was long and harsh, and none can view the history of black and white relations during Reconstruction and the last years of the nineteenth century without dismay.

This does not mean that the black personality was completely subjugated after the War and Emancipation. Black communities and black leaders developed a segregated society and a rich culture around their own homes and schools and especially their churches. This period of segregation was an imposed system brought about by Klans and legislation and social states of mind that lasted for a hundred years. Because African-Americans lacked the former "protection" of the slave owners and later protection of civil rights legislation, during these Jim Crow times blacks were in a socio-legal limbo, subject to lynchings and other atrocities committed on their persons and property without any legal means of redress. Sometimes "to read history is to weep."

Nor does this mean that all black-white relations were bad. Many blacks and whites were bonded by love and mutual dependence during that time, and many survived because they helped each other.

The tattered times of Reconstruction had its own roll of dynamic Negro personalities. The efforts of such black legislators as George Ruby, Meshac Roberts, and Morris Cuney to effect a peaceful social change during Reconstruction was certainly the stuff of heroes, in spite of the overwhelming resistance which they met.

A notable group of African-Americans made their mark in West Texas. The western part of the state was opened to settlement through the protection of the black Ninth and Tenth Cavalries, the Buffalo Soldiers, so called by the Apaches because with their black curly hair they looked like bull buffalos, which, by the way, became their insignia. In an official report of an expedition against the Apaches, one of their commanding officers wrote, "I cannot speak too highly of the conduct of the officers and men under my command. They were always cheerful and ready, braving the severest hardships with short rations and no water without a murmur. The black troops know no fear and are capable of great endurance."

The opening of the west Texas range to cattlemen afforded blacks another occupation in which men of color achieved distinction. Mathew

"Bones" Hooks was considered the champion bronc buster in a Texas full of busters. Al Jones went up the trail thirteen times, four times as the trail boss. "80 John" Wallace was a cowboy who bought land and stock and established a 7,600-acre ranch that his daughter has increased to 15,000 acres; Colorado City's integrated high school is named after him. One of the most famous cowboys of the West is Bill Pickett, who invented bulldogging. He later rodeoed—with Will Rogers and Tom Mix as his hazers—in Madison Square Garden and became the first African-American in the Cowboy Hall of Fame.

In 1908 Jack Johnson of Galveston became the first black world champion heavyweight boxer. Scott Joplin of Texarkana gave the world ragtime. Huddie Ledbetter, "Leadbelly," disseminated the Brazos Bottom blues. Dr. J. Mason Brewer of Austin and the Texas Folklore Society became the nation's leading black folklorist.

These were the blacks of early Texas legend and history, the individuals whose personalities and activities were so dramatic that their stories became symbols, often larger than the lives they lived. Their names stood out in the Texas experience among people of all colors. Unfortunately, their names were unsung and their voices were silent in the academic records of their times and later. Texas textbook history was played out on a white, Anglo-Saxon, Protestant stage.

The study of African-American culture in Texas was from its beginning in 1909 an important province of the Texas Folklore Society. The Society's first publication was a 1912 pamphlet of Negro folk songs, and the first Publication of the Texas Folklore Society (PTFS I, 1916) contained a Negro folk tale. The first nineteen volumes, to 1944, contained thirty articles on Negro folklore. Many of these stories, songs, and beliefs were field-collected folklore that was published for the first time in Publications of the Texas Folklore Society. Field collections dropped off sharply after World War II, when Americans began to get more racially sensitive and self conscious. Thereafter the articles were usually studies about Negro folklore, as is this *Juneteenth Texas*, rather than illustrations of field collected songs and tales.

The twentieth century before World War II was a time of discovery of black culture and of blacks themselves, who had been slaves-chattel-aliens for many years and were just a few years beyond Emancipation. Their culture was only beginning to take shape as a growing, independent, and vital part of American culture. The study and appreciation of their folklore—their songs and stories, their culture and traditions and beliefs—were the first steps toward racial understanding and eventual integration.

On the national scene in the late nineteen and early twentieth centuries, Negro art forms—usually filtered though the white perspective—were becoming accepted fare in all levels of society. Joel Chandler Harris with his Uncle Remus tales might have done more than anyone to bring the richness of black life and culture into white consciousness. Harris was widely known, read, and loved throughout the United States, and his gentle, obedient, and unthreatening Uncle Remus was a comfortable character to come into white homes. Roark Bradford's *Ol' Man Adam and His Chillun*, from which Martha Emmons got her "Adulteration of Old King David" and Marc Connelly got his Pulitzer Prize winning *Green Pastures*, was written in the same spirit.

These paternalistic depictions of blacks, happily working for Ol' Massa on sunny Southern plantations, seem romantic and unreal to our present generation. They continue the slave-oriented Uncle Remus stereotype, and they proliferate other demeaning stock characterizations that hinder rather than help racial understanding. But, at the time, they began to narrow the gap between two cultures that were chasms apart.

The Fisk Jubilee Singers were international performers of Negro spirituals, and they impressed white audiences with the beauty, the seriousness, and the depth of feeling of a race which had long been singularly out of the framework of consideration.

Amos and Andy, Molasses and January, Hambone, and Rochester—all of whom were much loved by white audiences during the Depression Thirties—were in the vanguard of the civil rights movement, whether they were meant to be or not. Even post-Civil-War minstrelsy, with its stereotypes and romanticized "darky" songs, played a part in integrating black culture into the dominant white society. Hambone, of the syndicated newspaper cartoon "Hambone Sez," was quoted for his wisdom during the Depression almost as much as Will Rogers. One reason for the popularity of these entertainers was that their characters reinforced traditionally white-conceived stereotypes of always-happy, lazy, childlike blacks. This is not an acceptable concept by modern black activists—or white activists, for that matter. But these were positive images to white Americans during their times and were personalities who were fondly taken into white homes.

Blacks in popular culture are still stereotyped, and Jack Benny's Rochester becomes today's sardonic butler Benson. And Sanford and Son and friends at the junkyard take the place of Amos and Andy and Madam Queen at the taxi stand. No white man in his right mind would do a Step'n Fetchit imitation for Spike Lee, but hours of black television sitcoms present such characters as J. J. of *Good Times* and George Jefferson, the black Archie Bunker, both of whom are artistically flat, nondimensional characters. Attitudes and perspectives have changed over the past half century, but some of the results are the same.

The Texas Folklore Society from its beginning to World War II was involved in the exploration and discovery of black culture. Its first publication, in 1912, was Will H. Thomas's monograph, "Some Current Folk-Songs of the Negro." Dorothy Scarborough presented Negro folk music studies at meetings and published in *Coffee in the Gourd* (PTFS II, 1923), her important study of Negro blues as folk songs. This was before John Lomax began his serious work with black folk music. Spiritual singers regularly were featured performers at TFS meetings. And when Harvard's George Lyman Kittredge made his first visit to the TFS in 1913, Lomax took him to hear Negro preaching and singing at an Austin church (PTFS XXXIII, 6). Among later contributors, the best known collectors and tellers of Negro tales in the Society were Martha Emmons, A. W. Eddins, and J. Mason Brewer. John Henry Faulk studied and wrote about Negro church and religious life. Hardly a meeting went by before WWII without some presentation in the field of Negro folklore, and the Society regularly carried Negro folklore in its publications. Because Negroes' position in society was in a state of flux at the time, the attitudes of the presenters were similarly various (Abernethy, 1992, see chapter appendices).

Dobie recognized this variety of attitudes toward blacks in his preface to *Rainbow in the Morning* (PTFS V, 1926, 4) and said, "The editor disclaims any responsibility for the opinions and information set forth by the varying contributors on the subject of negro folk-songs printed in this publication. If one wants to spell negro with a capital N and another with a little n, the editor has nothing to say; if one considers the negro as a shining apostle of sweetness and light, another as a gentle old darkey, and still another as 'phallic kinky,' it is none of the editor's business" (PTFS V, 4). This is the same Dobie who in his political escapades twenty years later—and post WWII racial attitudes are different from pre-WWII—fell into disrepute among some Texans because of his liberalism, particularly because he espoused voting and education rights for Negroes and stated that they should be allowed into the University of Texas.

Editorial distancing such as Dobie's, especially in an academic journal, would be unacceptable in our present ethnically enlightened times, as would most of the attitudes toward blacks found in the Society's first thirty years of presentations. But we must not forget that we are talking about a different historical time, and social historians must never forget that they cannot judge past moralities by present-day standards. This is called generational chauvinism, the belief that only the values of one's own generation are valid. The old Roman Cato, who had lived beyond his conditioning over two millennia ago said, "It is not easy to render an account of your life to an age other than the age in which you have lived."

Dobie and most TFS readers and writers were the most educated and sophisticated people of their time and culture, but they were still products of their times. Scotus and Aquinas believed in a geocentric universe, Thomas Jefferson had slaves, and respectable western folk of the nineteenth century believed that society would collapse if women got the right to vote. Abraham Lincoln did not believe that slaves should be given citizenship, and he denied the doctrine of social equality for blacks (Randall, 118). And many educated ante-bellum southerners had no more guilty consciences about the presence of slavery than our own parents and grandparents of the Twenties and Thirties had about the presence of Jim Crow laws. Jim Crow was status quo, a fact of life, even though to some, sometimes, it seemed as peculiar as the previous stage of black servitude under that "peculiar institution."

Thus, much of that early writing in the realm of African-American folklore is perceived much differently today from the way it was seen and written over fifty years ago. Fifty years of racial social revolution has changed perspectives. The condescension and paternalism and stereotyping of those early folklorists are obvious and glaring in light of today's social and racial attitudes. But even today whites still have problems writing about black folklore. Much writing by whites about African-Americans is touched with racial romanticism. Some whites see blacks and their culture as they wish them to be, carriers of "pure" folk culture in black music and art, unsullied by the commerce and materialism of the more affluent white culture. Only the black world knows how close white writers are to reality.

Color does not separate individual members of the races; culture does. We are all children of Eve, the seed of some australopithecine mother of a million years ago. Those who sing the same songs, tell the same stories, worship the same gods, and dress alike and decorate their bodies alike are bound together by a cultural cement, color and racial differences notwithstanding. Those who say *crick* instead of *creek* and *you'se* instead of *y'all* are separated in spite of similarities of color, unless they can find compensatory folkloric and customary similarities. The purpose of this publication and of previous publications of the Texas Folklore Society is to acquaint members and readers with other cultures, to find the humanity that binds all children of Eve into a sympathetic and understanding people—to narrow culture gaps that can be as socially divisive as the Mason-Dixon Line.

I conclude with an animal tale in the Uncle Remus-style, black, folk tradition. Frank Dobie published this in his first PTFS (II) in 1923. This tale is typical of the African-American folklore that was collected and published in those early days of the Society. It was collected from the oral tradition and written down nearly seventy-five years ago by A. W. Eddins, a San Antonio school teacher and white writer who was following in the steps of white journalist Joel Chandler Harris. This is a classic dialect joke, funny because of its intellectual wit and its universal wisdom. The dialect personalizes it (at the same time that it stereotypes it) in the same way as do the Sut Lovingood tales or the José Jimenez monologues or Pat O'Brien's Irish jokes or Alan King's Jewish jokes. Black or white, any reader who has found himself as a goose in a den of foxes easily identifies with the teller of this tale. But in our society, then and now, the speaker must be a black man for the tale to have social significance.

Ole Sis Goose wus er-sailin' on de lake, and ole Brer Fox wus hid in de weeds. By um by ole Sis Goose swum up close to der bank and ole Brer Fox lept out an cotched her.

"O yes, ole Sis Goose, I'se got yer now, you'se been er-sailin' on mer lake er long time, en I'se got yer now. I'se gwine to break yer neck en pick yer bones."

"Hole on dere, Brer Fox, hold on, I'se got jes as much right to swim in der lake as you has ter lie in der weeds. Hit's des as much my lake es hit is yours, and we is gwine to take dis matter to der cotehouse and see if you has any right to break my neck and pick my bones."

En so dey went to cote, and when dey got dere, de sheriff, he wus er fox, en de judge, he wus er fox, en der tourneys, dey wus foxes, en all de jurrymen, dey was foxes, too.

En dey tried ole Sis Goose, en dey 'victed her en dey 'scuted her, en dey picked her bones.

Now my chilluns, listen to me, when all de folks in de cotehouse is foxes, and you is jes er common goose, der ain't gwine to be much jestice for a pore nigger.

Bibliography

Abernethy, Francis E. *Legends of Texas' Heroic Age*. Boston: American Press, 1984.

___. *The Texas Folklore Society 1909–1943*. Vol. I. Denton: University of North Texas Press, 1992.

Buckley, Eleanor C. "The Aguayo Expedition into Texas and Louisiana, 1719–1722." *The Quarterly of the Texas State Historical Association*, XV, No. 1 (July 1911): 1–65.

Campbell, Randolph B. *An Empire of Slavery: The Peculiar Institution in Texas 1821–1865*. Baton Rouge: Louisiana State University Press.

Dobie, J. Frank. *Coffee in the Gourd*. PTFS II. Austin: Texas Folk-Lore Society, 1923.

___. *Rainbow in the Morning*. PTFS V. Austin: Texas Folk-Lore Society, 1926.

Prince, Diane. "William Goyens, Free Negro on the Texas Frontier." Thesis. Nacogdoches, Stephen F. Austin State University, 1967.

Handbook of Texas. Walter P. Webb et al, eds. Austin: The Texas State Historical Association, 1952.

Randall, J. G. and David Donald. *The Civil War and Reconstruction*. Lexington, Mass: D. C. Heath and Company, 1969.

Sance, Melvin. *The Afro American Texans*. San Antonio: Institute of Texan Cultures, 1987 rev.

All day singing at Pine Grove Baptist Church, Nacogdoches County. (Courtesy, F. E. Abernethy.)

Black Sacred Harp Singing Remembered in East Texas

By Judge Donald R. Ross

One sad commentary about Sacred Harp singing in East Texas has been our lack of concern for the preservation of the traditions of this historic and unique musical expression of faith, praise, and celebration. The story of Sacred Harp singing among black people in East Texas illustrates what can happen when these traditions and this music are taken for granted. And it illustrates what can be lost by not preserving it for the interest and enjoyment of future generations.

Soon after I took up Sacred Harp singing in rural East Texas in the 1950s, I became aware that this musical tradition was also appreciated by some black people in several communities around where I grew up. My first personal experience of singing Sacred Harp with blacks was at a small Baptist church in an all-black community called Mayflower, in Rusk County.

The summer night was hot, and I thought I was early arriving at the singing. As I approached the church, however, it became apparent that I was late. The crowd was so large that I had to park my car a considerable distance from the church. As I walked toward the church down that country road with cars parked on both sides, I could hear familiar a cappella harmonies, sung in a somewhat different style than I

▼

was used to hearing, streaming from the open windows of that old clapboard church house.

When the church came into view, I could see that it had standing room only. Every pew was filled, and people were standing along the walls on the inside and gathered around the open windows on the outside.

It did not take long for word to reach the persons in charge that a white visitor had arrived, and I was promptly escorted inside and to a seat on a front pew that someone had been obliged to vacate for me. The singing did not break up until somewhere around midnight. Needless to say, I was greatly impressed by the considerable enthusiasm shown for Sacred Harp singing at Mayflower.

As my general involvement in Sacred Harp singing developed, I made it a point to attend as many black singings as possible. It was apparent from that first exposure at Mayflower that there were some very noticeable differences in the way black people carried on this musical tradition from the way white people did. For example, I eventually learned that the reason the singing in Mayflower went on until midnight had to do with the way they called their song leaders. At a black Sacred Harp singing, there was no Arranging Committee to call the leaders. Instead, the leaders were called by the Convention Clerk, with whom the leaders were required to "enroll" before the start of the singing. The way one enrolled was by paying a requisite fee. At that Mayflower singing the enrollment fee was twenty-five cents. At the last all-black singing I attended, in the late 1970s, this token had doubled. Further, it was not only the leaders who were allowed to enroll. Anyone who had the required enrollment fee could sign up with the Clerk. If a person enrolled who was not a leader, when the Clerk called his name this person could designate any leader of his choice to lead in his place. And he could even pick the song! The duration of the singing then depended on the number of leaders enrolled. When everyone enrolled had his or her turn, that session of the singing was over. This might be only thirty minutes after the singing started, as was the case at that last singing I attended, or it might be midnight, as it was at Mayflower that night, all depending on how many leaders had enrolled.

This contrast in the number of leaders at Mayflower in the 1950s and the few at that last singing I attended in the late 1970s demonstrates the rapid decline of Sacred Harp singing among black people in East Texas. Today, there are no black singings, and to my knowledge, only one living black singer, an octogenarian who suffers from Alzheimer disease and is unlikely to ever sing again in this life.

The demise of the Sacred Harp singing tradition among black people in East Texas is regrettable not only for what it took away from subsequent generations, but also because of the loss of a distinctive singing tradition. Characteristics of the black style of singing that were unique to their culture and that greatly enriched this old musical art form are now lost. For example, these black singers always sang at a much higher pitch than the whites would ever attempt. It seemed to me that the black keyer tried to pitch the song just a tad higher than the best treble singer in attendance could reach. When he knew that treble singer would have to strain to reach the highest note in the song, then it would be keyed just right! Admittedly, the songs were keyed out of my range about ninety percent of the time.

Also, black people did not get in a hurry about anything at their singings, including pitching the song. It would not be unusual to key a given song four or five times before settling on the key that was "just right." Once the right key was secure, they would sing with an intensity of feeling and emotion that I have not seen or heard since. They sang with great spirituality and from the depths of their souls.

In their Sacred Harp tradition, there was no option about singing the notes; it was mandatory. If the chorus had a repeat, observance of that repeat was expected for the notes and for *each and every* verse. In regard to mood, if the song were particularly sentimental, it would not be unusual to sing the chorus softly the last time around. They seemed to do this instinctively, without any direction or instruction from the leader.

Not getting in a hurry was also the norm for the tempo. Most songs were sung much slower than whites sing them. Once when an older black singer attended the East Texas Convention around the mid-1970s and was called on to lead a song, he announced, "Number 106" and then gave these instructions: "I want to sing this song at a T-Model pace. Don't you white folks carry me too fast."

So far as East Texas is concerned—and I was never aware of black Sacred Harp singing in any other part of this state—there were two main annual conventions: the Rusk County Convention and the Panola County Convention. Both used the Cooper edition of *The B. F. White Sacred Harp*, rather than J. Jackson's *The Colored Sacred Harp*. Both conventions met during the summer months and moved from one rural community to another. I personally attended sessions of the Rusk County Convention in the following communities: Mayflower, Springfield, Chapel Hill, and Waters Chapel. I also attended the Panola County Convention when it met at Holland's Quarters and at Beckville. For many years these conventions were led by two brothers whose last name was Mitchell. After the death of these two outstanding singers, the leadership passed on to two equally talented brothers, John and Marvin Fite. One of the last of the black singers, the one who led "Ecstasy" at "a T-Model pace," was Mr. Jerry Brown of Panola County.

The one black singer who stands out in my memory most vividly was a man who lived in the same community where I was reared and whose name was Henry Hatchett. I never remember hearing Mr. Hatchett called "Mr. Hatchett" or even "Henry." It was either "Hatchett" or "Henry Hatchett." Unfortunately, Mr. Hatchett was mentally retarded and, because of his handicap, was the object of cruel practical jokes on occasion. However, he was very tolerant and friendly and loved by all. In spite of his fairly severe retardation, Mr. Hatchett was blessed with an extraordinary gift of singing, and the only way I ever heard him express this gift was in singing Sacred Harp. Even though he was unable to read or write a single word, not even his own name, Mr. Hatchett would attend every Sacred Harp singing he possibly could and sing from memory the notes and the words to every song. His favorite was #58, "Pisgah," and I have observed him lead this song, straying from the hollow square, walking in rhythm up and down the center aisle of the church, and making everybody happy, especially Henry Hatchett.

Henry Hatchett had no means of transportation of his own and was always dependent on someone else to furnish him a ride to the singings and back home. Sometimes when these rides failed to materialize, his desire to attend a singing would be so strong that he would walk many miles to get there. Typically, these singings would be held in country churches located in the backwoods off unpaved, tree-shaded roads. If the singing lasted into the night, this meant that Mr. Hatchett would have to walk some dark and lonely roads to get back home. One such road he frequently traveled by foot passed near my home. Many times I have heard Henry Hatchett in the late hours of the night singing "O Lord, remember me" as he walked down a long hill on this dirt lane toward his home.

It is interesting to speculate about how blacks in East Texas came to sing Sacred Harp in the first place. It is known that many settlers in this part of the state who came from Alabama and Georgia brought their Sacred Harp song books with them. It is also true that some of these settlers were slave owners. Therefore, it is logical to assume that some of these slaves learned to sing Sacred Harp from their white masters. On the other hand, it could also be that, having first heard it sung by whites, they then learned to sing it all on their own, perhaps even after emancipation. However it got handed down, we know that it was *not* an exact duplicate of the way the whites did it. There were too many practices, in style and procedure, that were unique to their culture to say they copied Sacred Harp singing exactly from the whites.

Unfortunately, no one—including myself—taped, filmed, or photographed the sounds and sights of these black Sacred Harp singings, and they now exist only in the memories of a few of us. True, there may still be black Sacred Harp singers in East Texas, but I do not think I will ever again hear it sung the way they sang it at Mayflower that night.

Rev. Henry E. Truvillion

Henry Truvillion of the Big Thicket: A Song Worth Singing

by Jesse Truvillion

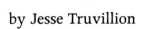rowing up in the Big Thicket of southeast Texas endowed one with a sense of awe about life and living that marked one's character. The Thicket gave distinctive meanings to words like *work, love, family, home, hope, truth, joy, pain,* and *education.* The day-by-day teachings of my parents etched onto my thinking the importance of being productive with hands and heart, so that I could matter, be useful, and find God's purpose for my existence. In their judgment, Macbeth was wrong; I had more to do than to just "live and die."

My father, the Reverend Henry E. Truvillion, stood before me like a giant tree, helping to decorate the evergreen forest of the Big Thicket—tall in physical stature and character. He was a man who made ethics more important than comforts and a contribution more important than popular credit. He walked the way he was built—with long strides that made walking in his footsteps difficult. As a little boy, I tried to step in his tracks. As a man, I discovered I could not.

More than thirty-five years after my dad's death, I visited the church where he had been funeralized. A stange thing happened. I had walked from the home of the deacon whose funeral was that day to the Mount Hope Missionary Baptist Church. I carried a second pair of shoes—the dusty roads made this necessary. This was common practice during my dad's years as pastor.

I was putting on the second pair of shoes when a man came, stood over me for a few seconds and said, "Well!" He promptly left and came back with a woman dressed in white, a member of the missionary society. They both stood over me as I tied the string of the last shoe. "Yes, that's Reverend Truvillion's little boy all right," she said. I was forty-two years old.

My dad made footprints in the sands of Newton and Jasper counties that the winds of time and change have not erased. His stories live on after him—always of the Bible, if not always in it. Talking on pitch at work, at home, or in the pulpit, he called out orders, or addressed principles with intent for exactness. I can hear him now on the railroad scene:

> Line them up, men,
> Line them up solid—
> Tamp them up, men,
> Tamp them up solid—
> So they won't come down—
> No, not ever.

The railroad tracks my father and his crews laid all across the south and southwest did not come down, ever.

Dad was counter-culture in attitude and practice. The civil liberties that characterize my adult years were denied him. He courted danger to encourage human decency.

My father was a man full of the Thicket, abundant with life and laughter. He seldom spoke a discouraging word. He always read aloud and slowly, so that listening, I could predict the Bible story we would hear from the pulpit on an upcoming Sunday. His notes were brief and sometimes written in the margins of his Bible.

Henry Truvillion was a lover of children, everybody's. He took the upbringing of children personally—beginning with his own five. Children would line up after Sunday School classes and march toward the pulpit where he would give each one a nickel so they could "give unto the Lord" in the morning offering. "Never come before the Lord empty-handed," he taught. He made a big example with his giving to children and to the larger community.

Henry Truvillion was himself a song worth singing, "A Ballad of the Big Thicket," singing to his work crews—"Head high, throw it away!" His "holler" and his "blow" were known throughout the Emancipation Communities of Deep East Texas. I still use his auto horn blow—two longs followed by two shorts. There was music in his accent and love in his song.

Music was to him a bridge to understanding, crossing barriers during rigid segregation, always concerned to leave "a safe crossing" for his children. He and my mother were truly *one* with the precepts and examples we were raised by: "If you want plants to grow, give them fertilizer," Dad often said, "but if you want children to grow up well, give them high ideals."

It was not until 1974 that the United States Congress established the Big Thicket as a National Preserve. By this time I was a college and seminary graduate, and a pastor in the New York City area. I knew of the Thicket's importance long before the United Nations designated it a "Man and the Biosphere Reserve" in 1981, attesting to the worldwide significance of the Thicket's resources. It was in 1973, during the trauma of the Kennedy assassination, that I was awakened to my dad's role in the Big Thicket folklore era, and to the richness of his contribution.

I was living with a white family in upper Ridgewood, New Jersey, when an unbelieveable discovery was made. I was waiting for the Presbyterian manse (big word for a pastor's residence) to be made ready in Jersey City, New Jersey, since the Baptists in Ridgewood "put me out" for having gone and become a Presbyterian.

It was the afternoon of President Kennedy's funeral, and needing a lift from the dirge-sounds and sights of that sorrowful drama, we cut off the television and went into the music room of their spacious and lovely home. The husband host, proud of his collection of folk music, wanted to share some of his favorites. He played a recording of Josh White, and I responded, "That sounds like one of my daddy's songs."

Picking up the record jacket he read a notation: "For the original of this song see Library of Congress Number . . . by Henry Truvillion."

"Do you know this man, Jesse?" my host asked.

"Yes, he's my father," I responded.

An intense discussion followed. I remembered recordings being made in my home in Texas, along Highway 87, in Newton County, and I remembered the white man who came to our home several times and set up his recording machine with the "dog listening to his Master's Voice." His name was John Avery Lomax. Sometimes Mrs. Lomax came with him, sometimes his son Alan came also. Stories were told by Daddy, songs were sung, questions were answered in great detail, and issues were discussed with raw frankness, as only two friends would.

Some of the recordings were made in our living-room, where a Marine finish graced the hardwood floor and oriental rugs enlivened the sitting areas. John Lomax sat in the rocker during the long recording sessions. My dad facing him in a overstuffed comfortable chair. The machine made a long roll of hair-like shavings as it recorded. Mr. Lomax, as we all called him, gave me a buffalo nickel to "clean up the hair" the machine left on the floor. The amount of black hair was considerable, but I think my mother was the one who actually swept it up when the sessions were over. The nickel was a gift to me.

John Lomax was likeable. He liked Daddy, and he, on several occasions, gave gifts to our entire family. I particularly remember some Christmas gifts from Mrs. Lomax, although I don't remember the years. They were people we liked and they liked us. Mr. Lomax gave Daddy a copy of one of the recordings. It was a twelve-inch disk, and it was recorded in the woods on the job site, with my dad directing his men in unloading rails and tamping ties.

On several occasions hands who had worked with Daddy came to visit, requesting the playing of the record so they could hear my daddy call out their names. This was a big thing in those years. Never did we know the role of the Library of Congress. The discovery in the music room in Upper Ridgewood surprised me, and when I called my mother in Texas that night, she, too, was quite surprised.

I told my mother that I would call the Library of Congress in the morning, Tuesday, November 26, 1963, and ask how the recording got there. The Folk Lore Department of the Library of Congress informed me that there were fifty-two recordings of Henry Truvillion there, and that his family was deceased, for no response had been given to their attempt to contact descendants of "the subject."

"I am Henry Truvillion's son," I exclaimed, "and my mother, and her five children are very much alive."

I was asked a few questions. Then I was asked to speak to another person, who asked the same and more questions. They became convinced that I was who I said I was. My mention of John Lomax and the Library of Congress number on the Josh White recording sealed the matter. I was then given a "state of the recordings" report. It appeared my phone call was made just in time to save the recordings. They were made on very fragile material and were all twelve-inch records. They could stand one more "playing," then they were done.

The recordings needed to be transferred onto reel-to-reel tape, and the policy was (based on congressional law) that a member of the family had to give permission and pay for the transfer. Thirty dollars was needed, and my signature.

I took a train to D.C. the next day, listened to several of the recordings, and was able to assist in correcting some of the transcriptions the staff had made of the recordings. I was shown a form on which my father was supposed to have made an X on the signature line.

"He couldn't write," they told me.

"That's not true," I replied.

I was shown a copy of a book by one of the curators of that department in which material from some of my father's recording was included.

"We made reasonable effort to find a family member," he said, "but we could find none."

"All the while there existed my mother and her five living children," I said.

I followed up that visit with two others in the spring of 1964. I was asked to look at a lot of photos taken by John Lomax in Deep East

Texas. I found among them a picture of my mother and my dad standing in the family garden. My dad was holding onto a turning plow, it being hitched to a mule for plowing. My mother was wearing her deep smile and a plain white working dress. My dad was vested in overalls and a black hat with the red bandanna about his neck. Texas Highway 87 was clearly seen in the background. The photo was taken in late fall or very early spring; the two seasons looked a lot alike. Evergreens defy seasonal attire, and the plowing my dad was about, in the picture, appeared to be breaking ground, the first plowing of that land. The picture appeared to be of a celebration visit by John Lomax marking the purchase of the new Truvillion land and home site and the end of Daddy's railroad career. It may well have marked the last time the two men, dear friends as they were, saw each other.

This transitional picture was taken then of Daddy's last days of working on the railroad and his first days as the owner of a tract of land and becoming a farmer. A stump is visible in the background. I remember it. It kind of symbolized the forest mourning its loss, having to give way to clearings for farms, fields, and factories.

I left the Library of Congress with a copy of the picture and a receipt for the preserving of the recordings of my dad's work songs, field hollers, conversations with John Lomax, his stories of his own childhood years in Mississippi, his stories of laying railroad track in the Thicket, the story of his Call to the Ministry, and his defense of his Christian doctrine. I left the proud son with a new dimension, a new awareness that my father, with my mother's affectionate support, had made a meaningful contribution to the folklore of America; that he had been indispensable to the track-laying ventures of the Wier Long Leaf Lumber Company; and that his contributions had gone beyond the railroad tracks of Newton and Jasper Counties—beyond the homes and churches of the Piney Woods of East Texas.

Hearing his voice and laughing at his satire in 1963, helped me focus more clearly on the meaning of his last years and dying days in 1948. He and John Lomax had both been men on a mission. Each had served the other well, considering the raw segregation of the years of their sojourn. Lomax had been in search of folklore riches; Dad had been a meaningful resource. They were indebted to each other. Together they preserved for us roots in the Thicket, of its human life and labor, the songs and stories, the strengths and soul, the down-to-earthness, and the transcendence of the people. Neither man was purely ordinary. Lomax was not your ordinary white man, and Henry was not a colored nobody. Their trusting affection helped them relate on a plane beyond the limits of the racial faith of their days. Neither man was a saint, unstained by time. Both John and Henry gave their times a redeemable existence. John was in search of ballads, of the lore of America. Henry was a ballad that John found—"a song worth singing." In 1920 on a site near Wiergate, Texas, he sang,

> Gather around the rails here, boys
> We are going to unload now
> When I deal the rail
> You catch my deal—
> Don't let me hold it here a year.

> All along—Walk—
> Walk on and don't you stumble,
> Don't let me hurt anybody
> This is a safety first company.

Henry E. Truvillion was born on Christmas Day, 1886, in the red hills of Brookhaven, Mississippi. From his stories, we know that his mother was named Caroline, called by the church and community "Aunt Caroline." His father was named (or called) Henry Truvillion. His father's middle name or initial is unknown to me, though there had to have been one. I did not learn until the 1970s that my father's name was slave coded: Henry Truvillion's property. With the help of my secretary (while I pastored in New York City), I was able to trace my dad's lineage to a slave owner named, of all things, Henry Truvillion, through records found in Jackson, Mississippi. The man was first listed in the Mississippi Census of 1840, entering from France with several slaves listed among his belongings. He was deported, but entered again, as the 1850

Census showed, but this time from Spain. Thus the French and Spanish sound in the name. There are various spellings of Truvillion; the slaves relied on the sound for the spelling.

It appears the first born male's descendants all were named Henry, with a middle name, or initial, to set them apart. So it was, without knowing it, the family continued the slave owner's name. Dad's name was Henry Eddie. His first born son was named Jim Henry. I am the fourth child and second son. I named my own son Mark Henry. My son was ten years old before I realized I had continued the slave owner's name. I had prayerfully named my son to honor his paternal grandfather, the Reverend Henry E. Truvillion, whose life journey ran from Brookhaven, Mississippi, to Burkeville, Texas. When I learned about the slave owner's bit, I was fit to be tied.

To my knowledge and according to Lomax's writings, my dad's travels with the railroad took him as far north as upstate New York and as far west as California. He never returned home to Brookhaven. His laboring adventures made him a well-traveled man with a mental storehouse of many stories. His songs were stories in themselves—sermonic in character. In telling his stories and singing his songs, he painted on a mental canvas living situations that engulfed his hearers. "Long ago" and "after a while" were made to be right now. He had discovered America "one rail at a time," and he made the working experience sound like church: in tune, on pitch, and in good rhythm.

Henry Truvillion's work crews became an extended family to him. Each man was called by his full name. Elbert Peacock was not referred to as "boy" or "man." He was referred to, way out there in the Thicket on the right-of-way of a railroad, as the person he really was, by the sacred name of his parents' whispering—"Elbert Peacock." Even if the men were being scolded, their full names were embraced. This was a crucial matter. Notice that at the great March on Washington in 1963, black laborers (with others) carried signs reading, "I am a Man." No person likes to be referred to as "nobody"; each person wants to be "somebody." Who, being old enough to remember, can ever forget the eighth round of a prize fight in Houston's Astrodome (during the Civil Rights years) when Mohammed Ali taunted Ernie Torrell, saying to his opponent, "What's my name?" Mr. Torrell had boasted that he was going to whip Ali until he said Cassius Clay, his slave name. For the African-American male, this is crucial. Way back there in the Thicket, Henry Truvillion's laborers were not boys, things, or property. Each man was a man—"a somebody."

Working on the railroad then was a pioneering venture, and living out there wasn't easy. Listen to this song sung by Henry while the crew was tamping ties (recorded in 1940 by John Lomax):

Well—Work don't hurt me
Don't care where
Or the weather
I'll go
Work don't hurt me
At the early rise
Work don't hurt me
'Cause I've got singing
Right in my side
Right in my side
Right in my side

There were no walkie-talkies out there on the railroad, no CB's or beepers. A man was known by his holler, a loud call that sounded through the forest. My dad had a holler that communicated directions, signaled a message or a distress cry. Developed over years on the railroad, it could be heard while I was in the field working the farm; in the woods while driving cattle; when a hunt was over; when it was just time to go home; and I heard it in his preaching. There was a quietude in the woods that caused a holler to carry a long way. The talking drum was gone before he was born, so the holler was heard instead of a bell, a whistle, a horn, or a drum.

I was very young when I discovered its value. I had been sent into the forest to pick blackberries. I rode my horse, a gift from Dad, and I carried two syrup buckets for my berry pickings. This was a special assignment, and I was proud, for with these berries, pies would be made for a special occasion. What an honor for a kid!

My horse was named Bill; "Old Bill" he was called. Grand was the day he arrived at our house on State Route 87 on a truck that carried cattle. He walked down the ramp, and the driver of the truck gave my dad the rope that was tied to Old Bill's halter. The whole family was out front for the occasion. He was our first horse. We'd had a mule before. I was surprised when my dad led Old Bill to me and said, "He's yours, Son." He dropped the rope, picked me up and sat me on his back. He then handed me the rope, and said, "Ride him, Son, he's your horse." I had never been on a horse before, but with a slight touch of my feet on his side Old Bill trotted toward the gate that led into our front yard and I quickly got off, frightened stiff.

Time and sugar made me and Bill the best of friends. I rode him with no bridle, just the halter. We owned no saddle, ever. He and I went berry picking often, but this day had "fate" written in its script. I was told to be home before noon, so the pies could be made for whatever the occasion was.

I ventured into the Piney Woods in a carefree spirit, thinking the only dangers out there were snakes (some snakes have two legs and human hands, though). Where there were clearings in the forest there were berries, especially along the Yellow Bayou and the pastures near it. In short order, I picked two buckets full of blackberries. Old Bill stayed near me while I picked, looking carefully for snakes. The horse would not come near a snake, so I knew not to tread where Old Bill signaled fear.

I hung the filled buckets on a tree limb, mounted my horse, proudly collected my buckets and headed, I thought, for home, directing my horse with word signals. There were no trails nearby, so the sun told me where home was. I followed for a long while, wondering why I had not reached Highway 87. All I needed to do was find the highway and take it north, cross the Yellow Bayou, and I would be home in no time. But the woods were thick, and dark, and deep, and except for an occasional bird call, there was silence, no sound from the highway—just lots of silence.

Old Bill was walking. One did not run a horse in this thickness, unless on a trail. By the sun I knew it was mid-afternoon when I first heard Daddy's loud holler: "My son, ho!!"

My reaction was one of concern for Daddy. "I didn't know he was coming out to pick berries, too," I said to Old Bill. "Let's stop here and let him catch up with us." So we waited a while and Daddy hollered again. "My son, ho!!"

"I think Daddy is lost, Bill. Let's turn back and find him." Very soon he hollered a third time, but with distress in his call.

"My son, ho!"

"Daddy is hurt," I said. "Let's trot, Bill. Come on, I may waste a few berries, but we need to hurry to help him." Going toward the sound and coming to a clearing, we found him leaning on a post, crying like a child. Only in church had I witnessed him cry before.

"Hand me your buckets and get down off your horse, Son."

There was a fence there of barbed wire. We let Old Bill jump over to where Daddy was. Then we sat down on the ground until he stopped crying.

"Do you remember crossing the Yellow Bayou, Son? Did you not see the fence near the water?" He went on to mention a certain white man who vowed to shoot any black man seen on his property.

"For the last few hours, you've been on that man's property, Son." Then we started home. Old Bill walked behind us. "Look at the sun. Home is not that way, Son. Home is back this way. You've been lost a long time."

I thought *he* was lost. When I found him, I discovered that *I* was lost. But I had discovered more than the way home that day. I had discovered something of the measure of a father. I was a boy unknowingly lost in the Piney Woods. Even a mean white man would have thought twice about harming a little black boy on a horse with two buckets of blackberries. But a full-grown black man was a different matter. With a sure knowledge of the danger to himself, that man came into the woods looking for his son, knowing by the amount of time that child had been gone, he had to be lost. There would be other times, too, but on that summer day, Henry Truvillion, the railroad section foreman, showed me the stuff a father is made of. There was no shame in me, telling my brother, Jim, seven years older, that I had gotten lost in the forest today, and Daddy came and got me.

It was great fun riding in the car with my mother and dad to Wiergate, crossing lovely Cow Creek, then up the last hill to the railroad track, watching the Pine Knot Special (with the great black train engine) go from the sawmill out into the forest to bring back the logs on the rails that Daddy's crew had laid. He wore his red bandanna every day, but it always seemed new. He looked like "a man in charge," and my mother and I always waited to receive his wave, then it was back home for the day.

Wiergate was very busy in the 1920s, 1930s, and 1940s. High piles of logs, trains on the move, sounds of the big saws cutting logs into lumber, and lots of men working with gray gloves on. There was the Commissary, the company store, where everybody purchased their goods and shared their stories. There, too, was the big depot and the post office. It was a boom town in my early childhood years, and it was muddy, always muddy—red mud.

The first house finished for an African-American in Wiergate was built for Henry Truvillion, the foreman. He was outstanding as a track foreman, with his songs, his hollers, and that on-pitch speech that both directed and entertained. His railroad assignment took him far, and for seasons. In those years, time and distance were subservient to the task. The company's call was like an order from on high.

These were the "after years" of World War I and the "before years" of the great stock market crash. They were dancing in the Thicket. There were honkytonks and barrelhouses, moonshine whiskey, and homemade wine. While the "fear of God" flourished in the Thicket, the Devil moved about quite freely also. Henry Truvillion rediscovered his religious roots in those East Texas Piney Woods that, except for the thickness, looked a lot like his Brookhaven, Mississippi, countryside.

One of John Lomax's recorded conversations with my dad has Lomax remarking, "Now, he is the Reverend Henry Truvillion," going on to make extensive remarks about Dad's call into the gospel ministry.

There is amazement in Lomax's voice as he comments on the foreman for the railroad becoming a foreman for Jesus Christ. The conversation is soul stirring. It's a recording session with a folklorist in which a track-laying engineer is talking about being a foreman on the "straight and narrow," as found in the Bible. He would now be laying track for life's railroad, and a train on the main line, with Jesus Christ as the engineer. He would not even sing any of his old worldly songs. He had a new motto:

Things I used to do
I don't do anymore.
Songs I used to sing
I don't sing anymore.

Lomax's amazement was piqued when he asked the Reverend Henry Truvillion about the Lord's Supper. My dad had made some comments about race having no place in Heaven, so it had no place in church. He implied an inclusive and integrated church, one that should have nothing to do with color. The talk took place in the late 1930s, when racial segregation was a faith and racial practices were a religion—all backed up by Jim Crow laws.

Lomax asked, "What about the Lord's Supper, Henry? Would you serve the Lord's Supper to white people?"

"Sure," answered the new Servant of the Word and Sacraments. "The Lord's Supper protects itself."

I heard my dad enlarge on this "protects itself" declaration many times, and always with Biblical quotes. Church divisions and divisions in churches were, according to him "man-made and not God-intended." Those who serve the Lord's Supper are only servants, he contended. Jesus serves the real Supper, and it is all spiritual. When we take or serve the Bread and the Wine, we are expressing our willingness to receive His real "Spiritual Supper." Now *that* Supper cannot be blemished by sinful hands or hearts. For that which is in spirit received is beyond color—beyond male or female.

Henry Truvillion contended that spiritual order invades the natural order at its own will. He said so to Lomax, to his family, and to his new comrades in ministry. It shows up in his preaching. In one of three sermons preached at Big Sandy Baptist Church, north of Wiergate, on a particular Sunday, he made this interpretive point on the Red Sea Crossing:

Now when the children of Israel had
Crossed safely to the other side,
They were pursued by the Egyptian charioteers.
In the midst of the bed of the sea
One of the wheels of the chariot
Carrying the commander came off.
Quickly, the Egyptian engineers restored the wheel—
But the chariot would not roll—
    because the wheel was on backwards.
Off they took it—turned it over
And put it on a second time.
But, it was still backwards.
You see, Brothers and Sisters—
When you are working against God,
Everything you do is wrong.

As a preacher he was as much a storyteller as when he was on the railroad. He never pastored St. Luke, where the family held membership, but on occasion he preached there. On a Wednesday night, when I had become the person who opened the door, swept the church, and rang the bell of St. Luke Baptist Church, along Highway 87, he was the preacher. Electricity had come to the Emancipation Community. St. Luke was lighted with three hanging bulbs down the middle and one over the pulpit. It was spring. That bulb over the pulpit drew a thousand bugs. That may be the reason he preached from "the Table" instead of fighting the bugs flying about the pulpit.

His sermon was about light—Jesus was the True Light. His story began:

It was a Sunday night after church in my native Mississippi. I walked a lady home and then took a short cut to get back to my own home. It was very dark, but I was not afraid since, in those days, I traveled at night with a six-shooter in hand.

But I became lost, engulfed in bramble briars. I knew I was in a large pasture and there was a large pond of water in the pasture. I felt that if I moved I would fall into the water. In desperation, I cried out for help. "I'm lost!" I cried, several times.

A man opened his back door and yelled, "Wait a minute." I heard him cut splinters from a stump. I saw him light them. When they were burning good he held them up, and said, "Can you see this light?"

"Yes," I answered, "but isn't there water between you and me?"

"No, just briars, lots of them. Don't stray to the left or to the right; just come straight to this light."

Now this Bible I'm holding up here is God's splinters; the Holy Spirit is the fire. My job here is to hold up this light. Now, is there anyone lost here tonight? I invite you to come to the light.

That's the night I became a Christian, making my decision to follow Jesus. Standing up "amidst the briars," I walked straight to him, shook his hands, and said, "I want to give my life to Jesus Christ." He jumped up, danced about, and shed a tear or two. In short, he was happy.

When the singing stopped, he was supposed to listen to a deacon present me, and then they would take a vote and set a date for my baptism. Instead, he proceeded to talk to the Light, saying, "Lord, this is my son."

My father's ministry was strongly supported by my mother, Oneal Bluitt Truvillion, the fourteenth child of Lillie and Jerry Bluitt of Magnolia Springs (still in the Thicket, but in Jasper County). They were married in 1927. He called her "Sweet" and she called him "Hon."

Henry E. Truvillion was himself a kind of Light to those he led on the railroad and to those he shepherded in churches. Some of the churches he pastored had Big Thicket names: Toledo Bend, Cedar Creek, Sandy Creek. Others had Biblical names like most indigenous African-American churches: St. John's and Mount Hope. The *Newton Herald* (our county newspaper) called him "a prominent minister," at the time of his death, adding that he "was loved and respected as a good man and a number one citizen and Gospel preacher."

Henry Truvillion had been a star find for John Avery Lomax, as that folklorist chronicled the lore of one romantic American era.

Both Henry and John died in 1948. Dad was the first of his railroad crew to die. Two of his men still survive: Elbert Peacock and Otis Hawthorne. In the spring of 1995, those two men, their families, and I shared memories of my dad as a railroad foreman and a foreman for Jesus Christ. John Lomax, the white man who took pictures and made recordings, was remembered too. We were gathered in Shankville, Texas, at the Peacock Family Reunion. At the same time in Meridian, Texas, the third annual John A. Lomax Gathering was taking place—complete with the singing of songs of the Lomax Collection.

My dad counted his last days for us. "I've got nine more days," he told Mother. He kept counting down to three more. That was Sunday. No more words were spoken. He died Wednesday morning, May 5, two days before his first grandchild was born. I remember when the heavy breathing stopped, the silence, and then Mother screamed.

I ran to the door of his bedroom and I saw him stilled. I had seen others dead, but this was Dad. "We need a man here," an attending woman said. "Son, go get your Uncle Wiley."

I ran, as fast as a twelve-year-old boy could, the two hundred yards to my uncle's store and reported, "Mrs. Holmes said 'Come quick'."

He said, "Lord, have mercy."

I turned then to return home and suddenly realized I was a fatherless child in the Thicket. The steps going back were heavy. Death had inflicted a new reality upon us as a family and as a community. The stories and the songs; the sermons and the sayings; his holler and his laughter had all ended. He was to me both Dad and pal. I would miss his vocalizing as we drove to church on Sundays that sounded like a train whistle blowing and the rumbling of the wheels on the tracks he and his men had laid. There was both pride and thanksgiving in the tears that I shed that morning.

Mother's Day, May 9th, was Henry Truvillion's burial day. Sunday funerals were common in the Thicket, and it seemed that all persons were present from the surrounding Emancipation Communities. I remember every song, each of the readings, but most of all the sermon. The Moderator of the Lone Star Baptist District Association, The Reverend Harvey Peacock, the same man who had presided at Dad's ordination and who later presided at my own ordination, eulogized him.

One sentence from the sermon summed it up for me:

"A man who preaches three different sermons to the same congregation on one Sunday, and received seventy-five cents as an honorarium, is a big man."

My horse, Old Bill, seemed to understand what was happening as the long line of cars left the church heading for the cemetery at Magnolia Springs. As Dad's body passed home for the last time, Old Bill approached the fence that paralleled Highway 87 and followed along as far as the pasture would let him. Then he stood on his hind legs, screaming a cry, and pounding the air with his forelegs. I had never seen him do that before.

Daddy had never ridden him. Old Bill was a gift to his youngest son. He and Daddy were affectionate. On that Mother's Day, Old Bill joined in the mourning.

That night I heard my mother pray an unforgettable prayer. Her husband had been a railroad man, whose job played out. They were left with no benefits, no pension, and most of their savings spent on medical and hospital bills.

I guess she thought we were all sleeping. She stood before the dresser in her bedroom—using it like an altar. She lifted all the money she had left as high as her arms would let her, and said, "Lord, what am I going to do with all my little children?"

She had less than twenty dollars left. With it and faith in God, she started over. What a love story she lived until she died on January 7,

1990. Her children graced her grave with the same words that grace her husband's, Henry Truvillion's:

> She gave her life in Service
> to God and her neighbors.

Henry and Oneal Truvillion plowing a spring garden.

Saturday night in the Fourth Ward. (Courtesy, Joseph F. Lomax)

Houston's Fourth Ward

by James Thomas Jackson

Once Upon a Time

In Houston's black Fourth Ward, I grew up in a cul-de-sac.

My street, Crosby, dead-ended with our house. Unasphalted, it stayed that way until well after my eighteenth birthday when I entered the armed services during World War II. Our tiniest black ghetto—five wards in all and listed numerically—was Watts, California-sized, perhaps: 2 x 2 x 2 miles, and downtown Houston's eyesore of a backyard. It was still pretty much that way when I left it for Los Angeles, California, in August, 1965.

Our ghetto, because of Houston's downtown nearness, was ever a mass of contradictions in social, commercial and even cultural mores. We could "trip" from the sublime to the ridiculous in an instant, depending on how one kept score. A black customer could be refused use of a restroom, while a black employee—male or female—not only cleaned them but used them at will, even though double bathrooms were installed within the major premises. On our jobs, both domestic and residential, we entered by rear doors and had possession of the places all day during our chores. At evening tide we departed through the same rear doors. These double-standard confusions were many, varied, and blew our black minds for as long as it took to "adapt"—if we wanted to survive race prejudices—without going plumb nuts in the process. Our ghetto was our saving grace: in our combined blackness, faith in our churches, and trust in eventual overall justice, which was made manifest in our striving for entity—through the front door.

I have fond boyhood memories, though. Horses from Phoenix Phil's Dairy were kept in a large corrugated-tin barn just around the corner from our house. Their clip-clopping and clanking milk bottle clatter, both empty and full, mornings and afternoons, sufficed as timepieces to in- and out-of-house patrons more than any Woolworth, Schultz-United, or J. C. Penney alarm clock. One morning a horse driver's car engine caught fire, parked right in front of our house. The white owner (blacks cleaned the stables, tended the horses) tried using my father's water hose but to no avail. Another white, a passing derelict a short block away on our Cleveland cross street, rushed back to assist. Snatching the hose out of the frustrated driver's hand, he was yelling "Sand! Sand! Sand!" Grabbing handfuls of it he splayed it all over the car fire. In an instant the fire was extinguished. He, alone, of all of us was blest with knowledge of so handy an expedient, and we had a whole city block of the stuff.

Conversely, Phoenix Phil's Dairy was located at the last edge of the street, ending a Fourth Ward boundary, becoming the foot of this part of Houston's downtown commerce. It faced a portion of poor white and struggling metropoles taking up where we left off. On the roof and high above the dairy's white brick edifice, where our milk was daily bottled and loaded into an early dawn's horse-drawn truck, was a huge Phoenix Phil sign. A colorful commercial sign of a white, pink-cheeked boy-child of three, wearing an outsized, deliveryman's cap of white crown, black bibbed, and dressed in striped blue overalls. The right strap of them hung down unfastened. In one hand he was carrying a giant quart of white bottled milk. The tot's commercial name was "Phoenix Phil." This logo told us Fourth Warders in particular, and all persons entering and departing this area in general, that this milk was baby-pure good. I went away to serve my country remembering that particular sign, as did, I'm sure, many of my black and white playmates (who lived on our fringes), and always expected it to be there when we returned. Sometime in the late fifties, the sign and the old ownership went. "Phoenix was sold to Foremost," was the word we all received.

Back to Crosby Street. Over the wooden and very tall fence of Crosby Street lived some white folks—as they did, always near the edge of Fourth Ward's perimeter. This house, a two-story, painted white, had a large tree which offered much shade deeply planted near its back stairs. I remember the middle-aged couple's name as the Benfords. They appeared to live coolly and quietly. Sheriff Benford was a no-nonsense man in his job. (To this day I see him only a decade removed from a Texas Ranger.) He was reputed to "kick asses and take names," indiscriminately. Our high fence limited association, except for my occasional day's work inside their light, bright and airy home doing some cleaning chores, in which case one or the other was nice as pie to me. A-okay. Sheriff Benford's presence "over the fence" just might have dispelled many burglary attempts from our humble abode, and nothing but respect passed back and forth from our good neighbor fence.

The Benfords' house also greeted the end of Calhoun, where it curved out, became Baldwin, and headed south past well tended shrubbery, umbrella trees, and white, early plantation houses well to the rear. Presenting a moody but wealth-accrued quietness, Baldwin seemed the most sedate street of my childhood. And at Christmas time, peeking through a key-holed fence, it looked forebodingly fetching with bright lights streaming through moss and shrubbery alike. It gave my young mind all sorts of wistful thoughts of a quiet, comfortable culture that never seemed to come our way.

One summer when I was ten or eleven, my new next door black neighbor, D. J. (Dan Johnny) Houghton and I started out walking from Calhoun's end. Adventurous in every way, we hopped and crawled over the eight-foot-high fence and started hiking up Calhoun's then unpaved street, taking turns carrying an empty five-gallon bucket, going "crawdad" hunting. ("Cray fish," the shrimp's bastard kin, living in bottoms of shallow creek water.) It would be a five-mile walk each way, a hot Texas summer with bristling heat, and the distance to Bray's Bayou and our foraging end mattered not one whit. The area was white folks' suburbs (then) whose occupants showed no inclination to bother us, and certainly we had no intention of bothering them. Houston then had places in white areas we blacks weren't about to go, especially those inhabited by poor whites who were mean as hell to "niggers." Those we encountered that day were simply indifferent. Plus, luck being with us, we hand-caught a whole bucket full of this muddy creek fish delicacy.

D. J. and I struggled the whole way back with our "catch," using a broken broom handle to equalize the bucket's water added weight. (D. J.'s cleverness: not wanting to ruin our bounty by stupidity.) I credit myself for being eager and adventurous, but D. J. was my own black Davy Crockett. We rested quite a lot and changed arm grips. We even used people's hydrants for fresher water in our return odyssey, and our catch was unspoiled when we reached home base. Once back home we were instant heroes. Black folks' love for "exotic" foods combined with a "mean" Depression made the crawdads a godsend, and from kids our age! Our neighbors said we had "pluck."

Both our parents had us distribute our goodies to as many in our block as possible. Fried crawdad odors permeated our area that night. Both D. J.'s and my plates were huge from our parents' frying: heaps of home-fried potatoes accompanied the now golden devils, along with our staple "Happy Jack" cornbread, skillet fried, and all the ketchup we wanted. I asked my mother if we should offer the Benfords' some, but a wagging maternal finger warned me against it. It seemed white folks had a thing against black folks giving them things. "Not to white folks," the wagging finger said. It was also the first time I heard the old saw, "like bringing coals to Newcastle," and later, one I was ever trying to comprehend, that black people were "inferior to white." No matter, D. J. and I would eat now and think later, having lots of growing up to do. So we ate our "exotic," muddy creek crawdads with ravenous relish and laughed like two fools at absolutely nothing at all.

A Black Family's Unusual Visitor

My mother was a God-fearing woman who loved roses. Her husband and children (myself included) also loved roses and feared God. In our family, the two went together, ever so nicely, at most times. But it was left to my father to teach me something about compassion.

Both Mother and Father had, it seemed, an almost innate understanding of the fact that people often failed as well as succeeded through no action of their own. My mother, in particular, thought of human lives as she thought of the roses that grew in the front yard: sometimes they wilted, sometimes they almost died, yet with a "little loving care," a "little gentleness," a "little concern," those roses always bloomed again.

When I was growing up during the depression years, we lived in the southern latitude of a pronouncedly black ghetto in Houston—a fact that never distracted us for long. Life was sometimes a hell or, at best, a restricted pleasure. There was often much hunger among our neighbors and those whom my mother called "the less fortunate." That expression of hers drove me to a multitude of soul searchings—who, I wanted to know, could be "less fortunate?" After all, we were already black, already deprived of innumerable economic advantages. Even then, at my tender age, I knew that we were scorned, derided, hated for our immutable blackness.

For a long time, though, I was proud of our black "freedom." We had, at least, blackness in common. And it was so beautifully black! For instance—

The blind man next door to us who delighted me with stories even more engrossing than those I read to him from the Holy Bible.

The elderly spinster three houses down, whose lawn I cut once a month for a few quarters. (I always used a hoe and botched it each time—but she forgave me.)

The Pullman porter, next door to her, who on departing for work carried that distinctive-looking, black "doctor's" bag, with the bold watch chain slung across his stomach; who worked on the Santa Fe and had a pretty wife.

The woman fortune teller down the street, with her many mysteries that held all of us children in an ever-circumspective awe.

The gospel singer with the peg leg who lived around the corner, who got outrageously drunk every Saturday night and gave a one-man soul-show in his backyard.

Such was the beauty of our isolated black land. It was our domain and only rarely was it broached by the appearance of either youthful white faces who wanted to play with us, or the curious sight of a white journeying mendicant, invading our black ghetto with flimflam wares.

Why, I thought, if we were so inferior, so unequal, so unfit to mingle with whites—why should they come to our part of town to peddle? They had removed us from their dominant scenes and restricted us from associations within our mutual city, leaving us with only wistful looks at an expanding and growing place which, even then, my own hod-carrying father was sweating to help build.

They made us ride buses in the one small section allotted us—packed black sardines, well to the rear, like slaves on some ship from African shores, bound for shores like these.

The word was that we were smelly, wore the same clothes all the time, had no culture, no intellect, couldn't think. That our cooking pots reeked with the pungent odors of chit'lin's, red beans and neck bones. That our bodies—when we bathed— smelled of Octagon, Ivory or the even more disinfecting odor of Lifebuoy. That our streets and gutters ran rife with the litter of empty whiskey bottles. That our houses bled and flaked with a blatant cry for paint.

Then the picture changed. This man came. This white man in tatterdemallion clothes came to our black ghetto. His last recourse. He was raggedy as a twenty-nine-cent mop in a Baptist church in '32. He looked real bummy, and my mother fed him. That day she was cooking red beans and rice, collard greens and neck bones. The collard greens came from our own back yard.

My father arrived home early that day, smelling of mortar—a "perfume" I had learned to love the smell of. It meant prosperity, really. Mother fixed a big plate. (The white man's was big but no bigger than Father's—never bigger than the breadwinner's.) We all ate as though nothing unusual was happening. Washing all the food down with Poly-Pop, a watery strawberry flavoring with lots of sugar.

At the dinner table I studied the mighty symbol of authority. White face, blue eyes, blond hair, badly in need of a shave and hungry like a dog. He was too hungry to smile.

After the meal Father gave the man a pair of pants, a shirt, one of his hats and two cigars. My mother filched about $1.90 from our "don't go" money bank. He looked like a new man when he left: shaved, cleaned up some with pomade perking up his hair. I almost hated to see him go. There was so much I wanted to know. So much I wanted him to tell me.

Father understood that I was curious, and talked with me later. I can remember his words today.

"James," he said, "he is a white man with problems. He is not wanted. He is hated and despised among his own people. He is what is known as po' white trash. That sounds bad and, for him, it is bad. But that's the way things go.

"He is a white man with nothing. But in this house he is treated with kindness and understanding . . .

"Now," he added, done with his seriousness, "Don't you think your mother's rose bushes could use a little water? It seems to me they haven't had a drop to drink all day."

It was time to lay a "little loving care" elsewhere.

Used with permission from *Waiting in Line at the Drugstore and Other Writings of James Thomas Jackson* (Denton: University of North Texas Press, 1993).

Annie J. (Mother Davis) Davidson, (1874–1973) midwife of the Cedar Grove Community (Courtesy of Clyde Daniels)

Daniels residence, across from Cedar Grove (Courtesy of Clyde Daniels)

Where The Cedars Grove

by Clyde E. Daniels

My lineage is that of slaves and the sons and daughters of slaves who endured unconscionable deeds. And for that, I give them the honor and God the glory.

I am the descendant of East Texas Piney Wood natives extending six generations, with roots that spread from the Red River bottoms to Cypress Bayou.

Paternally, George Daniels was a slave and skilled mason from the Judge Daniels Plantation north of New Boston, Texas. George built the first courthouse in Bowie County. I now reside on property purchased by my grandfather, Willie Daniels.

Maternally, Frank Hall was a slave on the Hall Plantation near Hallsville, Texas.

Wreath of Laurels
　　—for my African-American Ancestors

To the old trailblazers,
Who laid the foundation
By the grace of God,
In Whose shadow I stand,
Whose path I trod;

To the old trailblazers,
Who tilled the soil
And took the whip,
Whose bleeding festering sores
Reflected their scarred souls,
And weathered calloused hands
Mirrored calloused hearts;

To the old trailblazers,
Whose hope of a sun-filled day
Was spoiled by the rife eclipse
That taunted them;

To the old trailblazers,
For *all* their untold stories
And forgotten accomplishments . . .
For *all* the years of being
Toiled into the soil,
I humbly bestow—this
　　Wreath of Laurels.

At midnight, Mother Davis was already tired, but her night was far from over. For she would deliver two babies before two o'clock. I was barely born when my uncle stepped out into the night. "Over here, Mother Davis," he shouted across the field, for his wife's time had come.

Two families waited in anticipation as twin cousins were born, and the autobiography of this poor-boy had just begun. We were twin cousins, for we shared our birthday, but I had the birthmark.

The Mark

—1:25 a.m. 19 March 1956
    across from Cedar Grove Church

Standing behind the midwife,
The ladies inquired
"What is it?"
"Is it a cotton ball?"
"Or a ball of fire?"
"Looks like a radish
to me."
"No, it's a beet,
or maybe—a turning plow."
"I think, no! I'm sure,
it's a mustard seed."
"No! no! Why, anybody
can see it's a fish."
"It's fire!
Or could it be a lion's
mane?"
"No—It's a teardrop,"
Mother whispered,
"That marks my baby boy—
For I wept sorely."

Genealogy

A little bit of Indian,
A little bit of Mexican,
A whole lot of African,
And maybe a little White,
But that's all right,
I'm American anyway.

For me and most of my
Folks are a mix—
Not unlike my native
Land . . .
For wasn't "US" made
From the dust of many
Lots . . .
This melting pot?

Negro Survival Kit . . .

Button Box and a Bible,
Never seen a home in the
'Hood without it!
All we ever had was a
Stitch and a prayer.

On August 9, 1941, World War II was in full swing overseas. As a tactical ploy, the War Department, with the approval of Congress, opened Red River Army Depot. It was carved out of 116 family farms and ranches covering more than 19,000 acres between the Red and Sulphur Rivers, and cotton-picking days were over in Bowie County.

Activating the Depot created a wave of people fleeing the river bottoms and backwoods some five-and-a-half miles north of Hooks, Texas, to go to work at the plant. People moved off the bottoms, to "up on the road," closer to their jobs. Thus, Cedar Grove was born, mushrooming out of the old Burns settlement into a "boom town" community, the product of wartime prosperity.

Our Town

The world didn't revolve
Around Cedar Grove,
But our lives did.
For this was our nest,
Our niche in the universe.
Yet, less than a neutron—
In an atom—in a molecule
Of dust—in eternity.

Cotton educated me; I picked it only one day, and I knew there had to be a better way to make a living. When I grew up, cotton farming was just about over, though the tales and lore surrounding it were far from over. In fact, they had just begun.

Hybrid Cotton
on the
Red River Bottoms

Raising cotton on the Red
River bottom had been
Revolutionized,
Sharecropping on the thirds
With a hybrid seed.
"Color-coded cotton," folks
Were saying. "Well, what will
They think of next?"

Coded cotton to make the
Tallying easier.
'Cause 2/3 was regular white
Seed cotton,
And 1/3 was hybrid, *Brown*
Seed Cotton.
At harvest time, all the white
Cotton would go to the Anglo,
And all the brown cotton to the
Negro . . .

Though at harvest time,
The WHOLE crop—
Was "NEGRO COTTON ! ! !"
Great googly-goggly!
M-E-R-C-Y! And mo' mercy!
Mercy—mercyyy—mercyyyy!!!
There was pandemonium in the
Camp.
"A deal is a deal is a deal,"
Some folks were saying.
'Cause nobody knew, but they
Sure found out,
Though much too late,
That hybrid cotton—would
Cross-pollinate!

So, folks that thought they
were raising cotton were
Actually *Raising Cain.*
Though when everybody cooled
Off and settled down.
The cotton was split the way
It was supposed to be.

But! *The Man Upstairs* knows
There ain't never, ever, been
A single grain of that *dominant,*
Brown Seed Cotton in them bottoms
Since—
"Not nar" seed.
'Cause the boss man said
While speaking straight and on
The level,
"Ain't gone be no mo'
Brown Seed Cotton—EVER!"

When I was growing up in Cedar Grove, I had a stable full of horses: a black stallion, an appaloosa, a palomino, a Shetland pony, a quarter horse, and a pinto. O-h-h-h, I had a fine mess of horses, stick horses, that is. Growing up in Cedar Grove, we were no worse or any better off than most folks. Like most kids, we only got toys at Christmas time. And kids being kids, the toys didn't last long, usually 'til about January, especially if they were battery operated. So the rest of the year, we used our imagination or played games that were passed down from generation to generation.

Under the Post Oak

". . . 98. 99. 100. Ready or not.
Here I come."
Playing tag, hide and go seek,
From morning 'til evening and
Into the night, where we'd play
By the glow of the front porch
Light.
"Y'all kids better not play too
Far from the house, in that tall
Grass," Mother would say.
"Better stay up here by the house,

'Round this light.
Lord knows y'all kids gon' get bit
By a snake, way y'all out there
In the dark a-rippin' and runnin.'"

"All right! Y'all gon' get bit by
a snake," Mama was forever saying.
"Ahh, let the kids play.
Snakes won't bite this month,"
Papa would often say.
"They won't bite this month, but
They will sure as heck bite you,"
Mother always replied.
Papa gave his routine chuckle,
And we'd play on.

Tired of tag, caught lighting bugs
A while.
They were so intriguing to our
Eager minds, and even more
Fascinating was the fun derived
From nabbing them.
For they'd light here, then
Disappear.
Light up over there, then vanish
In thin air.
Here he is . . .
      No! There he is . . .
          No! Here he is . . .
Could be heard throughout the
Neighborhood as our voices echoed
In the air of a dewy night.
We'd eventually catch a few
Put 'em in a fruit jar,
Oooh and ahhh, then let 'em go.

If nothing else to do, we'd go
Crazy counting stars.
Rarely getting past a half
Dozen or so.
Getting all mixed up and
Having to start over again,
And again, and again,
'Til, alas, we thought it wise
To leave the stars to another
Night.

When the dew grew thicker, our
Eyes grew weary.
And time had come to depart our
Play,
To rest from our travail.
Then, as always, at going home
Time, the *"Boogie-Man's"* name
Would somehow surface out of the
Dark and dewy atmosphere.
Of course, not a soul would dare
Concede to even the slightest
Notion of fear.
But just to be on the safe side,
We'd walk our playmate-cousins
Half way home.

And as we walked, we'd reminisce
Of the fun we had and the games
We played . . .
At the *great divide* we said our
Good-byes, and sprinted our half
Back home.
Upon our return we were worn out,
Utterly exhausted.

For it had been another fruitful
Summer's day.

And as we'd drag into the house
The old screen door would screech,
Then flop behind us.
"Wash your feet, say your prayers,
And go to bed," Mother would say.
. . . And tomorrow was another day,
Under the post oak.

P.S. Yes, we'd go *"grit and all."*

How You Can See Forever

When I was just a boy,
We'd set out at night.
Papa'd smoke a pipe,
And I would gaze the stars,
Flirting with the stars,
The Milky Way, and all the
Rest,
Billions of brilliant
Glittering grains of sand . . .

Celestial bodies times
Infinity,
Where the face of God
Prevails.
Where man beholds the
Universe and loses sight
Of self . . .

Even today, years and years
Hence,
Whenever I get the chance to
Pause and take a break,
On a calm and clear night,
I stop, behold the stars,
And see forever . . .

Chicken Snake

I chased that chicken
Snake from the hen house
To the plum thicket
A many a times,
Where Papa would say,
"Let 'im go boy.
He'll Swallow the wrong thing
One of these days."
And one day he did.
It was that ole white
Porcelain doorknob
That Grandpa gave to Papa
After Grandma died.
Ole bogus egg is all it was.
Of course we weren't the
Only ones to use 'em.
Everybody had 'em.
Some folk were even well
Off enough to afford the
Real McCoy, a glass egg.

When an ole snake would
Finally take the bait,
It was always my job to

Get a grubbing hoe and cut
The doorknob out,
So we could use it again.
And as a child it *never*
Ceased to amaze me,
How it was so, that the
Preacher was always talking
About the serpent—and how
Shrewd and subtle he was.
How he was so crafty and
Cunning, that he beguiled
Eve.
As a child, I just couldn't
See! The ole serpent being
That smart—
"A slickster at his job."
And didn't know an egg
From a doorknob.

Work wasn't all we did in Cedar Grove, but we did a lot of it. I wasn't a child prodigy or anything, but at the tender age of ten, I earned my Ph.D. (post hole digging). Work was usually a group activity, whether it was milking, canning, washing, plowing the fields, or digging post holes. If we were too young to carry weight on the main chores, we had to carry water to those who could, 'cause living under Papa's roof, the rule was, "if you could walk you could work."

Male Bovine

Anything fun—
Like playing dominoes
And checkers,
Will send you straight
To hell.
That's what we were told.
Ohhh but hard labor
Is good for a growing
Boy!
Pulling up bitter weeds
By the roots,
Digging post holes,
And planting 'taters . . .
The Farmer in the sky
Will bless you—
By-n-by.

The church has been the center of the Black community since slavery. And the most well thought of people in the community were church-goers. But no matter how good you were or how well you had done, there were certain rules in the church you didn't break. If you did, sooner or later, you had to pay.

Church Do's

They buried Widow Thompson
Last Saturday forty years
Ago.
But I guess folk never will
Forget the eulogy Reverend Rivers
Gave.

Folk still *talkin' 'bout* how
He praised that woman something
Fierce.
He told how good a woman she
Was—at church every Sunday!
Never missed a day unless she
Was some powerfully sick.

He talked about the savor of her
Blueberry cobbler, and her sweet
Potato pie.
And u-m-m-m them golden nuggets
Of chicken—
On Sunday she'd always fry,
That made your mouth water,
And was tempting to the eye.
Ohhh, he praised how she raised
All her children,
Being a mama and a papa, after
Her husband's untimely demise.

Oh he so eloquently expounded
On the nature of her virtues,
Articulating the very essence of
Her charming personality.
With lavish praise, he went on
And on and on . . .
Finally concluding that she
Was just an all 'round good
Woman!
One we could pattern ourselves
After.
For she'd lived a life worth
Emulating . . .
Except! Her Church dues wasn't
Paid!!!

Lord have mercy!
Some forty years ago and folk
Ain't never, ever, never,
Forgot that eulogy.

So the rankest back-sliders
And the best of saints,
Are mindful of this—
That if you don't want your mama,
Papa, brother, sister, aunts, uncles,
And that *"Host of nieces and
Nephews"*
Embarrassed something bad,
You had better ante-up!
'Cause you can be *Prayed Up*
All you want to,
But if you ain't *Paid up,*
The preacher's gonna talk.

So the church do's are on
This wise.
As far as attending church,
You can go or you cannot.
But one thing you do—
Is pay your dues.

Music and song acted as a solace, an outlet for the stress and pain of everyday life. The long meter sung in the Black churches gave it a soul and rhythm effect unique to its culture. The long meter also tends to be melancholy, having a blues effect. The sad melancholy sounds heard in the fields, at home, and at church, allowed folks to experience an outpouring of emotions without an impeachment of their dignity, because they were singing and mourning to their God. When they really had the blues, they'd only moan. 'Cause the old folks said, "When you moaned, the devil didn't know what you were talking about."

"R & B"

Rhythm and Blues is what
The old folks used,
When good times were hard
To find.

'Cause from time to time
Ole trouble would come
Their way.
They'd go down to the
River.
And in that red sandy clay,
They'd bend their knees
And stay all day.

The Master always answered.
Though in answering—
He'd sometimes pull the
Thorn that pricked their
Side.

Other times the thorn was
Left to fester.
And he'd fix what was wrong
By sending a melody and a
Song.
And that's why my people
Sing the blues.

So make no mistake . . .
Don't even hesitate.
When you see a brother
Singing the blues,
He's a blessing in disguise.

'Cause he's singing . . .
To keep from having runny eyes.

Tales were told everywhere. But the best tale-telling seemed to be at large gatherings which fostered an atmosphere for stories. Many tales surrounded Cedar Grove, but some of the most intriguing, mysterious, and entertaining were about dead folks, spirits, and ha'nts. And here is a tale told for truth.

The Biggest Tale Ever Told

The biggest tale ever told 'round
Cedar Grove
Was when the mortal dead came to
Life.

"They say." The preacher was so
Reverently reading The Consecrated
Scripture,
While friends and family viewed
The body.

The body was lying as usual,
Parallel, separating the preacher
And the pulpit from the rest of
The congregation.

When all of a sudden, the body
Arose. "What all y'all looking
At me for?" he asked.
Talk 'bout a congregation
Dispersing!

"Aunt Heggie's chullun" tore that
Church house up!
Folk were ripping and tearing,
Pawing and clawing,
Climbing over and under pews . . .
Pushing and shoving, shirking
And jerking.
Oh, it was an awesome mess,
'Cause they did some powerful
Carrying on!

Folk were rushing the front
Entrance of the church like a
Defensive line on the gridiron.
They flat turned—church—
Outtt!!!
Leaving none in the building
'Cept the preacher and the corpse.

The preacher was looking at the
Body that was looking at him.
Preacher glanced over his right
Shoulder, turned his head slowly
And peered over his left.
Then turned back, looked at the
Corpse and said,

"What the hell kind of carpenter
Would build a church house
Wit' out a back door!"

Washday at Cedar Grove. (Courtesy of Clyde Daniels)

Mance Lipscomb. (Courtesy, Ed Badeaux, Houston, Texas)

Mance Lipscomb: Fight, Flight, or the Blues

By Glen Alyn

In 1895, on April 9—about the time when Texas rivers are swelling up with rain and the creek bottoms are rising, getting washed clean of winter debris and bringing down a whole new set of branches, topsoil, leaves, earthworms, and all manner of aquamarine mysteries fish love to feast on—a little baby boy began to cry for the first time outside his mama's womb, staring into a hung-together sharecropper's shack not far from the north bank of the "Navasot" River in Brazos County, Texas. His mama and papa named him Beau D. Glen Lipscomb, and he became known as "Mance."

As little Bodyglin grew up in these parts and through a set of names that included Crackshot and Mance, he would come to know this section of Texas ninety miles northwest of Houston, 120 miles east of Austin, and thirty miles south of Texas A&M University as his "precinct." Before his Go-along would end on January 30, 1976, Mance Lipscomb would become the ace gittah player in his precinct. He would cast a net of music on dancers in this three-county area, and the net would spread out into the USA in the 1960s to include white fans of the Vietnam era and the Flower Generation, then flow over the world through the ears and fingers of musicians who recognized, appreciated, and attempted to emulate his mastery of the guitar and the blues genre.

Mance's reputation would ebb and flow in the undercurrents of the media and in people's hearts, til it weaved its way back to his father's homeland, where the colorful ghost of Mance Lipscomb would appear on a "History of the Blues" postage stamp series in Gambia, West Africa, around what would have been Mance's ninety-eighth birthday in 1993. That was a few months before his life story, in his own words, would be published by W. W. Norton, and go on to win the highest national award for a music book, plus some others. A month after his hundredth birthday, Da Capo Press's paperback release of *I Say Me For a Parable* joined international ranks with the vinyl records and CDs of Chris Strachwitz's Arhoolie Records (whose first release was Mance Lipscomb's first album), the award-winning Les Blank documentary entitled "A Well-Spent Life," and subsequent video, film, and audio releases by others. Begun by an African-American fiddling father and a half-Choctaw Indian mother who could dance while balancing big baskets on her head, Mance Lipscomb's River of Time flows on long after his death.

Mance's papa Charles was a slave in Alabama, likely coming from the same West African Voodoo tribes that came to populate Haiti. At age eight, Charles, his papa and his siblings were sold and made their way on a steamboat or overland to New Orleans, where they were put on a slave ship to Galveston. Mama was left behind somewhere, sold or had died. Sold on the block to the Lipscomb family, they were brought up to Hempstead in a wagon and lodged on the family plantation, where they were rechristened the Lipscomb family—like all the other slaves on the Lipscomb plantation.

Some time after the Civil War, little Charlie took up the fiddle, meandered north ten miles up to Navasota, and became the ace fiddler in the precinct, playing the Saturday Night Barn Dances and Reels of the Reconstruction and pre-World War I era. Intoned by the blue notes of the African tradition, on a non-fretted instrument that could escape the European twelve-tone scales, many of Charlie Lipscomb's tunes were nevertheless structured European folk melodies. Charlie's fiddling ac-

companied dance steps resembling the reels and square dances preserved today by white country-western dancers. These dance steps
shuffled alongside more African-based dances like "Breaking the
Chicken's Neck" and the "Shimmy-She-Wobble."

Charlie passed his fiddling talent on to his son, and Mance was
around twelve when he got his first guitar. Papa Charlie quickly taught
young Mance how to play bass behind him, following up with basic
chords so he could stand on a soapbox and back his papa on Saturday
nights. On the other genetic hand, Mama Janie Pratt didn't play an
instrument, but she was a gospel songster and a half-Choctaw, who remembered at least enough of her native tongue to scream it out whenever she was angry. She frightened Mance into never learning a word of
it because he only heard it when his mama was likely to flail into him.
She and the church provided Mance the gospel music and songster influence.

By "songster," Mance meant a person with a big stout voice, some-
one who could be heard for a mile or two when they sang field shouts
across the turnrows, someone who relied on their voice more than the
instrument they played as their primary instrument of communication.
Mance Lipscomb referred to all these people as "songsters"—Mama
Janie Pratt who sang gospel songs in church in a big loud voice;
Peckerwood who sang field shouts heard from two miles away; Blind
Lemon Jefferson, Taj Mahal, Lightnin' Hopkins, BB King, his sister Annie
Lipscomb, Mahalia Jackson, Aretha Franklin, Janis Joplin, Muddy
Waters, and Howlin' Wolf—all folks with big loud throats. Mance never
referred to the following people as "songsters," but he did call them all
"clair pickas" (clear pickers): Mississippi John Hurt, Mississippi Fred
McDowell, Buddy Guy, Elizabeth Cotten, and Mance Lipscomb.

Besides singing gospel songs, Mama Janie was quite a dancer. She
could even balance big baskets or buckets atop her head, leaving her
hands free to sway with her body and express other rhythms, while the
white audience requesting her to do her "basket trick" would throw
pennies and nickels at her. She often made more money accepting such
requests than the fifty cents a day she might earn for doing the white
folks' laundry. Mance may well have come to understand the relation-

ship of the dance to the music through his mother. Whatever the origin, Mance shared this in common with flamenco guitarists: They watch their dancers, and everything they do is for the expression of the dance rather than the attention of the soloist. Mance played all night long for the Saturday Night Suppers, often from eight or so at night until after church was out on Sunday around noon. He was the undisputed ace man in his precinct for nearly forty years. Had he not understood and prioritized this relationship of the music being for the spirit of the dance, even his musical prowess and varied repertoire may not have allowed him such longevity.

Then there was working from "Caint ta Caint," the field shouts and hollers that may have started before the sun came up, and the field songs like "Hannah, hurry up an go on down" that were sung to lose the hours and fall into the rhythms of the day and the seasons. Until the tractor replaced mule plows in the 1950s, these songs influenced Southern African-Americans and anyone else around who happened to hear them.

These field shouts, call and response or no, were a keynote in Mance's musical upbringing. He heard them for sixty years, while he and his family worked the fields and the turnrows with mules, plows, cultivators, traces, singletrees, hoes, shovels, and cottonsacks through four generations.

Prison songs were a variation of these work songs, with themes more focused on oppression and incarceration than the songs of their origins—songs intended to establish work rhythms, rapport between man and beast, and some degree of satisfaction of one's relationship to work rather than antagonism toward it. When Mance was just beginning to handle his own plow and mule, an ex-convict worked long enough for Mama Janie for Mance to remember the prison song "Captain, Captain": "Well I asked my Captain, 'What time a day?' He jest lookt at his watch man, an he walked away. Wouldn mind workin, Captain, from sun ta sun. Ef you'd pay me my money, Captain, when payday come."

Mance, sometimes called "Crackshot," got his first glimpse of a guitar and earful of Devil Music from an African-American spectre named

Sam Collins, an embodiment of the strange meeting of two worlds whose facial features looked and voice talked like a black man, but who carried the white skin and red hair of an Irishman. Too scared to give away his position, Crackshot climbed through the ten-foot-high cotton stalks around Sam's shack in the after-work darkness and drank in the only guitar Mance saw or heard for years. Collins sat on his front porch, waiting for the evening breezes and playing a song called "Sugar Babe" enough so when Mance finally got his own guitar, it was the first song he learned on it.

Mance behaved similarly when he hid in the fields, crawling up as close as he could to the shacks of the Mexican migrant workers who had fled the fields of Pancho Villa's and Zapata's rebellions during what folks north of the Rio Grande called "the World War I Era," while down South the tongue spoke "El Tiempo de la Cucaracha." Mance carried back a lovely little waltz melody singing in his ears, set it to the Saturday Night Dance tempos and called it "Spanish Flang Dang." (For years before and after, over a dozen melodic versions were played in white folks' parlors throughout the South on pianos, banjos, and even string quartets.) And still Edison's Victrolas had not filtered into Mance's precinct.

Along about then, a blind man started stepping off the train on occasion in Navasota. He brought someone to help him down the busy streets, a guitar in a rough open tuning, a tin cup, and a bottleneck. He'd stand across the street from the bank, and belt out gospel-influenced songs to the other-worldly slicing echo accompaniment of his slide guitar. His name was Blind Willie Johnson. Mance had learned his second song by then, a nineteenth-century fiddle tune called "Take Me Back" taught him by Papa Charlie. Johnson soon found that Mance had a finer-tuned ear, so he'd ask Mance to tune his guitar for him whenever he came to Navasota. Mance would inch up through the crowd, tune up Johnson's guitar, and then scoot back and blend into the crowd like a cockroach. He soaked up that sound, learned Johnson's "Mother Had a Sick Child" and "God Moves on the Water (the Titanic)," and used a pocket knife and open tunings to develop other spirituals like "When Your Lamps Burn Out" and "Motherless Chillun Sees a Hawd Time When Their Mother is Dead."

By 1917, Mance had been bassing and chording behind his papa's fiddling for around ten years. Playing first for his peers at the children's and teen-agers' "Ring Dances" and such, Mance was steadily gaining a local reputation. He would soon fill his father's shoes as the second generation Lipscomb who was "the ace musician in the precinct." Married for four years, with one son, Mance had become a family man. The field work with its accompanying songs and rhythms continued along with what was becoming known as the Saturday Night Dances or "Satiddy Nite Suppas." Because the cotton got flooded out three out of four years from 1917 to 1921, Mance went north to his cousin Son Pratt's place south of Dallas near Waxahachie—before the cotton would have popped full open in Navasota—to earn some spending money. He and his cousin took the Inter-Urban Trolley and headed into Dallas to hear a big loud songster name of Blind Lemon Jefferson sing and play under a big live oak tree next to the railroad tracks in the Deep Ellum section of Dallas.

Jefferson was one of the early blues innovators. Later, through the development and distribution of Okeh and other race records, he would influence generations of first black and later white blues players. But Mance heard him first live and in the flesh. While that big black man sang and pounded away on his guitar, intimidating everyone he could with his booming voice and stunning guitar solos that went on for as many measures as Lemon thought he could have his way with, Mance creeped to the back of the crowd, drinking it all in right through his ears. He came away with "Out an Down," "See ta My Grave Kep Clean," and a wealth of solo guitar techniques he later incorporated into his steady dance-style blues. Sure enough, Lemon never knew somewhere in the back of the crowd stood a genius musician that could hear a song one to four times and go home and sing all the verses and play nearly every note. After 1921, Lemon was gone to Chicago, where after a few years of fame he froze to death alone on one of its streets.

Then there were the kids' games such as "Putting Them in the Dozens." "Yo Mama wears combat boots" was borrowed from that tradition. A technique used to test one's toleration for temper, it was a child's game and a survival game rolled into one. When the Bossman upbraided you, called you names and insulted your family, the best response wasn't to defend your honor. That could lead to death. So the Dozens was one way to learn how to take it. Although "Soap and Water Keep Yo Body Clean" is about the only song in this genre that survived in Mance's later recorded repertoire, he undoubtedly sang a few more in his teens and twenties.

Before the Edison cup records began to be discarded by Navasota whites in favor of the crank-up 78 rpm Victrolas, and so handed down to African-Americans along with the first worn out Model A and Model T Fords some time after World War I, two vaudeville musicians of note brought songs to Mance from other parts of the South. Native Navasotans, Richard Dean and Hamp Walker joined the Barnum and Bailey Circuses as barkers and tent teasers. For years, Dean and Walker would stump the South for six months, playing circuses and black vaude-ville, entertaining blacks and whites alike in places for the most part where they were allowed to play and dance but not urinate, and then return home for six months during the winter and spring off-season.

Maybe it was somewhere around Mance's late teens when he sat around a woodburning stove one winter, pleading with Dean and Walker to learn him the runs and structure of "She Flagged a Mule to Ride," "You Gonna Quit Me Baby," and "Shorty George." But learn them he did, and he never forgot the songs or their teachers.

Mance was fourth in the line of eleven children, all of whom had one musical ability or another. Charlie was four years older and Ralph two years older than Mance. They both preceded Mance as guitar play-ers, but once he got his own guitar in his hands, Mance took only a couple years to "pass them like a paycar passin a tramp."

Though phonographs appeared at the turn of the century and be-came very popular by the end of World War I, they didn't have an impact on Navasota's African-American community until the late 1920s, when "race records" filtered a whole new world of music through dog-eared Victrolas handed down to one house or another into the African-American sections of Navasota. Mance's favorites from the miracle of 78 revolutions per minute were Memphis Minnie and Bessie Smith, fol-lowed by Blind Blake and Clarence "Pinetop" Smith, and no doubt recordings of a man he'd previously heard in Dallas—Blind Lemon Jefferson. Mance added to his repertoire "Bumble Bee," "I Wanta Do Sumpm For You," "Careless Love," "Keep on Truckin," and numerous others. Victrolas and radio had commercialized the Blues. But long before that, the Blues had spread like rain throughout the South. It permeated because it was the voice of a people. It was theirs, and they knew it. It spoke of and to their lives and experiences. It was part of what Mance came to call his Life Story Songs and True Story Songs.

By the Depression, recorded music had developed into an organized, highly profitable industry with the promise of making and influencing millions. The role of the local musician changed as the domination of the music industry increased. Meanwhile, Isom Willis, Mance Lipscomb, his nephew T Lipscomb (A. C. Sims) and others like them continued to play the Saturday Night Suppers. Some of them survived into the juke joint era of the 1950s. But at least through the 1930s, their music was left essentially free to develop and be liked or disliked according to the preferences and tastes of the local musicians and populations of each independent community. By the 1950s, music had become a horse of a different color.

Prior to then, the blending of extemporaneous traditions of African music, Native American musical traditions absorbed by intermarriage and interbreeding of Africans and Native Americans, and structured European musical forms created the genre we now call the Blues. The west African griots and the Africans who developed the intuitive tradition of singing to their mules in the fields as a way of creating synchronous rhythms and more productivity. The couplet-like call and response tradition of Negro gospel songs and work songs. The prison songs that were a variation of field shouts and work songs. Native American rhythms, melodies, and vocal blendings of sounds of the natural world brought forth by people like Mance's half-Choctaw Indian mother. The European/Appalachian melodies and structures played at the Saturday Night Barn Dances. The black vaudeville songs created by African-Americans and transported on trains and carnival tents throughout the South. The formal musical training of African-American and mixed blood musicians in New Orleans and Memphis, such as W. C.

Handy and Jellyroll Morton. All of these musical influences mixed together in a backdrop of backwater rural cultures throughout the South.

And somewhere between 1870 and 1910, the Blues was born. I believe different variations of it were created nearly simultaneously in
several parts of the South, including the Mississippi Delta, the Texas
Bottoms, and the Carolinas. The black vaudeville musicians may have
had a hand in spreading musical ideas and letting this newly created
tradition fall back on itself, but over a relatively short period—considering the relative isolation of a myriad of plantation cultures—the Blues
came into being. It was this musical blending of world cultures, sexual
candor, and using authentic life experiences as the subject for themes
and stories in its songs, that give the Blues vitality and universal appeal
to this day. Who really knows for sure? All of the people who created
the Blues are long dead, and most of them were not able to write their
version of reality anyway. The roots of these answers lie in the realm of
oral history.

Mance's early brush with near-fame came in the 1930s, after Jimmie
Rodgers had already moved to Kerrville, attempting to recover from
tuberculosis. His performance in the bustling town of Navasota was
limited to twenty minutes. He needed someone to open and carry the
shows for him, and he had somehow gotten wind of Mance's reputation
and heard him play. Rodgers asked Mance to tour with him. Perhaps
due to Mance's commitment to being a family man, maybe from Richard
Dean's and Hamp Walker's tales of the delights of being on the road in
the midst of a bigoted society, or the spectre of a waning musical star
dying from tuberculosis, Mance declined the offer.

But the first white man to discover Mance's extraordinary character was, of all people, the legendary Texas Ranger Frank Hamer. Hamer
became the Town Marshall of Navasota on December 3, 1908, shortly
after the lynching of John Campbell for allegedly slitting a white man's
throat after that man threatened him with an axe handle inside a general store. Mance was just beginning to learn guitar then, so it wasn't
his musical prowess that caused Hamer to decide that little Crackshot
would become his guide in the Navasota precinct. For three years
"Mance's hands didn't fit no plow handles" while Mance would open

the back gates and show him around the plantations on the sly. According to Mance, Hamer was a formidable lawman and an exceptional storyteller. Somewhere on the buggy rides between town and plantation, Hamer told Mance many a story about his growing up days out in West Texas, with a fair sprinkling of Pecos Bill tales thrown in as God's Truth as sure as only a Texan can tell it.

With mentors like Frank Hamer, Mance's papa, and an oral storytelling tradition stretching back to the Anansis in Africa, Mance carried on the tradition of masterful storytelling as well as developing his mastery of the blues guitar. The Anansis ended up in Cherokee country. In the eighteenth century that was still the Carolinas and Georgia. Threatened with torture or death if they spoke their native language, escaping slaves mixed with the Cherokees and blended their creation tales with them, transforming their spiders who wove masterful tales into pesky jabbering rabbits while they transformed their tribal name into "Aunt Nancy stories." No wonder Joel Chandler Harris couldn't understand why Uncle Remus kept attributing his stories to an Aunt Nancy who was never around to tell them herself!

In Mance Lipscomb's amazingly broad 350-song repertoire, over a hundred of which were recorded, he personified the Texas version of the masterful blending of these musical traditions, cast together from a wealth of African tribes and European nations, clans and tribes clashing in a system of agriculture subjugating a newly-acquired land brutally wrested from its native inhabitants—agriculture based on a rural focus and an economic system supported by the institution of slavery, and the variations that came after it through the use of African-American, Irish, Mexican, or other immigrant labor. In Texas, the Hispanic element colored the development of Texas blues as early as the 1820s.

Field shouts, fiddle reels, gospel songs, children's songs, coupled epithets called the Dozens, work songs, mule songs, vaudeville songs and presentations, storytelling and hoorawing, patriotic World War I and other Anglo songs, Mexican tunes, and even the recording artists of the race record era—Mance brought them all to the Saturday Night Suppers inside his guitar, fingers and memory. It was there he blended them with the strutting feet and undulating bodies of the dancers to produce a style that is distinctly Mance Lipscomb's delivery of the blues genre.

The women commenced cooking on Friday evening, all the way into Saturday night. Sweet potato pie, black-eyed peas, fried okra, fried chicken. A whole hog parboiled and barbecued. Cornbread, sweetbread, cakes, candy, apples and oranges. Rabbit, possum, armadillo. Cushaw melons and watermelon. Homegrown tomatoes and collard greens. Three-day beer, moonshine, soda water. Not all of it at every Supper, but all of it at one Supper or another as the seasons passed into years. Whatever they had, they brought it to the Supper, and ate it and drank it till it was all gone.

And Mance played while they ate, drank, danced, strutted their stuff, gossiped, gambled, hoorawed, caroused, fought, and loved. When Mance arrived a little before sundown, the food would already be laid out on tables near the door. He'd go inside and set up by the window with the stiffest breeze. Then the crowds would begin to pour in, walking and riding to the one social function African-Americans had created for themselves to end a week of working from Caint ta Caint. Women and children would generally stay inside, where the music, dancing and gossip would carry on. The biggest room would be emptied of any furniture, while another room might have every spare bed crammed into it for those who needed a nap before daybreak or the brazen rock and rollers of the supine variety. But no farmer's shack could hold the hundreds who would gather for these weekly affairs. If there was no gambling shack, men would spread quilts out in the yard, dealing their cards and piling their money high enough for Mance to gaze out the window at it as he sat shirtless trying to catch a cooling breeze. The men would filter in and out between the dance room, the supper tables, the rings of "man talks" and the gambling games, sometimes meandering into the woods for their fair share of moonshine or homebrew after the three-day beer tops had been popped and sailed over the roof.

The food was usually gone by midnight, but the dancing, gambling and other activity would carry into daybreak and on past church time. Mance played and sang through all of it, taking a break now and then to eat a bite or relieve himself, flirt and jive, and stay on until two in the afternoon if the gamblers were still tipping him good. Mance's pocket-knife slide version of "Jack a Diamonds is a Hawd Cawd ta Play" (recorded by Blind Lemon Jefferson in 1926) came in handy on such occasions. As all of the food, money, and energy were spent, folks would drift back home and many would make it to church. Then, Mance would collect up to a dollar and a half for his efforts. No wonder Elnora put on her own Suppers with her own man during the 1920s and 1930s. She upped their profits.

White folks soon asked Mance to play their Friday night dances. These would only last till twelve or one o'clock, and Mance would make up to seven dollars a night. With an unmistakeable blues flair, he added white folks' songs to his repertoire: "Are You From Dixie?," "Shine on Harvest Moon," "You Are My Sunshine," "It's a Long Way to Temporary (Tipperari)," "Over the Waves," and the crossover minstrel song "Alabama Jubilee."

By the 1930s in Navasota, radio had made its way into some African-American homes, but it was still more of an exotic item than a commonplace one. Mance recollects the voice, humor and songs of Woody Guthrie, and a few of the dramatic programs. Otherwise, he mentions nothing that caught his attention on the radio waves. After all, it was a media geared almost entirely for white audiences.

With the abolition of Prohibition, juke joints began to appear on Mance's landscape in the 1930s and 1940s. One day during World War II Mance heard Big Bill Broonzy's "Key to the Highway," relating to it so that he put an extra nickel into the jukebox to learn it. Just as the nineteenth century reels and barn dances of Papa Charlie Lipscomb's era gave way and turned into the Saturday Night Suppers and Saturday Night Dances of Mance's four-decade span of around 1910 to 1950, so did the Suppers give way to the juke joints of the Depression era. As Prohibition ended in 1933, legalized liquor sales and a rapidly organized music industry formulated the rise of the jukebox, across-the-counter liquor joints, the country versions of the bars and saloons of the Old West and the barrelhouses of the East Texas oil boom era. As the noise and mechanical horsepower of tractors eclipsed mules and withered the spirit of the field song in the 1950s, the juke joints siphoned off the economic plunder of the Saturday Night Suppers from the communities who created them to corporate holdings somewhere in big cities never seen by those who bought the liquor and slid their nickels into the jukeboxes.

The new noises gradually crept into Mance's environment, but never totally overtook it. Radio, more automobiles, and the strident calls for attention and self indulgence from the cities crowded into Mance's audio environment as World War II came and went. The need for amplification began to impose itself on the rural environment.

In 1949, Mance picked up his first electric guitar and amplifier, and soon carried them into Nolan's new juke joint and dance hall across from Sammy Keys' BBQ shack in Washington County, and elsewhere. He was playing it when Mack McCormick and Chris Strachwitz walked up to his front porch by the West End Grocery in 1960, and handed him Chris's Harmony Sovereign acoustic guitar. White audiences wanted their folk singers to play "the old way," and so Mance obliged them by flawlessly performing over two albums of material that night on a guitar his fingers had never touched before. After his wildly successful first appearance at the 1961 Berkeley Folk Festival, the electric guitar stayed in Mance's closet, reserved for local appearances for his home folk around Navasota. In the 1950s, the sounds of tractors and the insistence by white landowners to modernize and so become more economically dependent on industrialized machinery and agricultural poisons finally stamped out the sounds of the work songs. By 1960, except for prison farms, the field song that helped spawn the Blues was gone forever from the rural American landscape.

I have often wondered why the Blues has had such a recurring universal appeal. Perhaps the attraction transcends the musical forms inside which its themes are expressed. When threatened, the natural instincts of all animals—*homo sapiens* included—cause them to flee or prepare to fight. Yet neither option was available to African-Americans. If they fought, they would be publicly flogged or killed. If they ran away, they were usually tracked down with dogs and vigilantes, beaten, whipped, and brought back. The blues may be the expression of a third response when fight and flight are denied. The Bible—a document

African-Americans wove their native religions around, embraced to a degree but never allowed its Anglicized interpretations to entirely dominate their spiritual expression—may have given them some inspiration. Over the centuries, Jesus Christ's intonement to "turn the other cheek" when struck by one's enemy has received a host of conflicting interpretations. What if Christ's words, rather than being paraphrased in football lingo as something like "Hit me again! Hit me again! But harder! Harder!," was instead a suggestion to look for a third response, a more spiritually mature response of moving through the experience rather than stamping it out or running away from it? Wouldn't it be a whimsical paradox if somehow all this "Devil Music" came into existence as a means to express the finer harmonics and dissonances of the soul trapped for a time in its human existence? As a way to accept and incorporate daily experience rather than denying it in favor of some never seen Beyond, where "Don't Worry—Be Happy" makes perfect sense?

Speaking of devils and Mojo Hands, Mance first met Lightnin' Hopkins in Galveston in 1938, while visiting his twin brother and sister, Coon and Pie Lipscomb. Born in Centerville some ninety miles due north of Navasota, young Sam Hopkins picked up the guitar not too long after he watched one of his cousins drown in a stock tank. By his twenties, he drifted south to Conroe forty miles or so due east of Navasota, and so skirted the boundaries of Mance's precinct. The barrelhouses and clubs of Galveston and Houston called Lightnin' further south. This rapidly developing urban environment was where Sam Lightnin' Hopkins formed his "precinct" as defined by how far and wide his reputation as a musician and carouser would spread. Mance and Lightnin' had heard of each other's reputations for years, but this was their first encounter. As usual, Mance stood off away from the music, with his ears wide open and acting like he couldn't hit a lick on a guitar. They would meet again in Houston around 1957, shortly after Mance had hightailed it away from a rural existence where he'd only made a profit as a farmer one year in his entire life. Inside the club, some of Mance's fans pleaded with Lightnin' to no avail. Lightnin' wouldn't agree to Mance playing his guitar. Though Mance learned Lightnin's "Mojo Hand" and picked up more than a few of Lightnin's licks through his keen ears, Lightnin' Hopkins wasn't to hear Mance Lipscomb until they shared equal billing at many of the folk and Blues festivals of the 1960s. During filming in the late Sixties of Les Blank's "The Blues Accordin to Lightnin' Hopkins," they brought Mance down to flesh out enough usable footage to finish the film.

Unlike Lightnin', Blind Lemon Jefferson, Robert Johnson, Son House, and scores of blues musicians who forsook family and farm to move to the bright lights and big cities, Mance remained a family man, at one time heading up sixteen family members across four generations. Except for two years in Houston from 1956 to 1958, he always lived within a ten-mile radius of Navasota. Thus, the subject matter and thematic content of his repertoire is distinct from, as well as a part of, those urbanized musicians who were recorded prior to 1960. Mance's followers danced to a different rhythm.

For Mance, Jimmy Reed personified the African-American guitar sound of the 1950s—the hopped up, electrified and simplified rhythms that paved the way for white rock and rollers to embellish their intricate flat-picked electric lead runs over. Rearranging "Rock Me Mama" to a Jimmy Reed style rhythm and renaming it "Rock Me Baby," Mance's hat tipped to Reed essentially marked the end of the development of Mance's repertoire, a song list spanning over a century of American music. By the time Elvis Presley, Jerry Lee Lewis, Conway Twitty, Roy Orbison, Chuck Berry, Fats Domino, the Everly Brothers, and Buddy Holly took over radioland, Mance had sealed off his repertoire that led straight to the development of their music. That is aside from riffs that he might have picked up from other players at shared performances during the sixties and early seventies, for Mance's ears never shut down and his fingers never stopped searching for new places until his final stroke and double pneumonia permanently closed his left hand on January 30, 1974.

How did Mance's reputation spread all the way to New York without the aid of phonograph recordings, radio or tv? The same way it spread to Los Angeles when Mance's brother Ralph (and many of mystery novelist Walter Mosley's characters) moved there during World War II, when prospects for better paying jobs and better treatment were much brighter outside of Navasota. With massive migrations of blacks and whites out of the country and into the cities from World War I through the 1950s, the texture of America's population shifted from mostly rural to predominantly urban. African-American Navasotans pulled up stakes and headed for Houston, Los Angeles, New York, Chicago, and elsewhere. With them went Mance Lipscomb's reputation, spreading across America in pockets of African-American communities.

White folks outside Navasota didn't discover Mance until 1961, when he played at the Berkeley Folk Festival. The way it came about is an apt demonstration of Mance's maxim, "Sometimes when a thang hapm to ya, when it hurtin ya its fur ya." Mance was discovered thanks to Tom Moore, owner of the 20,000-acre prison farm called Allenfarm in Mance's precinct and symbol of all that kept African-Americans "in their place." German folk enthusiast Chris Strachwitz was an avid fan of Lightnin' Hopkins. He traveled from the San Francisco area to Houston in 1960 to record Lightnin' Hopkins, only to find that John Lomax, Jr. had just taken Lightnin' to California for the 1960 Berkeley Blues Festival. Determined not to waste the trip, Strachwitz linked up with Mack McCormick in Houston. They were fond of Lightnin's recording of "Tom Moore's Blues," a field song Mance had set to music one Saturday Night Supper in 1929 right on the Moore Brothers Farm, where he first heard it from Yank Thornton. Why not go to Navasota and see if they could look up the real Tom Moore? From Hempstead, ten miles south of Navasota on, every person they asked, "Do you know any good guitar players around here?" replied, "Mance Lipscomb." Even Tom Moore. That evening, these two white men sat in Mance's house until they'd recorded over two albums worth of material. On the way back to Houston, Strachwitz related his disappointment that they hadn't found a big loud drunk-and-wild blues player like Lightnin'. By comparison, Mance's voice was delicate and his guitar picking far more subtle. More schooled in musicology, McCormick convinced Strachwitz of the unique find they had in Mance because his repertoire was broader than anyone's he'd ever heard recorded. Strachwitz went back to Berkeley and founded Arhoolie Records by issuing Mance Lipscomb's first album. As a result,

Barry Olivier invited Mance to the 1961 Berkeley Folk Festival, Mance took his first train ride from Houston all the way to Berkeley, and gained a national following of adulating white fans just when his music was eclipsing back in Navasota into "old folks' music."

Now that Mance had gleaned and developed from his predecessors a masterful guitar style, it was time for him to give back these roots to a whole new generation longing for something authentic. One of Mance's early (for that era) white fans was Frank Sinatra. Mance was one of the first artists recorded on Sinatra's new Reprise label handed him by Warner Brothers. Released in 1961, the title track "Trouble in Mind" also happened to get recorded by Frank Sinatra. Mance had fond memories of serenading Sinatra and whomever his lover was at the time on Frank's yacht. For two or three days, Mance ate more kinds of food over seawater than he'd imagined was fixable.

Bob Dylan and Joan Baez followed Mance around in the early sixties. Mance's first album is prominently displayed on a photo on the back of one of Dylan's early albums. Dylan reportedly trekked all the way to Navasota to hit a lick with Mance, one of hundreds of would-be guitarists and songwriters who wanted some of the magic Mance offered to rub off on them.

Taj Mahal stayed up nights picking and grinning with Mance. Taj's parents were from the West Indies, his father a drummer and mother a dancer. Though he grew up formally studying jazz in western Massachusetts, Taj had similar roots to Mance's and parents with similar talents. Whenever Mance was near Taj's home in Oakland and Taj wasn't touring, he'd ask Mance over. Taj played for the May 24, 1974, Armadillo World Headquarters Mance Lipscomb Benefit held in Austin.

Heard any movies lately with a soulful bluesy acoustic guitar score? It's likely Ry Cooder. He and Taj played together early on. Ry was another of Mance's students. Cooder came to Austin to the Paramount Theatre in December, 1975, for the last Mance Lipscomb Benefit.

Janis Joplin met up with Mance shortly after her arrival in Austin from Port Arthur, in 1962. He backed her up at one of her early performances at Threadgill's in Austin. When he did, Mance broke the "colored" barrier at this traditionally redneck bar and gas station where

Ken Threadgill often yodelled Jimmie Rodgers tunes and began to let the longhaired student hippies suck longnecks along with the cowboys. Mance and Janis developed a warm friendship. They got together for one last hooraw at the 1970 Threadgill Reunion, about three months before Janis died of a drug overdose.

Mance increasingly went on the road. To the Ash Grove in Los Angeles, to universities and colleges in the Midwest and Texas. He developed a hearty friendship with Mimi and John Lomax, Jr., as early as 1962. Soon, Bonnie Raitt's agent Dick Waterman would begin to book him on the East Coast, and later Sandy Getz would obtain West Coast bookings for him. Traditional Arts Services was created expressly to bring Mance and another traditional African-American blues player to Seattle. But none of these agents were to Mance what Lightnin's agent or Presley's manager were to them. No one really hyped Mance. His reputation simply continued to spread among musicians, among those who heard him at music festivals, among those who bought one after the other of Mance's Reprise release or Arhoolie records—eight albums in all—along with his contributions to anthologies such as Vanguard's "Best of the Country Bluesmen" series. He was not a Michael Jackson kind of media sensation. Mance was just a human being whose music and presence moved people to tears and rejoicing all in one night.

It wasn't until the late sixties that Mance and his wife Elnora placed a television into their house. Elnora soon became fascinated with the soap operas, and you could hear them emanating daily from the tv placed by the woodburning stove on the wall opposite Elnora's easy chair. It must have given her some satisfaction to peek into the lives of white America through what became in two decades its dominant form of mass media entertainment.

On the other hand, Mance had visited Hollywood and seen firsthand how the magical illusions were done behind the scenes. To him, television had no substance and little reality. He remained connected to his direct life experiences, and would often admonish Elnora for believing the characters projecting on the tube were actually in the room while she hollered a warning when one of them was in danger. I suspect even Elnora digested this new-fangled imagery with many a grain of salt.

Meanwhile, Mance was on the road from Miami to Seattle, from Boston to Los Angeles. Sharing folk and blues festivals with Sonny Terry & Brownie McGhee, Robert Shaw, Lightnin' Hopkins, Howlin' Wolf, Muddy Waters, Buddy Guy & Junior Wells, John Lee Hooker, Joseph Cotton, Elizabeth Cotten, Mississippi Fred McDowell, Mississippi John Hurt, Furry Lewis, Freddie King, BB King. Sharing folk festival stages with Pete Seeger, Jean Ritchey, Earl Scruggs, Doc Watson, Ramblin' Jack Elliott, and Arlo Guthrie. Opening concerts for Janis Joplin, the Grateful Dead, Tracy Nelson & Mother Earth.

Tary Owens came with Janis Joplin from Port Arthur to the University of Texas in 1962. He was there when Mance and Janis were first getting together, booked Mance at most of his Austin performances from 1963 to 1967, and followed Janis out to California when she made her move to Haight Ashbury. For a time, he was part of Tracy Nelson's Mother Earth Band, another great female songster influenced by Lipscomb. In 1968, Tary booked Mance to open for the Grateful Dead, with Tary's band to back him up so he could play his electrified songs. The Grateful Dead's soundman refused to change the presettings for the opening act. The first couple songs were a series of screeching feedbacks that would have done Jimi Hendrix and The Who proud. Faced with disaster, Tary and his band left the stage. Mance finished out the set with a pristine solo performance and saved the hour. Tary said Jerry Garcia was significantly influenced by Mance Lipscomb, but it was more Mance's recorded repertoire than any personal interaction with Garcia that impacted his band's music, especially evidenced in "Shake It, Shake It, Sugaree."

When Mance played at the Ash Grove in Los Angeles, he was constantly surprised that they would ask him to stop playing after only a half hour or so. He was just getting warmed up by then. But people in the audience didn't seem to know the difference. Jackson Browne, Mason Williams (author of "Classical Gas" and countless comedies on The Smothers Brothers TV Show), and Frank Reckard (Emmy Lou Harris's lead guitar player for ten years), were awed by Lipscomb. Though relatively unheralded in the press and other media, Mance's influence found its own path into people's hearts.

In 1969, John Lomax, Jr., long active in the Houston Folk Music Society founded by his family's activities, helped fund the shooting of Les Blank and Skip Gerson's film on Mance, entitled *A Well-Spent Life*. John and Mimi had formed a fond and lasting friendship with Mance that lasted from their introduction in 1962 until John's death in 1973. Blank's award-winning film brought Mance wider national and international audiences.

Mance's students and fans kept growing, coming to his performances, while some made the mecca to his front porch in Navasota—so much so that Mance's neighbors nicknamed him "Hippy Man." Few, even his family, comprehended that this frail-looking old black man would slip away in some "furriner's" car or on the bus, play out of town and out of state, and make a worldwide impact on other human beings and the music they listened to. Slip off he did. To the Berkeley Folk and Blues Festivals, Monterey Jazz Festival, countless clubs, colleges and universities, Newport Folk Festival, Miami Blues Festival, Ann Arbor Blues Festival, Eureka Springs Bluegrass Festival. One Dallas native was alerted to a Mance Lipscomb performance when she saw a hand-scrawled garage-sale styled sign stuck in the grass on a suburban street corner. She followed its arrow to a dirt floor garage, where Mance as usual played for hours to whomever could fit behind somebody's house.

Stefan Grossman grew up in New York City into an extraordinary guitarist. His main instructor was the Reverend Gary Davis. He later studied with Mississippi John Hurt, Mance Lipscomb, and others to get at the roots of their complicated acoustic guitar styles and rhythms. Grossman toured Europe and founded the Stefan Grossman Guitar Workshop that distributes Mance Lipscomb videos, CDs, and tablature books along with the same for dozens of other blues and traditional guitarists.

Dick Waterman remembers Mance influencing John Hammond, Paul Jeremiah, and rising Rounder recording artist Paul Rishell. There were dozens of other students whose flame of fame never fully ignited: Mark Spoelstra, Marc Benno, Billy Bean, John Vandiver, Mary Egan, Cleve

Hattersley, Steve Mann, Kurt Van Sickle, Mark Bouliane, Tary Owens, Glen Alyn, and Bruce Willenzik.

Bruce Willenzik was Mance's self-designated chauffeur from 1972 through 1974. On January 30, 1974, Bruce took Mance to a Dallas hospital on the way to Mance's last scheduled gig, at Midwestern University in Wichita Falls. Three weeks later, after Mance had been transferred to Brackenridge Hospital in Austin, Bruce stepped onto the elevator as two fellow longhairs shuffled in behind him. Jimmy Vaughan introduced himself to Bruce, pointed to the shy kid next to him, and told Bruce he was taking his younger brother to see Mance. Bruce said Stevie Ray Vaughan acted toward Mance as if he were an icon. Years later, Bruce's brother Alan met some folks in Hawaii who had gone to Mance's funeral with Stevie Ray Vaughan a week after Mance's death on January 30, 1976. Though we were all there together in the early spring's taste of February Texas warmth, we were just longhaired white boys who all looked alike.

Which brings us to the time that Mance and I, his biographer, met. Being a Vietnam Veteran, if even a bearded one who looked more like a mountain man than a twentieth-century patriot, I must've looked like a security guard to Rod Kennedy. I'd met Mance for the first time earlier that sweaty afternoon in May of 1972 and was mightily impressed. After giving me specific instructions for handling the west side door for the evening performance at the Kerrville Municipal Auditorium, Rod Kennedy disappeared up front and in walked around thirty casually dressed men in white shirts, ties, slacks, and dress sport coats. With little metal antennas sticking out of their coat lapels a foot past their short haircuts, it wasn't difficult to spot them in the Flower Child crowd of folk music lovers mixed with some cowboy hat-and-boot locals in their Levis. There were yellow ribbons with "Reserved" marked on the first three rows of seats. One of the Secret Service Antennamen came over to me and said, "When I tell you, open the door and let the guests pass."

When I opened the door, in walked Lyndon Baines Johnson, Lady Bird, Lynda Bird, Darrell Royal and their entourage. When LBJ passed within inches of me, looked into my eyes, smiled a big old wrinkled

Texas grin and said, "Howdy," I remembered my thoughts one night on guard duty in Vietnam when all I could see was the infra-red coming off my hand and fingers along with the constant images of my worst fears. I vowed if I ever got close enough to the man who came to symbolize the Vietnam War, I'd kill him. Instead, when I looked in his eyes, I thought I saw a broken pain deep enough to match my own. Something in me knew that anything I could inflict on him wouldn't top the suffering he had already endured. I mumbled an awkward, "Hello," and let him pass like the dutiful soldier I no longer was.

Mance outlived LBJ, and I went on to write a book about him. Mance Lipscomb, that is. LBJ had met Mance at the Smithsonian Folklife Festival in 1968, and invited him to appear at "that little Hemisfair thang I put together" in San Antonio. Rod Kennedy told me the former President had come to Kerrville on the festival's opening night expressly to hear Mance Lipscomb. But now, was that the President of the United States, or just another one of Mance's fans?

Mance Lipscomb grew up as the blues popped up out of the countryside and took shape. Thanks to his life's experience, his eclectic tastes and musical genius, he carried forward a living musical legacy that allowed a generation of folk and pop music lovers to witness history in the making at every one of his performances. Thanks to his recorded repertoire and the dozens of musicians he influenced, his music lives on, feeding today's music directly through its roots.

Bibliography

Alyn, Glen (as told to & compiled by). *I Say Me For a Parable: The Oral Autobiography of Mance Lipscomb, Texas Bluesman*. New York: W. W. Norton and Company, 1993 (hardcover) and New York: Da Capo Press, 1995 (softcover).

Alyn, Glen. "A Musician and a Farmer: Mance Lipscomb's Life & Music." Insert for "Mance Lipscomb in Concert" video: Vestapol (division of Stefan Grossman Guitar Workshop), distributed by Rounder Records, Cambridge, Massachusetts, 1994.

Bingham-Bouliane, Nancy. Mance Lipscomb paper for University of Texas Folklore Department, 1970. See the Lipscomb/Alyn Collection, Center for American History, University of Texas at Austin.

The Lipscomb/Alyn Collection, Center for American History, University of Texas at Austin, contains extensive research material on Mance Lipscomb, including original manuscripts, hundreds of hours of interview transcripts and taped interviews, and photographs.

This article contains extracts of interviews by Glen Alyn with the following: Mance and Elnora Lipscomb, Lipscomb family members, Beck and Georgia Lee Wade, Ed and Lillie Lathan, Mark and Nancy Bouliane (all from Navasota); Dr. Roger Abrahams, Dr. Stanley Alexander, Les Blank, Guy Clark, Shirley Dimmick, Dr. William Ferris, Skip Gerson, Jimmie Dale Gilmore, Lightnin' Hopkins' cousin Steve James, Rod Kennedy, Lynn Lenau (member of Hempstead's Lipscomb family [Anglo]), Alan Lomax, Taj Mahal, Tary Owens, Frank Reckard, Gayle Ross, Chris Strachwitz, Kurt Van Sickle, Townes Van Zandt, Dick Waterman, Alan Willenzik, Bruce Willenzik, Lucinda Williams, and Mason Williams, among others.

Filmography

Les Blank. *A Well-Spent Life*. Sound by Skip Gerson. 45 min. Flower Films, 1970. Filmed in Navasota. Mance also appears in Blank's *The Blues Accordin' to Lightnin'*.

Institute of Texan Cultures. Film of Mance Lipscomb at 1968 Hemisfair, in San Antonio.

Stefan Grossman Guitar Workshop. *Mance Lipscomb in Concert*. Videotaped in Austin by Bill Arhos in 1969. 1 hour.

Stefan Grossman Guitar Workshop offers several videos on which Mance is represented.

Discography

Chris Strachwitz. Seven record albums, two CDs, and a collaborative CD and songbook with Stefan Grossman and Mel Bay, all recorded between 1960 and 1973. Arhoolie (Mance also represented on six other records).

Mance Lipscomb: Trouble in Mind. Reprise, Pop Series R-2012A and B10,046 & 10,047, 1961. Recorded in Los Angeles.

Tary Owens. Two CDs: Catfish CTF1003 *Rough Stuff: The Roots of Texas Blues Guitar* (Mance appears on three songs) and CTF1004 *Mance Lipscomb: At Home in Texas* (18 songs + additional monologues), 1993.

Glen Alyn. *Tellin' Stories, Sangin' bout Suppas.* (CD) Dawn, 1995. Glen Alyn reads seven stories from *I Say Me For a Parable* and performs his arrangements of eight Mance Lipscomb and three Alyn songs.

Mance Lipscomb. (Courtesy, Ed Badeaux, Houston, Texas)

A 'possum to go with the 'taters. (Courtesy of La Salle County Historical Society, Cotulla, Texas)

More Than Just 'Possum'n Taters: Texas African-American Foodways in the WPA Slave Narratives

by T. Lindsay Baker

"Ration time was Saturday night. Every slave get enough fat pork, corn meal and such to last out the week. I reckon the Master figure it out to the last bite because they was no leavings over."[1] So remembered John White from his life as a slave on the Presley Davenport farm near Linden in Northeast Texas.

White was one of several hundred elderly African-Americans who shared memories of slavery in Texas with field workers from the Federal Writers' Project of the Works Progress Administration during the hard days of the Great Depression. The slave narrative project, undertaken in sixteen states in 1937–39, was an outgrowth of the larger Federal Writers' Project. The latter effort had been conceived in 1935 both to provide jobs for unemployed writers and to prepare guidebooks for the various states. The writers undertook other history-related efforts, including impressive oral-history interview projects throughout the United States. As they fanned out over the country to seek elderly Americans with memories to share, many of the field workers interviewed aged blacks with memories of slavery days. This examination of Texas African-American foodways is drawn from the remembrances of former

▼

slaves in the Lone Star State who were interviewed both in Texas and in Oklahoma.[2]

The diet for Texas slaves mirrored the diet for the majority of southerners. It consisted principally of "the three Ms"—meat, meal, and molasses. These staple ingredients in various forms provided sustenance to most southerners from the initial settlement of the region by Euro Americans and African-Americans in the seventeenth century through the middle years of the twentieth century. Irella Battle Walker, a former slave in Travis County, Texas, remembered the "three Ms" this way: "De week's rations for a growed person run like three pounds bacon and a peck cornmeal and some homemade 'lasses."[3]

Perhaps the greatest factor in determining what foods Texas slaves ate was how they obtained their food. Judging from the evidence in the WPA slave narratives, most Texas slaves received regular rations provided by the masters. From the sample of 168 informants who discussed foodways, seventeen specifically described rations; ten of them described the food provided as adequate, four described it in general without comments on amounts, and only three described them as insufficient. In the slave households in which the families received rations, women added cooking to their duties for the master in the fields, at the looms, or in the big house. Betty Powers remembered, "Mammy and pappy and us twelve chillen lives in one cabin, so mammy has to cook for fourteen people, 'sides her field work. She am up way befo' daylight fixin' breakfast and supper after dark, with de pine knot torch to make de light."[4]

Many Texas slaves ate meals which were served communally, with nine of the interviewees remembering meals having been provided for groups of slaves. Mattie Hardman related, "The cooking was done all up to the general kitchen at Master[']s house and when slaves come from work they would send their children up to the kitchen to bring their meals to their homes in the quarters."[5]

It was fairly common practice on Texas plantations for children's meals to be prepared by one particular cook, who might also have childcare responsibilities while parents were at work elsewhere in the fields or at the master's house. Former slave Rosina Hoard remembered that on the Pratt Washington plantation in Travis County an old woman named Aunt Alice held both jobs: ". . . she done all the cookin' for de chillen in de depot. Dat what dey calls de place all de chillen stays till dere mammies come home from de field. Aunt Alice have de big pot to cook in, out in de yard. Some days we had beans and some day peas. She put great hunks of salt bacon in de pot, and bake plenty cornbread, and give us plenty milk." Ann Hawthorne, formerly a slave at Jasper, remembered, "Us all eat outer one big pan. Dey give each . . . a big iron spoon and us sho' go to it."[6]

Food for "house servants," those slaves who worked as domestics in the homes of the masters, might be far superior to that available to the field slaves. Hagar Lewis, a slave near Tyler, in a kindly manner related that her mother cooked for the master's family as well as for her own: "We ate the same, when the white folks was finished." Abe Livingston was more straightforward when he said, "When de white folks has et, we gits what lef." Perhaps even more candidly Tempie Collins related, "I gathered up scraps the white chillens lef."[7] A number of the ex-slaves interviewed, however, asserted that they ate the same foods as their masters.[8]

Being a cook carried both its advantages and its own liabilities. John White remembered from slavery days as a cook in Northeast Texas that when other slaves' rations ran short, "sometimes I'd slip some things out from the kitchen," noting "single women was bad that way." He then added, "Then they favors me—at night when the overseer thinks everybody asleep in they own places!" Working under the close scrutiny of the master or mistress, however, presented its own special problems. Easter Wells's mother cooked for her master in slavery in Texas, and his rule of the kitchen was that "iffen you burnt de bread you had to eat it." One day her mother did burn the bread, and to avoid the punishment she ran off to the woods for several days before returning, whereupon "old Master give her a whipping" but was "glad to git her back."[9]

For most Texas slaves, "meat" meant pork. The hog was the preeminent meat provider for the South, and either fresh or salted pork supplied the bulk of the meat consumed by southerners black and white.

In the WPA slave narratives, pork is overwhelmingly the most frequently mentioned meat, with fifty-four informants mentioning it in general, with even more references being made to specific cuts. John White's comment that every slave received "fat pork, corn meal and such to last out the week" was repeated in different words by other interviewees time and again. Impressed by the number of swine in his master's hog droves, Teshan Young, formerly a slave in Harrison County, added, "De marster have hawgs on top of hawgs on dat place, for to make de meat."[10] Because food occasionally or even chronically ran short on some farms and plantations, pig theft by slaves occurred from time to time. Interviewee Richard Carruthers, who grew up in slavery in Bastrop County, instructed his field worker on how successfully to steal a hog: ". . . grabbin' a pig sho' 'nough problem. You have to cotch him by the snoot so he won't squeal, and clomp him tight while you knife him."[11]

If pork and meat were synonymous for most Texans, bacon and pork were almost as close in meaning. Bacon for these foreparents of present-day Texans was not the same thin, semi-translucent product purchased in stores today. Instead, coming from the huge swine of the past century, this side of meat might measure nearly a yard long, two feet wide, and three to four inches thick. Cut into chunks or broad slices, it provided real substance into which to sink one's teeth. Because it was cured in salt, like most of the rest of the meat on the hog, many of the WPA informants not only used the terms "pork" and "bacon" inter- changeably, but they also used "salt pork" the same way. "Bacon" and "salt pork" are mentioned as having been regular food by twenty-one of the interviewees.[12]

All parts of the hog provided sustenance for early-day Texans. Of- ten hog butchering day, which almost always took place during the wintertime because the cold helped to preserve the meat, was the time when people ate the fresh organs like liver or lungs. All the meat that could not be preserved through curing had to be eaten or it would spoil during the next warm spell, so the days immediately following the hog killing might become almost an orgy of pork eating for all concerned. Chitterlings, deep-fried strips of small intestines, usually were prepared the next day or so when the hog fat was being rendered down in big iron pots for lard, as was "cracklin' bread," which consisted of crack-lings cooked in cornbread. Another treat soon after hog butchering which Texas ex-slaves remembered was souse, or "hogshead cheese." Of such foods consumed just after hog slaughter, Abram Sells, a slave near Jasper, remarked, "Then we kilt lots of hawgs and then talk 'bout eatin! O, them chitlins, sousemeat and the haslets, that['] s the liver and the lights all biled up together."[13]

The lard rendered up from the hog provided cooking fat that could be preserved for weeks and even months, and both masters and slaves considered the lard and the additional grease that cooked out of meats to be important food sources. Van Moore remembered his mistress near Crosby in eastern Harris County giving out rations on Sundays, when she would "fill up de big wood tray with flour and grease and hawg meat." The grease served non-culinary purposes as well, as evidenced by such informants as Wash Wilson of Robertson County, who remem-bered his mother doing laundry at night by the light of a crude lamp illuminated by burning hog fat, and Josie Brown of Victoria, who de-scribed slaves using lard as a hair dressing.[14]

Once the pig was killed and butchered, the work of curing began almost immediately. Slaves and others rubbed down the hams, shoul-ders, and sides of bacon with salt, and then typically buried the meat in salt for about a month. After the salt treatment ended, the meat then went into the smokehouse, where it received smoke curing for flavor. Mandy Morrow, who later cooked for Texas Governor James H. Hogg in the executive mansion in Austin, remembered from her childhood in slavery near Georgetown that her duties included tending the smokehouse fire. She noted that although most people used smoldering wood to make their smoke, her owner, Ben Baker, had her burn corn-cobs instead, and that "dey makes de fine flavor in de meat."[15]

Some of the WPA interviewees reported eating cured meats from the smokehouses as regular parts of their diets, but most often slave meat consisted of bacon or lesser cuts. Some former Texas slaves men-tioned eating ham or sausage, but these must have been exceptions, with these meats generally going to the masters' tables.[16] Jowls from the neck of the hog, which did not cure especially well, seem to have appeared on the slaves' tables with some frequency. Easter Wells reminisced that "We allus had hog jowl and peas on New Years Day 'cause iffen you'd have dat on New Years Day you have good luck all de year."[17]

One form of pig meat which appears in the Texas WPA slave narratives as generally festive food is roast pork. On occasions such as Christmas the masters might give their slaves a hog to butcher, roast, and eat as part of the general celebration. Another somewhat unexpected festive use of the hog typically also took place at Christmastime. "De men saves all de bladders from de hawgs dey kill, blows 'em full of air and lets 'em dry," related Teshan Young of Harrison County. He further explained, "De young'uns puts dem on sticks and holds 'em over a fire in de yard. Dat makes 'em bust and dey goes 'bang' jus' like a gun. Dat was de fireworks."[18]

"De corn feed both de critters and de niggers," stated WPA interviewee Henry Probasco, formerly a slave in Walker County, explaining "'cause de main food for de niggers am de corn and de corn bread and de corn mush."[19] Indeed corn in its various forms, particularly as ground corn meal, served as the staple food in the Texas slave's diet. From the 168 informants studied who had remembrances of Texas foodways, twenty-nine specifically mentioned cornmeal, while even more noted foods like cornbread, ashcake, and hoecake which were made from this ubiquitous foodstuff.[20] Cornmeal is made by grinding or pounding dried corn. In ante-bellum Texas this most often was done at home or on the plantation. "Dere warn't no mill to grind corn," remembered Amos Clark from slavery days in Washington County, "so de boss carpenter, he hollows out a log and gits some smooth, hard rocks and us grind de corn like it was a morter."[21]

Almost a quarter of the interviewees considered in this study listed cornbread as having been a major element in slaves' diets. Made from cornmeal combined with water or milk, lard or salt, and perhaps some leavening, cornbread typically was cooked in iron skillets or Dutch ovens. Jordan Thompson, a Texas slave in Rusk County, told his interviewer at Fort Gibson, Oklahoma, "I still likes the cornbread with fingerprints baked on it, like in the old days when it was cooked in a skillet over the hot wood ashes."[22]

Not all the breads made from cornmeal were necessarily as sophisticated as cornbread. Ashcake, for example, generally consisted of cornmeal mixed with water and maybe some grease. Instead of being cooked in a skillet or Dutch oven, ashcake instead was cooked on the hot hearth of the fireplace or the heated ground at the edge of a campfire. Ben Kinchlow remembered from his slavery days in Wharton County, "Now, ash cakes, you have you dough pretty stiff and smooth off a place in the ashes and lay it right on the ashes and cover it up with ashes and when it got done, you could wipe every bit of the ashes off, and get you some butter and put on it. M-m-m! I tell you, it's fine!" Other cooks placed the batter on leaves or green corn shucks, placing more leaves or shucks on top to protect the dough from ashes. Jeff Calhoun, a slave in Austin, told his interviewer, "we put one leaf down and put batter on dat and put another leaf over it and cover with hot ashes and by noon it was done." Fifteen of the informants considered in this study specifically mentioned ashcakes as part of their regular diet as slaves in Texas.[23]

Corn dodgers and hoecake are related but distinct cornmeal breads remembered by a number of the Texas former slaves. Both are prepared from cornmeal, water, and pork grease with possible additional ingredients for flavor. Made with a stiff dough or pone, corn dodgers are fried in a skillet, while hoe cakes are cooked on the blade of a hoe or shovel held over the coals of either an open fire or a fireplace. Browned on the hot skillet or hoe blade, corn dodgers and hoecakes were usually considerably harder and more difficult to chew than cornbread, so much so that they became the subject of a song that Harriet Jones remembered singing while cooking hoecakes in bondage on the Martin Fulbright plantation near Clarksville in Northeast Texas:

If you wants to bake a hoecake,
To bake it good and done,
Slap it on a nigger's heel,
and hold it to de sun.

My mammy baked a hoecake,
As big as Alabama,

She throwed it 'gainst a nigger's head,
It ring jus' like a hammer.

De way you bake a hoecake,
De old Virginny way,
Wrap it round a nigger's stomach,
And hold it dere all day.[24]

Cornmeal also served as the basis for a hot cereal at breakfast. Mixed with water and cooked over the fire, meal quickly became cornmeal mush. Whatever mush that might not be eaten in the morning could be fried up and eaten as "fried mush" for the next meal. Virtually every time that the Texas slaves ate, they had at least one food with cornmeal as one of its major components, whether it be cornbread, hoecake, ashcake, corn dodgers, or mush.[25]

The third M of the "three Ms" comprising the basic southern diet was molasses. Made by cooking down and evaporating the juice squeezed from sorghum cane, sugar cane, or another such cane, it is typically a thick brown syrup with a mild to strong, sweet taste. Not only was molasses something to pour onto cornbread or mush or to mix with hot bacon fat into "sap" for the same purpose, but it was also used as a "sugar" substitute to sweeten any foods and could even be mixed with hot water to make a tea-like sweet beverage. "'Lasses" was seemingly the frequent African-American pronunciation for molasses, and informant James Hayes shared a story about this word in his 1930s interview at Moser Valley near Fort Worth. His master had been killed fighting in the Confederate Army, and since that time,

De women folks don' talk much and no laughin' like 'fore. I 'members once de missy asks me to make a 'lasses cake. I says, "I's got no 'lasses." Missy says, "Don' say 'lasses, say molasses." I says, "Why say molasses when I's got no 'lasses." Dat was de fus' time Missy laugh after de funeral.

From his bondage near Crockett, Texas, John Love remembered a song that the slaves sang as they were squeezing the juice from cane to cook down into molasses:

Ain't no more cane on the Neches,
Ain't no more cane on de land;
Oh——ooooo——ooooo——oO!
Done grind it all in 'lasses,
Oh——ooooo——ooooo——oO![26]

The "three Ms" constituted the major foods for Texas slaves, as they did for almost all Texans in the mid-nineteenth century. The slaves in Texas did, however, eat other foods as supplements to this generally fat- and carbohydrate-rich but mineral- and vitamin-deficient diet. As might be expected in Texas, which even before the Civil War had comparatively large numbers of cattle, beef found its way into many slaves' diets, even if only as a festive food. Twenty-one informants reported some form of beef as having been a regular part in their diets. Having lived on pork, meal, and molasses in Georgia, Julia Francis Daniels was impressed with the beef she was able to eat in Texas.[27] For many Texas slaves, including seven informants in this study, festive occasions were the only times during slavery in Texas when they consumed beef. Many seemingly viewed beef as a "white man's food," considering themselves fortunate even to receive leftovers from the masters' tables. James Green, a slave at Columbus, remembered the words to that effect in this ditty:

Old marster eats beef and sucks on de bone,
And give us de gristle—
To make, to make, to make, to make,
To make de nigger whistle.[28]

Meat that appears unexpectedly frequently in the remembrances of Texas former slaves is wild game. With many of the interviewees having lived quite literally on the fringe of settlement, however, it makes sense that they and their masters would be using this important natural food source which later diminished as the frontier moved westward. Although the slaves were prohibited from using firearms, they themselves could trap or otherwise kill many small animals and catch fish, while the masters surprisingly often provided their bondsmen with food in the form of game which they had killed. From days in Texas immediately following the Civil War, Elige Davison reported, "Iffen the woods wasn't full of wild game us . . . all starve to death. . . ."[29]

The wild game most often killed by Texas slaves were small mammals like opossums, raccoons, rabbits, and squirrels, which could be trapped, hunted with dogs, or killed with rocks and sticks. From these animals, opossums predominate with thirty-three references in the interviews of former Texas slaves in the WPA narratives. Living in hollows and moving comparatively slowly, these marsupials "in season" in the late fall added tasty protein to many slaves' diets. "Us have a good possum dog, sometimes two or three," remembered Abram Sells from slavery in the Newton area in deep East Texas. "Every night you heered them dogs barkin' in the field down by the branch. Sho 'nuf, they git possum treed and us go git him and parbile him and put him in the oven and bake him plumb tender." From the Texas former slaves, perhaps the best instructions for opossum cooking come from Lizzie Farmer, who was interviewed as part of the Oklahoma Slave Narrative Project but who had grown up in bondage at Mount Enterprise, Texas:

> When we cooked possum dat was a feast. We would skin him and dress him and put him top de house and let him freeze for two days or nights. Then we'd boil him with red pepper, and take him out and put him in a pan and slice sweet 'taters and put round him and roast him. My, dat was good eating.[30]

In the menu of small mammals hunted for food by Texas slaves, rabbits came in second behind opossums in numbers of remembrances. Twenty-five of the informants recollected rabbit as a regular part of their diets in mid-nineteenth-century Texas. From her childhood in slavery in Cherokee and Houston counties, Julia Francis Daniels remembered her brother going rabbit hunting on Sundays. "He'd leave for the

swamps 'fore daybreak and we'd know when we'd hear him callin',' 'o -
- o-o o-o-o-da-da-ske-e-e-e-t,' he had somethin.' That jus' a makeup of
he own, but we knowed they's rabbits for the pot.'[31]

Raccoons and squirrels were next most frequently mentioned as
wild game food by the Texas ex-slaves, with thirteen and ten references
respectively. Both of these animals, more difficult to kill than opossums
and rabbits, also were hunted with dogs and caught in traps. Raccoon
preparation for eating was basically the same as that for opossums, while
that for squirrels was for either stew or frying. Living much of the time
high in trees, squirrels presented slaves with problems, for they were
difficult for unarmed blacks to hunt. A number of the WPA interviewees
revealed in their discussions of small game hunting some of their frustrations in the restrictions imposed on them as slaves. Millie Williams,
for example, remembered the words to a song that expressed such feelings:

> Rabbit in de briar patch,
> Squirrel in de tree,
> Wish I could go huntin',
> But I ain't free.
>
> Rooster's in de henhouse,
> Hen's in de patch,
> Love to go shootin',
> But I ain't free.[32]

Large game also played its part in the diet of many Texas slaves.
Usually the masters hunted these animals with firearms, but on occasion the blacks used simpler methods to "bag" the game. Twenty-one
of the interviewees listed venison as a regular food. Eli Davison, who
came to Madison County in 1858, remembered that his master planted
seven acres in corn but "all he did was hunt deer and squirrels," feeding his slaves on a regimen of cornbread and wild game. Carter J. Jackson, who came to Texas as a slave in 1863, reported to his interviewer
how the slaves in his household killed deer without firearms: "Deer

was thick in them days and we sot up sharp stobs inside the pea field and them young bucks jumps over the fence and stabs themselves. That the only way to cotch them, 'cause they so wild. . . ."[33] Former slaves also mentioned a handful of other large game animals as having been in their diets, with six references to feral hogs,[34] five references to bears,[35] two references to buffaloes,[36] and one reference to antelope.[37]

Wild birds also attracted the attention of Texas African-Americans during the middle years of the nineteenth century. "It was wild down in de Neches bottom den," remembered John Love, who mentioned finding there "all kind birds and wild turkeys." The latter were the most frequently eaten of the game birds, with seventeen of the interviewees remembering wild turkeys on the dinner table.[38] Other birds that some of the Texas ex-slaves remembered as foods included prairie chickens, ducks, geese, quail, doves, pigeons, and even blackbirds, crows, and hawks.[39]

For many slaves fishing combined a leisure activity with enhancement to one's diet. Twenty-three of the interviewees shared remembrances of eating fish, all of them relating to freshwater varieties. After emancipation Julia Blanks, formerly an urban slave in San Antonio, moved with her husband westward to the Adams Ranch, where the Frio River afforded many opportunities for pleasurable fishing parties:

> The men used to go up to the lake, fishin', and catch big trout, or bass, they call 'em now; and we'd take big buckets of butter . . . and lard too, and cook our fish up there, and had corn bread or hoe cakes and plenty of butter for ever'thing, and it sure was good. I tell you . . . we was livin' ten days in the week, then.[40]

Chickens, though present on southern farms, do not appear to have been a frequent food for Texas slaves. Instead, chicken was essentially a luxury meat for the master class. Only five of the interviewees studied in this research mentioned chicken as a regular food item,[41] while eight mentioned it as something eaten only at special events or festive occasions.[42] Six of the interviewees noted that chickens were raised on the farms or plantations where they as slaves lived but do not mention eating them,[43] and one interviewee stated plainly that where he lived in bondage in Grimes County, "we didn't get no chicken."[44] Chickens at the time were seen as valuable barnyard fowls, producing not only their own flesh but also eggs. Only two interviewees, in fact, mentioned eating eggs, though two others reported stealing them.[45] Theft of chickens, viewed by many slaves as "white folks' food," must not have been too uncommon, as nine of the informants related stories of chicken-stealing incidents. One interviewee even noted that after emancipation his old master willed his recently freed slaves livestock and "some chickens."[46]

Another barnyard fowl frequently mentioned by Texas former slaves is the domestic turkey, but this bird too constituted luxury meat mainly for the master class. Three interviewees in the sample studied noted that their masters owned turkeys, while three others referred to them as regular food (apparently after emancipation) and five informants mentioned turkeys as something that they as slaves consumed on festive occasions.[47]

Although cornmeal was the most common way that all Southerners, including African-Americans in Texas, consumed corn, this staple food entered the diet in other ways as well. Most Texas farms in the mid-nineteenth century raised corn along with other crops, for the food contributed greatly to self-sufficiency. Fresh corn from the field remained edible for only a comparatively short time, but it provided a welcome if brief change in the routine diet. Some cooks prepared the fresh corn in pots over the fire, while others roasted it in the shucks—roasting ears. In the latter preparation, the cook pulled the shucks back carefully to expose and remove the "silk." After the shucks were pushed back down, the ears were soaked in water for a few minutes before they were laid on a bed of coals with a few embers sprinkled on top. In this manner only five or so minutes were needed to steam the corn in its own shucks.[48] Some Texas slaves also parched dried corn kernels to serve as snacks, Easter Wells remembering, "We all kept parched corn all de time and went 'round eating it."[49]

After cornmeal, however, the most common way that Texas slaves ate corn was as hominy. This dish starts with a hard "flint" corn which had been allowed to dry on the cob and then had been shelled. As the dry kernels, it could be stored almost indefinitely if protected from vermin. The other key ingredient for making hominy was lye, in the mid-nineteenth century made by leaching water through wood ashes. As WPA interviewee Phyllis Petite, a slave in Rusk County, explained to her field worker, one combined dry corn, lye, and water in an iron pot. Then as she directed, "Let the corn boil in the lye water until the skin drops off and the eyes drop out." To remove the toxic lye, then "wash that corn in fresh water about a dozen times, or just keep carrying water from the spring until you are wore out, like I did." Then one placed the prepared hominy in a crock or other container kept in a cool place, and, as Petite related, "you got good skinned corn as long as it last, all ready to warm up a little batch at a time." Eight of the interviews in this study listed hominy as a regular food item in their diets, while another three mentioned grits. Made from hominy which has been dried and then ground or pulverized, grits was cooked in hot water like cornmeal mush and was served as a popular side dish in many areas of the South including parts of Texas.[50]

If cornmeal served as the staple ingredient of the slave diet in Texas, flour served as probably the most important dietary dividing line between slave and master. Produced by grinding wheat, flour is the principal ingredient in biscuits, white bread, cakes, and other baked goods—foods in many instances reserved for the master class. Among the respondents considered in this paper, ten reported eating flour products as ordinary food.[51]

With cornbreads residing on the bottom rung of the "bread ladder" of status in the South, biscuits occupied an intermediate rung, with "lightbread" and cakes standing at the top. In households well off enough to eat flour, including slave families provided flour by their masters, biscuits were very popular fare. Made with flour, grease, milk or water, and usually baking powder as leavening, biscuits generally were baked in the ovens of ranges or in Dutch ovens on the fireplace hearths. In the WPA slave narratives examined for this study, nine Texas former slaves reported biscuits to have been special treats, while only four report them as having been regular food. Peter Mitchell, a slave at Jasper, reported, "On Sunday dey gives us jus' one biscuit apiece and we totes it round in de pocket half de day and shows it to de others, and says, 'See what we has for breakfast.'" Because they were forbidden food for slaves in some households, the temptation to steal biscuits was very strong. Three of the interviewees reported stealing them, as did Ida Henry, a slave in Marshall: "I would put biscuits and pieces of chicken in a sack under me dress dat hung from me waist, as I waited de table for me Mistress, and later would slip off and eat it as dey never gave de slaves none of dis sort of food."[52]

Lightbread, made with flour, milk or water, leavening such as soda or salt, and possibly also including eggs, generally was mixed in the morning and allowed to "rise," being baked sometime around midday. Either the ovens of ranges or Dutch ovens might be used for cooking. Interviewee Lizzie Farmer was thinking of the latter utensil when she reminisced, "Our bread was baked in iron skillets with lids and we would set the skillet on de fire and put coals of fire on de lid. Bread was mighty good cooked like dat."[53]

Former slaves from Texas shared some additional remembrances of foods prepared with flour, but perhaps the strongest impressions in their memories came from the rare occasions in which they enjoyed cake. This luxury always appeared during times of celebration, such as Christmas, Independence Day, or the marriage of one of the master's children, and seventeen of the informants in this study had such memories. Sometimes the slaves received their treats surreptitiously, as reported by Katie Darling, a slave near Marshall, in telling about his master's daughter: ". . . on Christmas Miss Irene bakes two cakes for the nigger families but she darsn't let missy [the mistress] know 'bout it." Among the cake varieties mentioned are ginger, pound, molasses, and yellow cakes.[54] Occasional references appear in the WPA slave narratives for other treats made from wheat flour, including two for pancakes, one for waffles, and three for dumplings as a dessert.[55]

Vegetables punctuated the diet of Texas slaves. In season the bondsmen might enjoy a wide range of fresh vegetables, from either their own gardens or those of their masters; some of the vegetables might be kept in cellars or preserved dried well after the harvest.[56] Time and again the interviewees commented on the consumption of potlicker, the concentrated liquid consisting of water and vegetable juices often mixed with meat juices that resulted from the cooking of vegetables. Bert Strong, from Harrison County, reminisced, "I 'member once they's grumblin' 'bout what they have to eat and old massa come to the quarters and say, 'What you fussin' 'bout? They's a gallon good potlicker in the pot.'"[57]

Greens appeared numerous times in the remembrances of the Texas ex-slaves. Bert Strong remarked, "I's raised on greens and pork and potlicker and 'taters and ash-cake." Many of the informants recalled just that they had greens,[58] but some remembered specifically collard, mustard, parsley, and turnip greens.[59] Turnip greens often were raised, for they also produced the turnips themselves, which could provide valuable sustenance.[60] Some of the interviewees also remembered going to the woods and meadows to pick wild greens. John Sneed related from his boyhood as a slave south of Austin, "Us jus' go in de woods and git wild lettuce and mustard and leather-britches and poke salad and watercress, all us want to eat."[61] Another leafy vegetable reported by a number of the WPA interviewees was cabbage. Seven of the former slaves from Texas noted cabbage, with an eighth mentioning it in the form of sauerkraut.[62] Peas and beans, valuable sources of vegetable protein, also frequently appear in the remembrances of the Texas former slaves. Twenty of the WPA interviewees commented on eating peas, with three more identifying them specifically as blackeyed peas.[63]

Beans were mentioned by the Texas ex-slaves almost as frequently as peas. Eleven of the informants comment on beans in general, with three more mentioning specifically dried beans and two listing fresh beans as regular food.[64]

Of all the vegetables mentioned by the Texas former slaves, the most often recalled was the sweet potato. Tracing its origin to South America, this nutritious tuber traveled to Europe on Columbus's ships and from there came to North America during the colonial period. Easily storable well after the autumn harvest, the sweet potato became a major constituent in the diet of many southerners, as it remains to this day. Thirty of the WPA interviewees who had been in bondage in Texas shared their memories of sweet potatoes, twenty-two of them commenting on them as having been part of their regular diet. Mose Smith successfully ran away from his master at Paris, Texas, but after he had been gone some weeks, part of the time having little to eat, he remembered, "I was wishing to be back with the master and get full of them good baked sweet potatoes!" Six of the interviewees specifically noted sweet potatoes being cooked with baked opossum, all of them clearly relishing the taste. In a representative remembrance, Abram Sells, formerly a slave in the Newton area in deep East Texas, described that after the opossum had been parboiled and then baked to near done, "Then we stacks sweet 'taters round him and po' the juice over the whole thing. Now, there is somethin' good 'nuf for a king." For Sells, however, the memories of sweet potatoes blended with those of talk and dreams about freedom:

> I 'member how some . . . the oldes' niggers was settin' round the fire late in the night, stirrin' the ashes with the poker and rakin' out the roas' 'taters. They's smokin' the old corn cob pipe and homemade tobacco and whisperin' right low and quiet like what they's gwinter do and whar they's gwinter go when Mister Lincoln, he turn them free.[65]

A handful of the Texas former slaves also reported eating Irish or white potatoes as well.[66]

The WPA narratives from former Texas slaves contain small numbers of references to other vegetables. Perhaps the largest surprise in the evidence comes in the comparatively small number of references to okra, a food which came to the New World from Africa as a consequence of the slave trade and which frequently is associated with African-American cookery. Two informants commented on okra or okra seed as being parched as a coffee substitute and only one reported eating it as regular food. This suggests that okra may not have been commonly eaten by Texas slaves.[67] Other vegetables which have only occasional mention in the narratives include onions and tomatoes with two references apiece, beets and squash with one reference each, pumpkins with two references, and cushaws with one reference.[68]

Fruit also appeared in the diets of some of the Texas slaves, though the Lone Star State was not known for fruit production. Six of the WPA interviewees commented on fruit in general, with specific references to grapes, berries, figs, apples, and watermelons. From her life as a freed-woman at Leon Springs, Texas, Julia Blanks remembered particularly the wild fruit: ". . . they was grapes, dewberries, plums and agaritas, black haws, red haws. M-m-m! Them dewberries, I dearly love 'em! . . . We used to gather mustang grapes and make a barrel of wine." Three of the interviewees reported apples as having been special treats from the master at Christmastime. Watermelons, easily grown in the Texas climate, appeared in the narratives from seven of the informants.[69]

Many of the former slaves interviewed by the WPA field workers were children at the time when they were in bondage. This may help to explain the surprising thirty-one of them who reported milk as having been part of their regular diet. In a representative remembrance, Jacob Branch, a former slave at Double Bayou near Beaumont, related, "Dey have big jar with buttermilk and 'low us drink all us want." Similarly Alice Houston, earlier in life a slave near San Marcos, explained, "Ole miss, she have a big dish pan full of clabber and she tells de girl to set dat down out in de yard and she say, 'Give all dem chillun a spoon now and let dem eat dat.' When we all git 'round dat pan we sho' would lick dat clabber up."[70] Butter, likewise, appears in the remembrances of the Texas slaves more often than might be expected, with sixteen references appearing. Cheese, on the other hand, is noted only once as a food provided to slaves.[71]

Slaves in Texas had the same penchant for sweets as may be found in people around the world. The role of molasses as one of the mainstays of the slave diet already has been mentioned, but sweets in the ante-bellum Texas slave diet took other forms as well. The source of the juice from which molasses was made was cane, and five of the WPA informants included in this study noted sugar cane as a food source.[72] Eleven of the informants reported sugar as having been a normal food item, with five more reporting it to have been available on infrequent occasions. Mollie Watson remembered from her days as a child slave in the inn on the courthouse square in Centerville that when her mistress was away, "Ole Margaret, the cook[,] would give me lumps o' brown sugar to wash an' dry de dishes fer her."[73]

Either sugar or molasses might be used as ingredients in the preparation of candy, another sweet which appears in the former remembrances. Perhaps another index to the fact that many of the WPA informants were children as slaves, candy appears fifteen different times in the interviews examined for this article. Lizzie Hughes, born in slavery at Nacogdoches in 1848, remembered from her childhood this verse about homemade candy:

Master say, you breath smell of brandy,
Nigger say, no, I's lick 'lasses candy.[74]

Texas slaves from time to time enjoyed sweets in other forms as well. A natural sweetening available on the frontier of settlement was in honey from bee trees. Some pioneers not only plundered bee trees, but they also created hives for their own swarms of bees in order to have honey at their convenience. Texas slaves not only ate honey, but they also used it in curing tobacco, as reported by informant Henderson Perkins, formerly an urban slave in Centerville. "We takes de leaves [of tobacco] and cures dem, den place dem on de board and put honey 'tween 'em. We place a log on top and leave it 'bout a month," he told his WPA interviewer, adding, "White man, dat am t'baccy!"[75] Other references to sweets coming from the interviews with Texas ex-slaves include one mention of ice cream at a wedding party after emancipation and three mentions of puddings as desserts.[76]

The WPA slave narratives based on interviews with former Texas bondsmen contain only limited references to seasonings, suggesting a comparatively bland diet. The main seasonings mentioned are salt and pepper. During the Civil War Lou Smith in Texas experienced actual deprivation of salt. She reported, "We'd go to the smoke house where meat had been salted down for years, dig a hole in the ground and fill it with water," continuing, "After it would stand for a while we'd dip the water up carefully and strain it and cook our food in it." The interviewees reported both black and red pepper as being used in their cooking.[77]

The Texas former slaves reported drinking a number of different beverages, with the one most frequently consumed being water.[78] The most frequently reported hot beverage mentioned in the remembrances of the former Texas slaves is coffee, which seventeen individuals noted. Rose Williams remembered her first cup of coffee because of its circumstances. She and her family had been purchased by Hall Hawkins of Bell County, and their rations included not only white flour but also coffee. "I's never tasted white flour and coffee and mammy fix some biscuits and coffee. Well, de biscuits was yum, yum, yum to me, but de coffee I doesn't like." She learned that the enjoyment of coffee was an acquired taste.[79]

Both in bondage and later as freedpeople, many of the informants substituted other things for coffee because of its comparative high cost. Among the other foods which the informants reported parching to take the place of roasted coffee beans were dried corn, cornmeal, okra or okra seed, sweet potatoes, beans, rye, wheat, bran, and peanuts. One of the best descriptions of the preparation of such a coffee substitute came from Mollie Watson, formerly a child slave in Centerville:

> De coffee was made outen rye or corn meal or sweet pota-
> toes that was dried and parched. When dey made it from sweet
> potatoes dey would slice 'em and put 'em in de sun to dry lak
> dey did fruit or corn. When it was plum dry it was put in de
> oven and parched and den dey would grind it in a little hand
> mill. It made purty good coffee.[80]

Former slaves from Texas in this study mentioned commercial tea as a hot beverage only three times, though they also discussed herbal teas as cures.[81]

Whisky and combinations including it were the most frequently listed alcoholic beverages cited by the Texas ex-slaves. Easily produced with corn as its basis, whisky was very nearly the universal alcoholic drink in the South. The masters controlled or attempted to regulate whisky consumption, but even so Texas slaves seem to have gained access to the liquor at least during festive events such as corn shuckings,

weddings of masters' children, Christmas, and other celebratory occasions.[82] Eggnog, made with whisky, beaten eggs, milk, and sugar, was
reported by six of the Texas ex-slaves to have been prepared at the direction of their masters for slave consumption at Christmas or other
celebrations.[83] The WPA interviews with former slaves in Texas contain
a smattering of mentions of other alcoholic beverages being consumed,
among them three references to wine, three references to cider, one to
apple toddies, one to brandy, and one note on beer.[84]

One last category of information on African-American foodways in
Texas provided from the WPA slave narratives comes in discussions on
cooking and eating utensils. Almost uniformly the cooking described
in the interviews was done either on fireplace hearths or on campfires.
There the predominant cooking vessels mentioned are iron pots, with
ten respondents describing these utensils. It was not unusual for a slave
family to have but one cooking vessel—the iron pot—and this situation
led to the development of distinctive African-American one-pot meals.
Lizzie Farmer described such a meal vividly:

> When we went to cook our vegetables we would put a big
> piece of hog jowl in de pot. We'd put in a lot of snap beans and
> when dey was about half done we'd put in a mess of cabbage
> and when it was about half done we'd put in some squash and
> when it was about half done we'd put in some okra. Then when
> it was done we would take it out a layer at a time. Go 'way! It
> makes me hungry to talk about it.[85]

Skillets as cooking utensils were just about as common as iron pots,
according to the interviews with Texas ex-slaves. With either smooth
bottoms or with "legs" to hold them above the coals of a fire, the skillets could be used either to fry or to simmer most foods.[86] Skillets with
legs might be fitted with flanged lids to hold coals and consequently
become baking utensils called bake kettles or Dutch ovens. The key in
cooking with the Dutch oven was not to use too much heat in order to
avoid scorching.[87]

The most commonly mentioned eating utensil noted in the interviews with Texas ex-slaves was the trough or trencher. Dating from at

least the eighteenth century, these wooden troughs once were widely used for communal eating, although by the middle of the nineteenth century only slaves or the lower class whites used them. Nine of the informants in this study reported these troughs as having been used by the masters in feeding children, while four of them reported their use for communal meals by slaves of all ages. Adeline Cunningham had her own specific memories of the trenchers from which slaves ate on the Washington Greenlee Foley plantation near Hallettsville, Texas:

> Dey feeds us well sometimes, if dey warn't mad at us. Dey has a big trough jes' like de trough for de pigs and dey has a big gourd and dey totes de gourd full of milk and dey breaks de bread in de milk. Den my mammy takes a gourd and fills it and gives it to us chillun. How's we eat it? We had oyster shells for spoons and de slaves come in from de fields and dey hand is all dirty, and dey is hungry. Dey dips de dirty hands right in de trough an we can't eat none of it.[88]

Other eating utensils mentioned in the narratives from former slaves in Texas include tin plates and cups, mentioned six times, and two reports of oyster or mussel shells as "spoons." Elsewhere the informants reported such eating and cooking utensils as coffee pots, knives, spoons, flint and steel for fire starting, and outdoor ovens for bread baking.[89]

The old food preparation methods persisted well into this century, as noted by the field worker who about 1937 interviewed Lucy Lewis and her husband in their rural cabin in Brazoria County. The government employee jotted down that their cabin was furnished with "an enormous four poster bed and some chairs" and, as he noted, that "Pots, pans, kettles, and jugs hang on the walls. The fireplace has a skillet and beanpot in the ashes."[90] The foodways of old had survived almost unaltered. In more modern kitchens today with microwave ovens instead of Dutch ovens and with plastic wrap instead of corn shucks, the foodways of the former slaves still remain and will survive so as long as mothers fry bacon, bake cornbread, and pour molasses on top to make everything taste better.

1. U.S., Works Progress Administration, Federal Writers' Program, Slave Narratives, Texas, XVI, part 4, p. 124 (Irella Battle Walker), 124, Box A932, Manuscript Division, Library of Congress, Washington, D.C. The WPA Texas Slave Narratives preserved in the Manuscript Division of the Library of Congress are found in four large bound volumes of ribbon copy typescripts. Identified as Volume XIV of the Slave Narrative Collection, the four parts are located as follows: part 1 is in Box A930, parts 2 and 3 are in Box A931, and part 4 is in Box A932. Hereafter these materials will be cited as LC Texas Slave Narratives with their respective part numbers.

2. For background on the Federal Writers' Project and its component Slave Narrative Project see, among other sources, B. A. Botkin, "The Slave as His Own Interpreter," *The Library of Congress Quarterly Journal of Current Acquisitions* 2, no. 1 (July/September 1944): 37–63; Jerre Mangione, *The Dream and the Deal: The Federal Writers' Project, 1935–1943*; Monty Noam Penkower, *The Federal Writers' Project: A Study in Government Patronage of the Arts*; Norman R. Yetman, "The Background of the Slave Narrative Collection," *American Quarterly* 19, no. 3 (Fall 1967): 534–53.

    The interviews on which this paper are based, all generated by the Federal Writers' Project as part of its Slave Narrative Project, are available in original typescripts in either the Manuscript Division of the Library of Congress or in the Archives and Manuscripts Division of the Oklahoma Historical Society, Oklahoma City, Oklahoma. The Library of Congress holds 275 ex-slave interviews undertaken in Texas. In addition, the Library of Congress and the Oklahoma Historical Society together hold thirty-two interviews undertaken in Oklahoma but with individuals who earlier in their lives had been held in bondage in Texas. From the 307 interviews with Texas ex-slaves examined for this article, 168 included at least some foodways content, although the references varied from substantive to passing. The Center for American History at the University of Texas at Austin represents yet another storehouse for Texas slave narratives. It holds most of the same Texas interviews as the Library of Congress, although many are in different drafts, as well as preserving approximately three hundred additional Texas ex-slave interviews not examined in the preparation of this preliminary survey of Texas African-American foodways documented in the WPA slave narratives.

    The interviews cited here in the original typescripts in the Library of Congress are also available in imperfect facsimile reprints in George P. Rawick, ed., *The American Slave: A Composite Autobiography*, 41 vols. (Westport, Conn.: Greenwood Publishing Company, 1972–79), series 1, vols. 4–5, 7.

3. LC Texas Slave Narratives, part 4, 124 (quotation from Irella Battle Walker). For an overview of the care of slaves in Texas, see Randolph B. Campbell, *An Empire for Slavery: The Peculiar Institution in Texas, 1821–1865* (Baton Rouge: Louisiana State University Press, 1989), 134–52.

4. LC Texas Slave Narratives, part 1, 15 (Andy Anderson), 35 (Sarah Ashley), 112 (Harrison Boyd), 198 (Richard Carruthers), 257 (John Crawford); part 2, 75 (Andrew Goodman), 166 (Lizzie Hughes), 208 (Gus Johnson); part 3, 132 (William Moore), 190–91 (quotation from Betty Powers), 258 (Annie Row); part 4, 74–75 (Emma Taylor), 124 (Irella Battle Walker), 174–75 (Rose Williams); U.S., Works Progress Administration, Federal Writers' Program, Slave Narratives, Oklahoma, XIII, 317 (Easter Wells), 324 (John White), Box A927, Manuscript Division, Library of Congress, Washington, D.C., hereafter cited as LC Oklahoma Slave Narratives; "Eliza Elsey[,] Age 77[,] Fort Gibson, Oklahoma," 2–3, Slave Narrative Collection, Archives and Manuscripts Division, Oklahoma Historical Society, Oklahoma City, Oklahoma, cited hereafter with names of typescripts and designation OHS Slave Narratives.

5. LC Oklahoma Slave Narratives, 128 (quotation from Mattie Hardman), 270 (quotation from Harriett Robinson); LC Texas Slave Narratives, part 1, 45 (Joe Barnes), 215 (Sally Banks Chambers); part 2, 237 (Lewis Jones); part 3, 35–36 (Nap McQueen), 172 (Mary Anne Patterson); part 4, 76 (Mollie Taylor), 126 (John Walton).

6. LC Texas Slave Narratives, part 2, 120 (quotation from Ann Hawthorne), 142 (quotation from Rosina Hoard); part 3, 50, 55 (Isaac Martin), 189 (Ellen Polk), 220 (A. C. Pruitt); part 4, 124 (Irella Battle Walker).

7. LC Texas Slave Narratives, part 1, 264 (quotation from Tempie Collins); part 3, 5 (quotation from Hagar Lewis), 24 (quotation from Abe Livingston).

8. LC Oklahoma Slave Narratives, 17 (Lewis Bonner); LC Texas Slave Narratives, part 3, 41 (C. B. McCray), 89 (Tom Mills); part 4, 83 (Allen Thomas), 85 (Bill and Ellen Thomas), 118 (Lou Turner).

9. LC Oklahoma Slave Narratives, 135 (Ida Henry), 317 (quotations from Easter Wells), 324 (quotation from John White); LC Texas Slave Narratives, part 3, 134 (William Moore).

10. The WPA Slave Narratives relating to Texas which document pork in general as a regular part of diet include the following: LC Oklahoma Slave Narratives, 128 (Mattie Hardman), 324 (quotation from John White); LC Texas Slave Narratives, part 1, 14–15 (Andy Anderson), 45 (Joe Barnes), 73 (Jack Bess), 97, 104 (Julia Blanks), 123 (Jerry Boykins), 131 (Gus Bradshaw), 133 (Wes Brady), 174 (Martha Spence Bunton), 218 (Jeptha Choice), 264 (Tempie Cummins), 274 (Julia Francis Daniels), 279 (Katie Darling); part 2, 22 (John Ellis), 47 (Millie Forward), 75 (Andrew Goodman), 136 (Phoebe Henderson), 158 (Scott Hooper), 160 (Alice Houston), 166 (Lizzie Hughes), 180 (Carter J. Jackson), 215 (Harry Johnson), 238 (Lewis Jones), 247 (Lizzie Jones); part 3, 25 (Abe Livingston), 76 (Susan Merritt), 81 (Josh Miles), 83 (Anna Miller), 117 (Andrew Moody), 129 (Van Moore), 172 (Mary Anne Patterson), 206 (Henry Probasco), 233 (Elsie Reece), 258 (Annie Row), 263 (Gill Ruffin); part 4, 3–4 (Clarissa Scales), 11 (Abram Sells), 22 (Betty Simmons), 24 (George Simmons), 28 (Ben Simpson), 48, 50 (John Sneed), 52 (Mariah Snyder), 71 (Bert Strong), 84 (Allen Thomas), 116 (Reeves

Tucker), 126 (John Walton), 171 (Millie Williams), 174–75 (Rose Williams), 196 (Wash Wilson), 221 (Caroline Wright), 225 (Fannie Yarborough), 235 (quotation from Teshan Young); "Interview with Mollie Watson (Ex-Slave, Aged 83, Colbert, Oklahoma)," 2, OHS Slave Narratives. For an overview of pork in the southern diet, see Joe Gray Taylor, "The Food of the New South (1875–1940)," *Georgia Review* 20, no. 1 (Spring 1966): 19–23. For an archaeologist's analysis of comparative consumption of pork and beef in the South, see Joanne Bowen, "The Importance of Pork in the Southern Diet: An Archaeologist's View," *Food History News* (Isleboro, Me.) 5, no. 2 (Autumn 1993): 1–2, 8.

11. LC Texas Slave Narratives, part 1, 198 (quotation from Richard Carruthers). For other accounts of pig/pork stealing, see LC Oklahoma Slave Narratives, 191 (Lizzie Farmer), 136 (Ida Henry), 264 (Red Richardson); LC Texas Slave Narratives, part 1, 134 (Wes Brady); "Eliza Elsey," 1–2, OHS Slave Narratives; "Aunt Lizzie Farmer," 2, OHS Slave Narratives.

12. LC Oklahoma Slave Narratives, 17 (Lewis Bonner); LC Texas Slave Narratives, part 1, 35 (Sarah Ashley), 45 (Joe Barnes), 198 (Richard Carruthers), 257 (John Crawford), 262 (Green Cumby); part 2, 142 (Rosina Hoard), 169 (Mose Hursey); 208 (quotation from Gus Johnson), 232 (Harriet Jones), 292 (Silvia King); part 3, 10 (Henry Lewis), 139 (Mandy Morrow), 185 (Lee Pierce), 220 (A. C. Pruitt), 249 (Walter Rimm), 265 (Martin Ruffin); part 4, 68 (Yach Stringfellow), 124 (Irella Battle Walker), 148 (Emma Watson), 197 (Wash Wilson).

13. LC Texas Slave Narratives, part 1, 138 (Jacob Branch); part 3, 90 (Tom Mills), 117 (Andrew Moody), 248 (Walter Rimm); part 4, 11 (quotation from Abram Sells), 119 (Lou Turner), 148 (Emma Watson).

14. LC Oklahoma Slave Narratives, 237 (Phyllis Petite); LC Texas Slave Narratives, part 1, 164 (Josie Brown); part 2, 292–93 (Silvia King); part 3, 16 (Lucy Lewis), 129 (quotation from Van Moore), 247 (Walter Rimm); part 4, 48 (John Sneed), 196–97 (Wash Wilson).

15. LC Texas Slave Narratives, part 1 (215 (Sally Banks Chambers); part 2, 124 (quotation from Ann Hawthorne), 292 (Silvia King); part 3, 5 (Hagar Lewis), 139 (quotation from Mandy Morrow); part 4, 126 (John Walton); Taylor, "Food," 20–22.

16. LC Texas Slave Narratives, part 1, 243 (Harriet Collins); part 2, 128 (James Hayes), 292 (Silvia King); part 3, 5 (Hagar Lewis), 90 (Tom Mills), 139 (Mandy Morrow); part 4, 85 (Bill and Ellen Thomas), 107 (Albert Todd), 119 (Lou Turner), 196 (Wash Wilson).

17. LC Oklahoma Slave Narratives, 98 (Lizzie Farmer), 320 (quotation from Easter Wells); LC Texas Slave Narratives, part 4, 109 (Aleck Trimble), 197 (Wash Wilson).

18. LC Texas Slave Narratives, part 2, 99–100 (Pauline Grice), 86 (Austin Grant), 232, 236 (Harriet Jones); part 3, 82 (Josh Miles); part 4, 181 (Steve Williams), 237 (quotation from Teshan Young).

19. LC Texas Slave Narratives, part 3, 205–206 (Henry Probasco).

20. Ibid.; LC Oklahoma Slave Narratives, 324 (John White), 305 (Lou Smith); LC Texas Slave Narratives, part 1, 15 (Andy Anderson), 35 (Sarah Ashley), 112 (Harrison Boyd), 198 (Richard Carruthers), 221 (Amos Clark), 267 (Adeline Cunningham); part 2, 75 (Andrew Goodman), 208 (Gus Johnson), 215 (Harry Johnson), 238 (Lewis Jones), 264 (quotation from Ben Kinchlow), 293 (Silvia King); part 3, 16 (Lucy Lewis), 83 (Anna Miller), 89–90 (Tom Mills), 174 (Martha Patton), 189 (Ellen Polk), 190 (Betty Powers), 247 (Walter Rimm), 253 (Mariah Robinson), 258 (Annie Row); part 4, 50 (John Sneed), 76 (Mollie Taylor), 124 (Irella Battle Walker), 174 (Rose Williams), 235 (Teshan Young).

21. LC Texas Slave Narratives, part 1, 221 (quotation from Amos Clark); part 2, 264 (quotation from Ben Kinchlow); part 3, 89–90 (Tom Mills), 189 (Ellen Polk), 253 (quotation from Mariah Robinson).

22. LC Oklahoma Slave Narratives, 263 (Red Richardson); LC Texas Slave Narratives, part 1, 45 (Joe Barnes), 49 (Harriet Barrett), 103–104 (Julia Blanks), 128 (Monroe Brackins), 133 (Wes Brady), 172 (Madison Bruin), 215 (Sally Banks Chambers), 296 (Eli Davison); part 2, 72 (Mattie Gilmore), 120 (quotation from Ann Hawthorne), 142 (Rosina Hoard), 144 (Tom Holland), 169 (Mose Hursey), 183 (James Jackson), 185 (Maggie Jackson), 266 (Ben Kinchlow); part 3, 114 (Peter Mitchell), 183 (Daniel Phillips, Sr.), 185 (Lee Pierce), 189 (Ellen Polk), 191 (Betty Powers), 205–296 (Henry Probasco), 220 (A. C. Pruitt), 263 (Gill Ruffin), 265 (Martin Ruffin); part 4, 16 (George Selman), 24 (George Simmons), 52 (Mariah Snyder), 68 (Yach Stringfellow), 81 (J. W. Terrill), 148 (Emma Watson), 171 (Millie Williams), 197 (Wash Wilson), 221 (Caroline Wright); "Johnson Thompson[,] Age 84[,] Fort Gibson, Oklahoma," 2 (quotation), OHS Slave Narratives; "Lewis Jenkins[,] Age 93 Yrs.[,] Oklahoma City, Okla.," 4, OHS Slave Narratives; "Mollie Watson," 2, OHS Slave Narratives.

23. LC Texas Slave Narratives, part 1, 103 (Julia Blanks), 135 (Wes Brady), 185 (Louis Cain), 189 (quotation from Jeff Calhoun), 218 (Jeptha Choice); part 2, 6 (Anderson and Minerva Edwards), 180 (Carter J. Jackson), 247 (Lizzie Jones), 266 (quotation from Ben Kinchlow); part 3, 18 (Amos Lincoln), 117 (Andrew Moody), 247 (quotation from Walter Rimm), 71 (Bert Strong), 126 (John Walton), 197 (Wash Wilson); Sandra L. Oliver, "Joy of Historical Cooking: Bannock: Jonnycake, Dodgers, Ashcake, and Hoecake," *Food History News* 1, no. 3 (Winter 1989): 3–6.

24. LC Oklahoma Slave Narratives, 238 (Phyllis Petite), 270 (Harriet Robinson); LC Texas Slave Narratives, part 1, 262 (Green Cumby); part 2, 215 (Harry Johnson), 232–33 (quotation from Harriet Jones), 266 (Ben Kinchlow); part 3, 76 (Susan Merritt), 117 (Andrew Moody), 131 (Van Moore).

25. LC Oklahoma Slave Narratives, 270 (Harriett Robinson); LC Texas Slave Narratives, part 1, 135 (Wes Brady); part 3, 206 (Henry Probasco); part 4, 236 (Teshan Young).

26. Gilbert Fite, *Cotton Fields No More: Southern Agriculture 1865–1980* (Lexington: The University Press of Kentucky, 1984), 37; LC Oklahoma Slave Narratives, 239 (Phyllis Petite), 305 (Lou Smith); LC Texas Slave Narratives, 49 (Harriet Barnett), 133 (Wes Brady), 198 (Richard Carruthers), 215 (Sally Banks Chambers), 257 (John Crawford); part 2, 71 (Mattie Gilmore), 76 (Andrew Goodman), 127 (quotation from James Hayes), 158 (Scott Hooper), 166 (Lizzie Hughes), 208 (Gus Johnson), 233 (Harriet Jones), 238 (Lewis Jones), 286 (Mary Kindred), 292 (Silvia King); part 3, 10 (Henry Lewis), 27 (quotation from John Love), 83 (Anna Miller), 174 (Martha Patton), 189 (Ellen Polk), 190–91 (Betty Powers), 233 (Elsie Reece), 258 (quotation from Annie Row), 265 (Martin Ruffin); part 4, 76 (Mollie Taylor), 109 (Aleck Trimble), 124 (Irella Battle Walker), 174 (Rose Williams), 196 (Wash Wilson), 221 (Caroline Wright), 235 (Teshan Young).

27. Bowen, "Importance of Pork," 11–12, 8; LC Texas Slave Narratives, part 1, 14 (Andy Anderson), 73 (Jack Bess), 103 (Julia Blanks), 131 (Gus Bradshaw), 191 (Simp Campbell), 218 (Jeptha Choice), 274 (quotation from Julia Francis Daniels), 285 (Campbell Davis); part 2, 22 (John Ellis), 89 (James Green), 166 (Lizzie Hughes), 215 (Harry Johnson), 262–63 (Ben Kinchlow), 293 (Silvia King); part 3, 10 (Henry Lewis), 25 (Abe Livingston), 90, 100-101 (Tom Mills), 183 (Daniel Phillips), 222 (quotation from Harre Quarls); part 4, 148 (Emma Watson), 221 (Caroline Wright).

28. LC Texas Slave Narratives, part 1, 183 (William Byrd), 243 (Harriet Collins), 286 (Campbell Davis); part 2, 75-76 (Andrew Goodman), 86 (Austin Grant), 89 (quotation from James Green); part 4, 71 (Bert Strong), 82 (quotation from J. W. Terrill).

    Other informants who had remembrances of mid-nineteenth-century Texas foodways commented on additional domestic animals as food sources, with four references to mutton, two references to goatmeat, and one to horsemeat. LC Texas Slave Narratives, part 1, 188 (Jeff Calhoun), 286 (Campbell Davis); part 2, 262 (Ben Kinchlow), 293 (Silvia King); part 3, 51 (Isaac Martin); part 4, 71 (Bert Strong).

29. LC Texas Slave Narratives, part 1, 66 (Edgar Bendy), 300 (quotation from Elige Davison); part 2, 144 (Tom Holland), 251-52 (Toby Jones); page 3, 18 (Amos Lincoln), 26 (John Love), 50 (Isaac Martin), 81 (Josh Miles), 95 (Tom Mills); part 4, 48 (John Sneed), 70 (Bert Strong).

30. LC Oklahoma Slave Narratives, 98 (quotation from Lizzie Farmer), 237 (Phyllis Petite), 263 (Red Richardson); LC Texas Slave Narratives, part 1, 66–67 (quotation from Edgar Bendy), 73 (Jack Bess), 127 (Monroe Brackins), 218 (Jeptha Choice), 244 (Harriet Collins); part 2, 22 (John Ellis), 47 (Millie Forward), 72 (Mattie Gilmore), 83 (Austin Grant), 144 (Tom Holland), 160 (Alice Houston), 185 (Maggie Jackson), 234 (Harriet Jones), 247 (Lizzie Jones), 261–62 (Ben Kinchlow); part 3, 7 (Hagar Lewis), 10 (Henry Lewis), 18 (Amos Lincoln), 90 (Tom Mills), 131 (Van Moore), 167 (George Owens), 178 (Ellen Payne); part 4, 11 (quotation from Abram Sells), 24 (George Simmons), 48 (John Sneed),

83–84 (Allen Thomas), 180 (Steve Williams), 197 (Wash Wilson), 221 (Caroline Wright); "Lewis Jenkins," 4, OHS Slave Narratives.

31. LC Oklahoma Slave Narratives, 237 (Phyllis Petite), 263 (Red Richardson); LC Texas Slave Narratives, part 1, 127 (Monroe Brackins), 221 (Amos Clark), 274 (quotation from Julia Francis Daniels); part 2, 22 (John Ellis), 72 (Mattie Gilmore), 83 (Austin Grant), 144 (Tom Holland), 185 (Maggie Jackson), 247 (Lizzie Jones); part 2, 261–62 (Ben Kinchlow), 293 (Silvia King); part 3, 10 (Henry Lewis), 50 (quotation from Isaac Martin), 90 (Tom Mills), 132 (William Moore), 178 (Ellen Payne); part 4, 11 (quotation from Abram Sells), 48 (John Sneed), 70 (Bert Strong), 172 (Millie Williams), 221 (Caroline Wright); "Interview with J. W. Stinnett[,] Slave Born, Age 75, Route 1, Box 139, Muskogee, Oklahoma," 1, OHS Slave Narratives; "Lewis Jenkins," 4, OHS Slave Narratives.

32. For references to raccoons as a meat source for Texas African-Americans, see LC Texas Slave Narratives, part 1, 66 (Edgar Bendy), 73 (Jack Bess), 127 (Monroe Brackins); part 2, 47 (Millie Forward), 167 (Lizzie Hughes), 234 (Harriet Jones); part 3, 7 (Hagar Lewis), 18 (Amos Lincoln), 131 (Van Moore), 178 (Ellen Payne); part 4, 180 (Steve Williams), 197 (Wash Wilson); "Lewis Jenkins," 4, OHS Slave Narratives. For references to squirrels as a meat source for Texas African-Americans, see LC Texas Slave Narratives, part 1, 274 (Julia Francis Daniels), 296 (Eli Davison); part 2, 247 (Lizzie Jones), 293 (Silvia King); part 3, 7 (Hagar Lewis), 90 (Tom Mills); part 4, 11 (Abram Sells), 70 (Bert Strong), 172 (quotation from Millie Williams); "Interview with J. W. Stinnett," 1, OHS Slave Narratives.

33. LC Texas Slave Narratives, part 1, 49 (Harriet Barrett), 66–67 (Edgar Bendy), 104 (Julia Blanks), 131 (Gus Bradshaw), 188 (Jeff Calhoun), 296 (quotation from Eli Davison); part 2, 22 (John Ellis), 47 (Millie Forward), 180 (quotation from Carter J. Jackson), 261–63 (Ben Kinchlow), 293 (Silvia King); part 3, 26 (John Love), 90 (Tom Mills), 167 (George Owens), 172 (Mary Anne Patterson), 185–86 (Lee Pierce); part 4, 11 (Abram Sells), 70 (Bert Strong), 182 (Wayman Williams), 196 (Wash Wilson); "Lewis Jenkins," 4, OHS Slave Narratives.

34. LC Texas Slave Narratives, part 2, 261–62 (Ben Kinchlow); part 3, 95 (Tom Mills), 189 (Ellen Polk); part 4, 43 (Millie Ann Smith), 182 (Wayman Williams), 196 (Wash Williams).

35. LC Texas Slave Narratives, part 1, 188 (Jeff Calhoun); part 2, 293 (Silvia King); part 3, 26 (John Love), 172 (Mary Anne Patterson); part 4, 182 (Wayman Williams).

36. LC Texas Slave Narratives, part 1, 188 (Jeff Calhoun); part 2, 22 (John Ellis).

37. LC Texas Slave Narratives, part 2, 22 (John Ellis).

38. LC Texas Slave Narratives, part 1, 104 (Julia Blanks), 154 (Fannie Brown), 188 (Jeff Calhoun), 221 (Amos Clark), 246 (Andrew Columbus); part 2, 234 (Harriet Jones), 261 (Ben Kinchlow), 293 (Silvia King); part 3, 26 (quotation from John Love), 90 (Tom Mills), 189 (Ellen Polk); part 4, 11 (Abram Sells), 43 (Millie Ann Smith), 70 (Bert Strong), 182 (Wayman Williams), 196 (Wash Wilson); "Lewis Jenkins," 4, OHS Slave Narratives.

39. LC Texas Slave Narratives, part 1, 188 (Jeff Calhoun); part 2, 234 (Harriet Jones), 261–63 (Ben Kinchlow), 293 (Silvia King); part 3, 18 (quotation from Amos Lincoln), 90 (Tom Mills), 182 (Henderson Perkins); part 4, 70 (Bert Strong); 196 (Wash Wilson).

40. LC Oklahoma Slave Narratives, 237 (Phyllis Petite), 263 (Red Richardson); LC Texas Slave Narratives, part 1, 67 (Edgar Bendy), 103–104 (quotation from Julia Blanks), 185 (Louis Cain); part 2, 22 (John Ellis), 47 (Millie Forward), 72 (Mattie Gilmore), 76 (Andrew Goodman), 136 (Phoebe Henderson), 144 (Tom Holland), 185 (Maggie Jackson), 247 (Lizzie Jones); part 3, 189 (Ellen Polk), 95 (Tom Mills), 4–5 (Hagar Lewis), 10 (Henry Lewis), 15–16 (Lucy Lewis), 186 (Lee Pierce), 263 (Gill Ruffin); part 4, 48 (John Sneed), 176 (Rose Williams), 221 (Caroline Wright). One of the WPA interviewees mentioned eating fish in another form, that of tinned sardines, which as a child slave he purchased for five cents a can at a crossroads store near Paris, Texas. "Mose Smith[,] Age 85, Muskogee, Oklahoma," 1, OHS Slave Narratives.

41. LC Texas Slave Narratives, part 1, 14 (Andy Anderson); part 2, 223 (Mary Ellen Johnson); part 3, 76 (Susan Merritt), 97 (Tom Mills); part 4, 22 (Betty Simmons).

42. LC Texas Slave Narratives, part 1, 221 (Amos Clark); part 2, 76 (Andrew Goodman), 103 (Mandy Hadnot), 124 (Ann Hawthorne), 128 (James Hayes), 232 (Harriet Jones); part 3, 91 (Tom Mills), 117 (Andrew Moody).

43. LC Texas Slave Narratives, part 2, 136 (Phoebe Henderson), 160 (Alice Houston); part 3, 177 (Ellen Payne), 181 (Henderson Perkins), 255 (Mariah Robinson), 258 (Annie Row).

44. LC Oklahoma Slave Narratives, 263 (quotation from Red Richardson).

45. LC Texas Slave Narratives, part 1, 134–35 (Wes Brady), 247 (Andrew Columbus); part 3, 233 (Elsie Reece), 249 (Walter Rimm).

46. LC Oklahoma Slave Narratives, 136 (Ida Henry); LC Texas Slave Narratives, part 1, 35 (Sarah Ashley), 198 (Richard Carruthers), 212 (Jack Cauthern); part 2, 181 (Carter J. Jackson); part 3, 76 (Susan Merritt); part 4, 50 (John Sneed), 171 (Millie Williams), 186 (Wayman Williams).

47. LC Texas Slave Narratives, part 1, 14 (Andy Anderson), 104 (Julia Blanks), 243 (Harriet Collins); part 2, 124 (Ann Hawthorne), 232 (Harriet Jones); part 3, 25 (Abe Livingston), 117 (Andrew Moody), 177 (Ellen Payne), 255 (Marian Robinson); part 4, 49 (John Sneed), 183 (Wayman Williams).

48. LC Texas Slave Narratives, part 1, 49 (Harriet Barrett); part 2, 223 (quotation from Mary Ellen Johnson); part 3, 247 (Walter Rimm); part 4, 28 (Ben Simpson); "Johnson Thompson," 2, OHS Slave Narratives.

49. LC Oklahoma Slave Narratives, 317–18 (quotation from Easter Wells).

50. LC Oklahoma Slave Narratives, 237–38 (quotation from Phyllis Petite), 270 (Harriett Robinson); LC Texas Slave Narratives, part 2, 180 (Carter J. Jackson), 185 (Maggie Jackson), 266 (Ben Kinchlow); part 3, 189 (Ellen Polk), 248 (Walter

Rimm), 253 (Mariah Robinson); part 4, 85 (Bill and Ellen Thomas), 197 (Wash Wilson).

51. LC Texas Slave Narratives, part 1, 127 (Monroe Brackins), 198 (Richard Carruthers); part 2, 158 (Scott Hooper), 166 (Lizzie Hughes), 238 (Lewis Jones), 263 (Ben Kinchlow), 286 (Mary Kindred); part 3, 10 (Henry Lewis), 18 (Amos Lincoln), 76 (Susan Merritt), 83 (quotation from Anna Miller), 129 (Van Moore), 174–75 (Martha Patton), 186 (Lee Pierce); part 4, 48, 50 (John Sneed), 76 (Mollie Taylor), 116 (quotation from Reeves Tucker), 175 (Rose Williams), 185 (Wayman Williams).

52. LC Oklahoma Slave Narratives, 136 (quotation from Ida Henry), 303 (Lou Smith); LC Texas Slave Narratives, part 1, 174 (Martha Spence Bunton), 139 (Jeff Calhoun), 199–200 (Richard Carruthers), 264 (Tempie Cummins); part 2, 47 (Millie Forward), 126–27 (James Hayes), 183 (James Jackson); part 3, 114 (quotation from Peter Mitchell), 117 (Andrew Moody), 129 (Van Moore), 186 (quotation from Lee Pierce); part 4, 107 (Albert Todd), 109 (Aleck Trimble), 175 (Rose Williams).

53. LC Oklahoma Slave Narratives, 98 (quotation from Lizzie Farmer); LC Texas Slave Narratives, part 1, 133 (quotation from Wes Brady), 267 (Adeline Cunningham), 285 (Campbell Davis); part 2, 232 (Harriet Jones); part 3, 89, 95 (Tom Mills), 117 (Andrew Moody), 129 (Van Moore), 166 (George Owens), 222 (Harre Quarls), 265 (Martin Ruffin); part 4, 68 (Yach Stringfellow), 73–74 (Emma Taylor), 148 (Emma Watson), 236 (Teshan Young).

54. LC Texas Slave Narratives, part 1, 154 (Fannie Brown), 172 (Madison Bruin), 279 (quotation from Katie Darling), 286 (Campbell Davis); part 2, 47 (Millie Forward), 86 (Austin Grant), 105 (Mandy Hadnot), 124 (Ann Hawthorne), 127–28 (James Hayes), 152 (Larnce Holt), 232, 236 (Harriet Jones), 91 (Tom Mills), 117 (Andrew Moody); part 4, 49 (John Sneed), 181 (quotation from Steve Williams), 23 (Teshan Young); "Interview with Mollie Watson," 2, OHS Slave Narratives.

55. LC Texas Slave Narratives, part 2, 215 (Harry Johnson), 232, 236 (Harriet Jones), 293 (Silvia King); part 3, 14 (Lucy Lewis); "Aunt Lizzie Farmer," 3, OHS Slave Narratives.

56. LC Oklahoma Slave Narratives, 98 (Lizzie Farmer), 128 (Mattie Hardman), 263 (Red Richardson), 317 (Easter Wells); LC Texas Slave Narratives, part 1, 49 (Harriet Barrett), 73 (Jack Bess), 133 (Wes Brady), 182 (William Byrd), 191 (Simp Campbell), 262 (Green Cumby), 285 (Campbell Davis); part 2, 22 (John Ellis), 75 (Andrew Goodman), 128 (James Hayes), 180 (Carter J. Jackson), 183 (James Jackson), 247 (Lizzie Jones); part 3, 54 (Isaac Martin), 178 (Ellen Payne), 206 (Henry Probasco); part 4, 22 (Betty Simmons), 24 (George Simmons), 76 (Mollie Taylor), 84 (Allen Thomas), 113 (Aleck Trimble), 180 (Steve Williams), 185 (Wayman Williams), 221 (Caroline Wright), 235-36 (Teshan Young); Karen L. Simpson, "In Search of Our Ancestors' Gardens," *The Historical Gardener* (Mt. Vernon, Wash.) 2, no. 4 (Winter 1993): 4-5.

57. LC Texas Slave Narratives, part 1, 45 (Joe Barnes), 172 (Madison Bruin), 285 (quotation from Campbell Davis); part 2, 232 (Harriet Jones); part 3, 191 (Betty Powers); part 4, 10 (Abram Sells), 70–71 (quotation from Bert Strong), 16 (George Selman).

58. LC Oklahoma Slave Narratives, 17 (Lewis Bonner); LC Texas Slave Narratives, part 1, 45 (Joe Barnes), 131 (Gus Bradshaw); part 2, 120 (Ann Hawthorne); part 3, 16 (Lucy Lewis), 76 (Susan Merritt), 185 (quotation from Lee Pierce); part 4, 68 (Yach Stringfellow), 70–71 (quotation from Bert Strong), 197 (Wash Wilson).

59. LC Oklahoma Slave Narratives, 237 (Phyllis Petite); LC Texas Slave Narratives, part 1, 274 (Julia Francis Daniels), 279 (Katie Darling); part 2, 232 (Harriet Jones), 247 (Lizzie Jones); part 3, 18 (Amos Lincoln), 263 (Gill Ruffin), 10 (Abram Sells); part 4, 52 (Mariah Snyder), 109 (Aleck Trimble); "Interview with Mollie Watson," 2, OHS Slave Narratives; "Johnson Thompson," 2, OHS Slave Narratives.

60. LC Texas Slave Narratives, part 2, 136 (Phoebe Henderson), 247 (quotation from Lizzie Jones); part 3, 263 (Gill Ruffin); part 4, 48 (John Sneed); "Interview with Mollie Watson," 2, OHS Slave Narratives.

61. LC Texas Slave Narratives, part 3, 18 (Amos Lincoln); part 4, 28 (Ben Simpson), 48 (quotation from John Sneed).

62. LC Oklahoma Slave Narratives, 97 (Lizzie Farmer); LC Texas Slave Narratives, part 1, 131 (Gus Bradshaw), 174 (Martha Spence Bunton); part 2, 247 (Lizzie Jones); part 3, 184 (Daniel Phillips, Sr.), 220 (A. C. Pruitt); part 4, 10 (Abram Sells), 48 (John Sneed).

63. LC Oklahoma Slave Narratives, 320 (Easter Wells); LC Texas Slave Narratives, part 1, 112 (Harrison Boyd), 212 (Jack Cauthern), 244 (Harriet Collins), 279 (Katie Darling); part 2, 72 (Mattie Gilmore), 142 (quotation from Rosina Hoard), 158 (quotation from Scott Hooper), 169 (Mose Hursey), 180 (Carter J. Jackson), 185 (Maggie Jackson); part 3, 114 (Peter Mitchell), 166 (George Owens), 173 (Martha Patton), 184 (Daniel Phillips, Sr.), 191 (Betty Powers); part 4, 10 (Abram Sells), 24 (George Simmons), 171 (quotation from Millie Williams), 174 (Rose Williams), 235 (Teshan Young); "Interview with Mollie Watson," 2, OHS Slave Narratives; "Johnson Thompson," 2, OHS Slave Narratives.

64. LC Oklahoma Slave Narratives, 98 (Lizzie Farmer), 263 (Red Richardson); LC Texas Slave Narratives, part 1, 127 (quotation from Monroe Brackins); part 2, 72 (Mattie Gilmore), 142 (Rosina Hoard), 158 (Scott Hooper), 169 (Mose Hursey), 215 (Harry Johnson); part 3, 76 (Susan Merritt), 83 (Anna Miller), 184 (Daniel Phillips, Sr.), 191 (Betty Powers); part 4, 10 (Abram Sells), 174 (Rose Williams), 235 (Teshan Young); "Interview with Mollie Watson," 2, OHS Slave Narratives.

65. LC Oklahoma Slave Narratives, 98 (Lizzie Farmer), 264 (Red Richardson), 319 (Easter Wells); LC Texas Slave Narratives, part 1, 35 (Sarah Ashley), 127 (Monroe Brackins), 215 (Sally Banks Chambers), 218 (Jeptha Choice), 244 (Harriet Collins), 284 (Carey Davenport); part 2, 124 (Ann Hawthorne), 128 (James Hayes),

131 (quotation from Felix Haywood), 160–61 (Alice Houston), 223 (Mary Ellen Johnson); part 3, 166 (George Owens), 172 (Mary Anne Patterson), 190 (Betty Powers); part 4, 11–12, 14 (quotation from Abram Sells), 24 (George Simmons), 48 (John Sneed), 71 (Bert Strong), 75 (Emma Taylor), 80 (J. W. Terrill), 84 (Allen Thomas), 185 (Wayman Williams), 196 (Wash Wilson), 225 (Fannie Yarbrough); "Interview with Mollie Watson," 2–3, OHS Slave Narratives; "Lewis Jenkins," 4 (quotation), OHS Slave Narratives; "Mose Smith," 2–3 (quotation), OHS Slave Narratives.

66. LC Oklahoma Slave Narratives, 17 (Lewis Bonner); LC Texas Slave Narratives, part 1, 138 (Jacob Branch); part 3, 174 (Martha Patton); part 4, 10 (Abram Sells).

67. Carolyn Kolb, "Okra," in *Encyclopedia of Southern Culture*, edited by Charles Reagan Wilson and William Ferris (Chapel Hill: University of North Carolina Press, 1989), 514; LC Oklahoma Slave Narratives, 98 (Lizzie Farmer), 305 (Lou Smith); LC Texas Slave Narratives, part 2, 286 (Mary Kindred).

68. LC Oklahoma Slave Narratives, 98 (Lizzie Farmer); LC Texas Slave Narratives, part 1, 112 (Harrison Boyd), 155 (Fannie Brown); part 2, 41 (Sarah Ford); part 3, 18 (Amos Lincoln), 184 (Daniel Phillips, Sr.); part 4, 196 (Wash Wilson), 206– 207 (Willis Winn).

69. LC Texas Slave Narratives, part 1, 99–100 (quotation from Julia Blanks), 164 (Josie Brown); part 2, 103 (Mandy Hadnot); 210 (Gus Johnson), 236 (Harriet Jones); part 3, 233 (Elsie Reece), 255 (Mariah Robinson), 258 (Annie Row); part 4, 185 (Wayman Williams); "Eliza Elsey," 1, OHS Slave Narratives. For references specifically to apples, see LC Texas Slave Narratives, part 1, 243 (Harriet Collins); part 2, 103 (Mandy Hadnot), 152 (quotation from Larnce Holt), 291 (Silvia King), 215 (Harry Johnson); part 4, 71 (Bert Strong). For references specifically to watermelons, see LC Texas Slave Narratives, part 1, 55 (Harrison Beckett), 104 (Julia Blanks), 127, 129 (Monroe Brackins); part 2, 124 (Ann Hawthorne), 160 (Alice Houston); part 4, 83 (Allen Thomas), 186 (Wayman Williams).

70. LC Oklahoma Slave Narratives, 263 (Red Richardson); LC Texas Slave Narratives, part 1, 14 (Andy Anderson), 137 (quotation from Jacob Branch), 267 (Adeline Cunningham); part 2, 41 (Sarah Ford), 120 (Ann Hawthorne), 142 (Rosina Hoard), 158 (Scott Hooper), 160 (quotation from Alice Houston), 238 (Lewis Jones), 262, 266 (Ben Kinchlow); part 3, 14 (Lucy Lewis), 57–58 (Isaac Martin), 76 (Susan Merritt), 83 (Anna Miller), 166–67 (George Owens), 183–84 (Daniel Phillips, Sr.), 191 (Betty Powers), 233 (Elsie Reece), 263 (Gill Ruffin), 265 (Martin Ruffin); part 4, 76 (Mollie Taylor), 83 (Allen Thomas), 109 (Aleck Trimble), 124 (Irella Battle Walker), 148 (Emma Watson), 171 (Millie Williams), 174 (Rose Williams), 221 (Caroline Wright), 235–36 (Teshan Young); "Lewis Jenkins," 4, OHS Slave Narratives.

71. LC Texas Slave Narratives, part 1, 14 (Andy Anderson), 103–104 (Julia Blanks); part 2, 158 (Scott Hooper), 210 (Gus Johnson), 215 (Harry Johnson), 233 (Harriet

Jones), 238 (Lewis Jones), 262, 266 (Ben Kinchlow); part 3, 76 (Susan Merritt), 167 (George Owens), 233 (Elsie Reece), 253 (Mariah Robinson); part 4, 83 (Allen Thomas), 109 (Aleck Trimble), 221 (Caroline Wright); "Lewis Jenkins," 4, OHS Slave Narratives.

72. LC Texas Slave Narratives, part 1, 182 (William Byrd), 127, 129 (Monroe Brackins); part 2, 124 (quotation from Ann Hawthorne); part 4, 83 (Allen Thomas), 140 (quotation from Sam Jones Washington).

73. LC Oklahoma Slave Narratives, 239 (Phyllis Petite), 320 (Easter Wells); LC Texas Slave Narratives, part 1, 112 (Harrison Boyd), 164 (Josie Brown), 182 (William Byrd), 218 (Jeptha Choice); part 2, 103 (Mandy Hadnot), 158 (Scott Hooper); part 3, 10 (Henry Lewis), 16 (Lucy Lewis), 130 (Van Moore), 174 (Martha Patton), 220 (A. C. Pruitt); part 4, 76 (Mollie Taylor), 196 (Wash Wilson); "Interview with Mollie Watson," 6 (quotation), OHS Slave Narratives.

74. LC Oklahoma Slave Narratives, 239 (Phyllis Petite); LC Texas Slave Narratives, part 1, 12–13 (Saran Allen); part 2, 47 (Millie Forward), 76 (Andrew Goodman), 103 (Mandy Hadnot), 144 (Tom Holland), 152 (Larnch Holt), 157 (Scott Hooper), 167 (quotation from Lizzie Hughes), 288 (Nancy King); part 3, 122 (Jerry Moore); part 4, 69 (Yach Stringfellow), 71 (Bert Strong), 148 (Emma Watson); "Mose Smith," 1, OHS Slave Narratives.

75. LC Texas Slave Narratives, part 1, 14 (Andy Anderson), 164 (Josie Brown), 221 (Amos Clark); part 3, 172 (Mary Anne Patterson), 181 (quotation from Henderson Perkins), 191 (Betty Powers), 255 (Mariah Robinson).

76. LC Texas Slave Narratives, part 2, 105 (Mandy Hadnot), 223 (Mary Ellen Johnson), 293 (Silvia King); part 4, 85 (Bill and Ellen Thomas).

77. LC Oklahoma Slave Narratives, 98 (Lizzie Farmer), 304 (quotation from Lou Smith); LC Texas Slave Narratives, part 1, 35 (Sarah Ashley); part 3, 50 (Isaac Martin), 247–48 (Walter Rimm), 258 (Annie Row); part 4, 75 (quotation from Emma Taylor), 84 (Allen Thomas).

78. LC Texas Slave Narratives, part 3, 76 (Susan Merritt), 174–75 (Martha Patton); part 4, 67 (quotation from Yach Stringfellow), 81 (J. W. Terrill).

79. LC Texas Slave Narratives, part 1, 95 (Julia Blanks), 128 (Monroe Brackins), 279 (Katie Darling); part 2, 43 (quotation from Sarah Ford), 86 (Austin Grant), 157 (Scott Hooper), 170 (Mose Hursey), 232 (Harriet Jones), 263 (Ben Kinchlow); part 3, 91 (Tom Mills), 130 (Van Moore), 175 (Martha Patton), 225 (Eda Rains), 233 (Elsie Reece); part 4, 76 (Mollie Taylor), 171 (Millie Williams), 175 (quotation from Rose Williams); "Interview with Mollie Watson," 3, OHS Slave Narratives.

80. LC Oklahoma Slave Narratives, 305 (Lou Smith); LC Texas Slave Narratives, part 1, 198 (Richard Carruthers), 279 (Katie Darling); part 2, 43 (Sarah Ford), 47 (Millie Forward), 161 (Alice Houston), 183 (James Jackson), 215 (Harry Johnson), 263 (Ben Kinchlow), 286 (Mary Kindred); part 3, 174 (Martha Patton); part 4,

124 (Irella Battle Walker), 126 (John Walton); "Interview with Mollie Watson," 2–3 (quotation), OHS Slave Narratives.

81. LC Texas Slave Narratives, part 2, 157 (Scott Hooper); part 3, 174–75 (Martha Patton), 233 (Elsie Reece); part 4, 126 (John Walton), 175 (Rose Williams).

82. LC Oklahoma Slave Narratives, 264 (Red Richardson), 325 (John White); LC Texas Slave Narratives, part 2, 76 (Andrew Goodman), 86 (Austin Grant); part 3, 10 (Henry Lewis), 266 (quotation from Martin Ruffin); part 4, 90 (Lucy Thomas), 197–98 (Wash Wilson).

83. LC Oklahoma Slave Narratives, 264 (Red Richardson), 320 (quotation from Easter Wells); LC Texas Slave Narratives, part 1, 183 (William Byrd), 243 (Harriet Collins); part 4, 49 (John Sneed), 69 (Yach Stringfellow), 224 (Sallie Wroe).

84. LC Texas Slave Narratives, part 1, 100 (Julia Blanks), 164 (Josie Brown), 243 (Harriet Collins), 258 (John Crawford); part 2, 167 (Lizzie Hughes), 234 (Harriet Jones), 293 (Silvia King).

85. LC Oklahoma Slave Narratives, 98 (quotation from Lizzie Farmer); LC Texas Slave Narratives, part 1, 49 (Harriet Barrett); part 2, 142 (Rosina Hoard), 169 (Mose Hursey), 223 (Mary Ellen Johnson); part 3, 44 (Julia Malone), 220 (A. C. Pruitt), 223 (Harre Quarls); part 4, 52 (Mariah Snyder); "Interview with Mollie Watson," 2, OHS Slave Narratives.

86. LC Texas Slave Narratives, part 1, 49 (Harriett Barnett); part 2, 223 (Mary Ellen Johnson), 267 (Ben Kinchlow); part 3, 253 (Mariah Robinson); "Johnson Thompson," 2, OHS Slave Narratives.

87. LC Oklahoma Slave Narratives, 98 (Lizzie Farmer); LC Texas Slave Narratives, part 1, 45 (Joe Barnes); part 2, 266 (Ben Kinchlow); part 3, 222–23 (Harre Quarls); part 4, 73–74 (quotation from Emma Taylor), 84 (Allen Thomas).

88. LC Oklahoma Slave Narratives, 270 (Harriett Robinson), 318 (Easter Wells); LC Texas Slave Narratives, part 1, 172 (Madison Bruin), 267 (quotation from Adeline Cunningham); part 2, 120 (Ann Hawthorne), 178 (Wash Ingram); part 3, 83 (Anna Miller); part 4, 10 (Abram Sells), 16 (George Selman), 67, 69 (Yach Stringfellow), 76 (Mollie Taylor), 236 (Teshan Young); "Johnson Thompson," 2, OHS Slave Narratives.

89. LC Texas Slave Narratives, part 1, 45 (Joe Barnes), 112 (Harrison Boyd), 154 (Fannie Brown), 267 (Adeline Cunningham); part 2, 169 (Mose Hursey), 267 (Ben Kinchlow), 292 (Silvia King); part 3, 5 (Hagar Lewis), 76 (Susan Merritt); part 4, 68–69 (Yach Stringfellow), 83 (Allen Thomas), 148 (Emma Watson); "Interview with Mollie Watson," 2, OHS Slave Narratives.

90. LC Texas Slave Narratives, part 3, 14 (Lucy Lewis).

Nineteenth-century Negro home. (Courtesy, Houston Public Library; *Album of Houston, Texas)*

Sugar cane mill for making syrup. (Courtesy, Institute of Texan Cultures, San Antonio, Texas)

Upshur County Men's Chorus (Union Memorial Temple, Texarkana). (Courtesy, Jan Rosenberg)

Pearl Williams (light dress) offers selections, accompanied by members of the Harmonette Spiritual Singers (Union Memorial Temple, Texarkana). (Courtesy, Jan Rosenberg)

Giving Honor to God, the Joy and Salvation in My Life: The Appreciation Service in Song

by Jan Rosenberg

Throughout Northeast Texas' and Southwest Arkansas' African-American communities, gospel music musicians, singers, and lovers worship God in song and prayer. This particular kind of worship service is known as an appreciation program. It is a time to appreciate God and the contributions a musical group or singer has made to Him. It is an occasion orchestrated by the group or a soloist. For while the group is appreciated on earth, all praises go to God in Heaven.

On Saturday evening and Sunday afternoon, groups and soloists enter the worship hall and register their names. At an appointed time, each one will be called to the front of the room to say a few words about the host of the appreciation, and sing one or two sacred songs.

Participating gospel groups, such as the Silvertone Spiritual Singers, have been singing appreciations in the region since the 1950s. Some belong to the Arkansas Texas Quartet Union or the Arkansas Independent State Quartet Convention. In a border city such as Texarkana, home is not necessarily in Texas or Arkansas. State lines are blurred while the mission to God in song is solidly defined.

The appreciation is held in a facility that has been dedicated as a church by a minister and recognized as a house of God by the community. In Texarkana, that facility is the Union Memorial Temple. The Arkansas Independent State Quartet Convention has seven singing centers located throughout the state.

An appreciation has two distinct parts: the devotional and the service in song. The program is facilitated by an individual selected by the host of the appreciation. It may be a fellow singer; it could be a relative of the host. The only requirement is that he or she is a Christian.

J. W. Matthews was President of the Arkansas Independent State Quartet Convention from the late 1960s until his death in 1995. He explained the attitude one must have to successfully begin an appreciation program: "See, if you do a gospel program of any kind, it is for the Lord. Singing goes up. Gospel comes down. . . . So you've got to first ask the Lord in." (Interview, 15 July 1991)

The devotional is the time to get in the spirit, to give praise to the Holy Spirit, and ask It to enter the service. This turns program attendance into "a church." It starts with an a cappella song, initiated by a group of individuals who sit in the congregation. They may be facing the congregation or sitting within the group. These men and women are respected in the gospel community as singers of devotionals. Often they are members of their respective churches' Devotional Committees. Usually they are older members of the gospel community, experienced in singing the songs of their parents and grandparents.

Amidst decorations highlighting the appreciation, a singer like Mary Lindley will start to sing—unannounced—followed by those sitting by her side and in the worship hall. The following was transcibed 30 June 1990:

Oh, I know that Jesus is on the main line,
    you ought to tell Him what you want.
Whoa, oh, Jesus is on the main line,
    why don't you tell Him what you want.
Oh, Jesus he's on the main line,
    you ought to tell Him what you want.
You just call Him up, oh,
    and tell Him what you want.

Oh, you know that the line is never too busy
    to just tell Him what you want.
Oh the line is never too busy
    to just tell Him what you want.
Oh the line is never too busy to tell Him what you want
    You just call Him up and tell Him what you want.
    (Spoken) Amen

At the close of the song, one of the devotional leaders kneels to pray. God is invited into the worship place and the host is recognized. The prayer is spoken, chanted, and sung. The congregation responds freely (these responses are in parentheses), as in the following which was recorded on 1 July 1990:

This evening, our Heavenly Father (Yes, Lord, alright)
Lord, come on and see about us, please. (Yes, Lord)
Old Satan is on his rounds. (Oh, yes, Lord)
But if You come on, everything will be alright. (Yes, Lord)
Lord, it's once more time and again
That You look down on us all. Last night (Yes, Lord)
While we slumbered and slept, (Yes)
Lord, You told us what to think of love. (Yes, Lord)
And, and, and You abled our eyes to try to open (Yes Lord)
And witness a day when we'd never have could've seen before.
Now, now, now, Lord; [speech becomes chant]
Now, now, now, Lord (Now, Lord)
If you come on and see about us, (chant becomes speech)
Everything will be alright. (Yes, Lord)
You know, I know that Man have always kept
Your commands so well. (Yes, Lord)
But, but, but just by you being the God You is,
You look down on us, (Oh yes!)
And, and You forgive us,
And You give Your own begotten Son (Yes)
Who hung on the cross and bled and died. (Oh, Lord)

Lord, You tell me Jesus He hung on there
From the sixth to the ninth hour, (Yeah)
and the blood drained down to the ground
Now, now, Lord [chant] . . . Now Lord.
Tell me the sun refuses to shine
And the moon breaks away with blood.
[Sings] Oh Lord! (Oh Lord!)
Please come on and see about us this morning.
Bless these men who are trying to carry out Your program.
Lord, please look down on them. (Yes, Lord) . . .
Now please, Jesus, have mercy on us this evening.
These few words are said in Your priceless name,
Amen, Jesus.
[The devotional group comes in, and the group joins them.]
I'll be waiting up there somewhere,
I'll be waiting up there somewhere.
Come on up to bright glory,
I'll be waiting up there.

The gathering is now "a church." They are in the spirit and ready for the service in song. The emcee, Elder Smith, proceeds: "Everybody give the Lord a big hand for that. Thank You, Jesus, thank You. Hallelujah! We're here to have a hallelujah time tonight . . . and we are just here to magnify and lift the name of the Lord up tonight and sing His praise. We want everybody to get in the service tonight and just have a good time tonight. Amen. Let us say, Amen."

Elder Smith requests a welcome. This is a highly stylized statement fashioned from traditional phrases and the welcomer's speaking skills. Mrs. Justenor White is such a skilled purveyor of the welcome phrase. She stands, and turns to the church: "First giving honor to God, pulpit guest, members, visitors, and friends. It always gives me great pleasure to say to anyone 'You're welcome.' It's a privilege a queen would envy. She would not enjoy sitting on her throne if she did not feel welcome. 'Welcome' is a little word, and it serves to encourage those who are trying to carry on God's work. And speaking in behalf of the group in appreciation, if we had ten thousand tongues we would gladly use every one to say to you: 'You're welcome, welcome, welcome.'"

Elder Smith asks for a response from a visitor to the church. The response is not as stylized as the welcome, although it often begins, "Giving honor to God, the salvation and joy of my life. . . .'"

The emcee introduces the singers and groups who come one after another to take their place in the pulpit or stage area to sing. The singing becomes a mixture of spiritual expression in the older call-and-response spirituals and the modern gospel songs like Vera Bethea's singing of Thomas A. Dorsey's "Precious Lord:" on 16 July 1991:

Precious Lord, take my hand
Lead me on, and let me stand
'Cause I am tired, I am weak, and I am worn.
Through the storm, through the night
Lead me on in the light.
Take my hand, precious Lord,
Lead me on.

When my way grows drear'
Precious Lord, linger near,
When my life is almost gone
At the river, Lord, I'll stand,
God, guide my feet, Lord, hold my hand,
Just take my hand, precious Lord,
And lead me on.

Spirit in the appreciation is palpable. Participants and a singer may take a song and improvise on its words or rhythm to intensify the spiritual presence. This "drive" (see Allen 1991) is given in a variety of ways. The singer may insert a personal testimony into the song, like this gentlemen from Pine Bluff: "You can't do nothing but the spirit of the Lord! Say amen! . . . My Lord, I thank Him. . . . I saw a man lying in the doorway the other day. He said, 'I don't have nowhere to stay.' But, oh, we got a place to lay our heads. Somebody ought to tell him, 'Thank you!' (Sings) When praises go up, blessings come down. (Speaks) How many believe that? (Sings) When praises go up, blessings come down, hallelujah, hallelu, hallelu."

The musicians may join the singer, accentuating the phrasing with particularly driving chords. A singer like Vera Bethea, who has sung throughout Northeast Texas, might tell the church, "The Devil don't know what you're talking about when you moan," and proceed to hum "Precious Lord."

A love offering is gathered by the church and an invitation is made for those who wish to be saved by the love of Christ to do so in the spirit of this gathering. As the money from the offering will help pay the light and water bill for the facility, the salvation of Christ will help the man or woman whose spirit is burdened with trials and sin.

When the last groups have sung, the occasion winds down. Announcements of other appreciations are made, and a final prayer of thanksgiving for the appreciation occasion is offered.

Although the words of songs focus on a great day and a better world beyond, minds and hearts are focused on the time at hand. State lines, county boundaries, and city limits remain blurred as long as the focus on God is sharp. As Sister Dorothy Spinx of Dumas told me: "Only thing [we do] is lift up the name of Jesus. Well, you can tell them [in Texarkana] that we are praising God and if they get us over there, we'll do the same thing, praise the Lord! For He's worthy to be praised. Amen." (3 August 1991)

References

Allen, Ray. *Singing in the Spirit: African-American Sacred Quartets in New York City*. Philadelphia: University of Pennsylvania Press, 1991.

Baker, Benjamin S. *Special Occasions in the Black Church*. Nashville: Broadman Press, 1989.

Lornell, Kip. *Happy in the Service of the Lord: Afro-American Gospel Quartets in Memphis*. Urbana: University of Illinois Press, 1988.

Photographs by the author for the TRAHC Folklife Program.

The Silverton Spiritual Singers. (Courtesy, Jan Rosenberg)

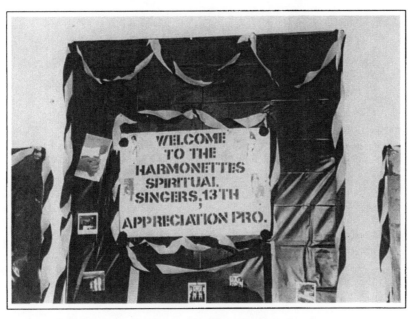

Union Memorial Temple, Texarkana. (Courtesy, Jan Rosenberg)

"Clifton Chenier, the King of Zydeco," (Courtesy, Joseph F. Lomax)

From Gumbo to Grammys: The Development of Zydeco Music in Houston

by Lorenzo Thomas

Appearing on television's *Tonight Show* in 1990, the popular Cajun accordionist Zachary Richard played a hot and slyly, charmingly risque song called "Somebody Stole My Monkey." The coy double entendre, reminiscent of the classic blues of Bessie Smith, sounded strangely innocent in these days when recordings are often "too live" for many listeners. And when he came over to the couch, Zachary Richard proved to be a true down home diplomat.

"Can you tell us about *zi-decko* music?" asked Jay Leno.

"Well," said Richard, "that's the New York pronunciation." And in the six seconds before the commercial he managed to give a pretty good definition and history of the real thing.

The brilliant, galvanizing music of Louisiana and Texas known as "zydeco" is interesting as a unique folk music that is also both popular and commercial. Zydeco is the music of a people who work hard for a living and play hard for fun; a music that has only one real purpose—to make you dance. It is also a syncretic form that belongs to a distinctive ethnic community; yet it has contributed to the musical vocabulary of "rock 'n' roll" which, in the late twentieth century, is nothing less than the popular music of the world.

▼

Zydeco is best and most properly defined as the dance music of African-American creoles in southwestern Louisiana. It is closely related to the Acadian or Cajun music of the same region and, in fact, shares the same song repertoire. Cajun music itself, based on late seventeenth-century French folk music, is identified with the fiddle and accordion/concertina traditions brought to Louisiana when French settlers were forced to leave Canada in 1755 due to early British victories in the French and Indian Wars.

The Cajun culture is rural and conservative but it has not been isolated from contact with French-speaking black people, or creoles, settled in the same area. The direct cultural links between white Cajun and black creole caused Tony Russell, in *Blacks, Whites and Blues* (1970) to call zydeco "a vivacious substyle" of Cajun music with a "repertoire of old French dance tunes, now much augmented by Western swing, blues, country ballads and pop" (79). The name *zydeco* was popularized by Houston folklorist Mack McCormick in a 1959 transcription of Dudley Alexander's performance of the traditional song "Les Haricots—Pas Sales," i.e. "The Snapbeans Have No Salt," an indication of poverty rather than health-conscious diet (Lomax 212–13). The word itself is quite interesting. "In Creole usage," says John Minton, "zydeco displays the same adaptability as the English word dance: as a noun it can refer to a social occasion involving music, dance, food and drink; to the music played at such an occasion; to a particular dance step, or to the tune that accompanies it—specifically, in the last two instances, to a fast, syncopated two-step."

Even if some listeners are unsure about the difference between Cajun and zydeco music, it is not hard to hear the element that makes zydeco unique and it is also clear that the two forms have influenced each other. The Cajun standard "Colinda" (supposedly the name of a pretty girl) is related to the West African calinda danced by slaves in New Orleans's Congo Square (Lomax 208–209), and while Cajun and zydeco musicians both perform the standard "Jole Blon," the zydeco band performs the traditional words and melody but adds African percussion in the guise of the *frottoir*, or "rubboard." The traditional Cajun percussion instrument is the triangle (which is also found in Caribbean merengue from

Haiti and calypso from French-influenced Trinidad). While the triangle can be a fierce instrument in the right hands, the zydeco band's corrugated washboard played by tapping and rubbing is capable of a wide range of polyrhythmic effects and seems to be utilized in a fundamentally African approach by performers such as Cleveland Chenier and Earl Sally. With such performers the *frottoir* has a function similar to the grooved quiro or bead-shrouded gourd (*chequeré*) used in Cuban and Puerto Rican salsa orchestras. In other words, zydeco may be understood as a doubly creolized or syncretized musical artform.

A folk idiom in music is usually, of necessity, a casual pastime and in rural Louisiana towns such as Lafayette and Opelousas that is what zydeco was. The best local players would perform for dances only on weekends. But there is also a stage in the development of an art form when it becomes possible for excellent artists to make a living. Accordionist Clifton Chenier and his band achieved that level in the late 1950s, but only by constant travel to the communities in Louisiana and East Texas that supported the music.

The spread of zydeco's audience is, of course, tied to the economic developments of the region. World War II industrial needs led to the relocation of many rural Louisiana people (black and white) to the shipyards of southern and central California and to oil refineries of the Gulf Coast. So it is that in cities like Oakland and Richmond, California, there is a strong tradition that accounts for the presence of artists such as Queen Ida, a Grammy Award-winning zydeco accordionist and vocalist. Similarly, in Port Arthur and Houston there developed strong black and white Louisiana-born communities that kept the music of the old home town vital in new surroundings. There was enough interaction and energy in Port Arthur that it could produce white blues artists such as Janis Joplin and Johnny Winter, or an Isaac Payton Sweat equally at home with Cajun and mainstream country & western, while also supporting the early career of the great blues guitarist and fiddle player Clarence "Gatemouth" Brown.

The black Louisianans who migrated to Houston during the war settled mainly in an area of the city's Fifth Ward called "Frenchtown" because it had been a destination for similar newcomers as early as the

1930s. A section of Houston's Third Ward and an area known as Sunnyside also attracted this population.

In his book *Houston: The Once and Future City* (1971), George Fuermann quoted folklorist Mack McCormick's description of the city in the 1950s: "an amalgam of villages and townships surrounding a cluster of skyscrapers. Each section of the city tends to reflect the region which it faces, usually being settled by people from that region. Thus the Louisiana French-speaking people are to be found in the northeast of Houston" (18). That is certainly a poetic explanation of real estate accident but it also underscored McCormick's deeper perception. "Each area," he wrote, "has gathered its own, and each group has in turn established a community within the city, which in itself has no cultural traditions, is rich in those it has acquired."

Blues singer Sam "Lightnin'" Hopkins noted that "everybody 'round here plays music or makes songs or something. That's white peoples, colored peoples, that's them funny French-talking peoples, that's everybody, what I mean. They all of 'em got music" (Fuermann 47). The music of the African-American "funny French-talking peoples," a style that Hopkins himself learned to play, was zydeco. By the 1960s there were small bars along Lockwood, Liberty Road, and near Sunnyside's Cullen Boulevard that featured zydeco trios (accordion, drums, and *frottoir*). There was also a weekly dance at the parish hall of St. Francis of Assisi Church on Dabney Street in Fifth Ward. Those Saturday evening dances, organized by Clarence Gallien, beginning in 1958, usually featured Clifton Chenier's band. Gallien, a native of Opelousas, settled in Houston in 1953 and continued to organize these affairs until his death in 1989 (Orlean 184–85). Today, St. Francis of Assisi and about five other churches form a network of rotating feasts sponsored by two or three promoters and church organizations with the result that there is a parish hall dance somewhere every weekend. The events are announced in the *Catholic Herald*, and the sponsors consult each other to avoid conflicts in scheduling.

"People of all ages come to the church zydeco show," wrote reporter Bill Minutaglio, "because they can do everything they can at a nightclub—smoke, drink and tell lies in the name of love—and they can do it under the relative safety of the big church umbrella" (16).

All of this activity—including two nightclubs (the Silver Slipper and the Continental Zydeco Ballroom) that present zydeco bands exclusively—depended upon the support of the French-speaking African-American community. *Houston Post* reporter David Kaplan explored the nature of that Fifth Ward neighborhood:

> Frenchtown was a tightly knit community. "They all built each other's houses," says retired blacksmith Charles Broussard, a 73-year-old Creole who grew up a half mile from Frenchtown, but spent a lot of time there.
>
> In its first few decades, Frenchtown had a country atmosphere. "There was good hunting, mostly quail and rabbit," says Broussard. (Kaplan F-4)

The cohesiveness of the Frenchtown community from the 1930s to the 1950s depended on sharing the language as well as family ties stretching from Houston back to Louisiana. It also depended upon Houston's rigid racial and economic segregation:

> Since the '50s, Frenchtown has been slowly dying. Many children of the settlers have moved out, into other Houston neighborhoods, while non-Creoles have moved in. Some of the younger generation left at the onset of integration. . . .
>
> "The younger generation moved to the suburbs," Broussard says. "Better jobs, better homes. Some of the property owned by their parents has just gone to waste." (Kaplan F-4)

This geographic decentering of the community—not an unusual urban development—was, of course, also accompanied by the total assault of commercial mass culture on the entire society beginning in the 1950s.

How then does zydeco music survive?

In one sense, the flourishing network of weekend parish-hall dances is a direct response to the fact that black French-speaking people (or their non-fluent children and grandchildren) are residentially scattered all over the city of Houston. The churches, rather than residential areas, are therefore the focus of this community. The dispersed audience has, in effect, created a new and decentralized venue.

There have also been significant changes affecting musicians. In the 1950s, Zydeco was very much a regional folk music and the musicians who held down the local bar gigs in the 1960s and 1970s were men who had other full-time jobs. At parish halls that featured Clifton Chenier and his Red Hot Louisiana Band, there would be neighborhood old timers who might play between sets by the star attraction. Unpaid but not unappreciated, their music would be entirely acoustic, usually performed on a small Cajun style "button accordion," a very different music than Chenier's electrified piano-keyboard Hohner and five-piece band.

Lonnie Mitchell, a native of Ames, Texas, perhaps exemplifies the history of zydeco music in Houston. Mitchell's father was also an accordion player and a weekend entertainer back in the 1930s. "White folks played the single-row button accordion," Mitchell told writer Aaron Howard. "When they'd break, they would throw the accordion away. My dad said black people would pick the accordion out of the trash, learn how to fix them and play them. The first accordion he found was in the trash, torn in half. So he took it, glued and taped it up and that's the accordion he learned how to play" (Howard, "Zydeco Connection" 14). Lonnie Mitchell didn't have to be quite as ingenious—he learned to play on one of his father's accordions.

Though he became a major figure in Zydeco music, Lonnie Mitchell remains a local musician. Unlike "Lightnin'" Hopkins and many others, Mitchell has never toured Europe even though he has been invited. He claims he was unable to leave Houston for economic reasons. "Anyway," Mitchell says, "Clifton Chenier told me that it takes several tours over there before a musician is able to ask for a good fee. I had a family to take care of." In 1990 he retired after thirty-three years as a body mechanic at a Cadillac dealership, but he continues to perform in several clubs. Because he did not play outside of the community, Lonnie Mitchell served the music in several ways. For several years he was owner and manager of the club now known as the Continental Zydeco Ballroom which, regardless of its many names, has been (along with Slim's Y-ki-ki Lounge in Opelousas) the Mecca of zydeco music since the 1940s. Mitchell also taught a large number of young musicians. Bassist Duane West and his brother, drummer Tall West, both play with the popular Wilfred Chevis and the Texas Zydeco Band and began their apprenticeship with Lonnie Mitchell at the ages of eight and ten respectively.

Most zydeco musicians, in fact, seem to have learned the music in this fashion. Herbert Sam, for example, played in the Fifth Ward clubs as a young man in the 1950s and taught all of his sons who now perform as The Sam Brothers Five and have recorded several fine albums. Leader Leon Sam, an accordionist who once wore long hair and a headband in homage to Clifton Chenier's trademark style, tends toward a brighter rock sound than his elders, but the band definitely has mastered the traditional music. Similarly, Lonnie Mitchell's Continental Lounge band included, for a time in the mid 1970s, three teenagers who practiced "soul music" riffs while warming up, but launched straight into the traditional zydeco standards when Mitchell gave them his cue. In August 1993, Mitchell's services to the artform were rewarded with a musical tribute at Houston's The Orange Show folk-art landmark. Hosted by bluesman Big Roger Collins, the twelve-hour show included performances by most of Houston's zydeco musicians.

The difference between traditional Acadian music and zydeco, according to Zachary Richard, has to do with "a musician named Clifton Chenier, down in Houston." Indeed, Chenier's innovative virtuosity in blending Louisiana heritage and blues sung in English propelled the form into the modern entertainment industry; but it is a musician like Lonnie Mitchell who helped keep the source of the music alive. Zydeco— as a folk music—could only survive by being transmitted through the family band, master musicians such as Mitchell, and a devoted audience. An incentive to play this music, of course, might be the desire to emulate Clifton Chenier—an artist who achieved international renown. Such, in fact, is the case with Leon Sam, with the current "King of Zydeco" Stanley Dural (known internationally as Buckwheat), and

Chenier's own son, C. J. Chenier, who has taken over leadership of the Red Hot Louisiana Band.

Until quite recently, zydeco has been a form that fits the classic definition of folk music very precisely. It is casual, related to a specific social function, has a traditional repertoire that is also traditionally transmitted in a master/apprentice mode that, more often than not, exists within the family. The music is also, as we have pointed out, directly associated with a French-speaking African-American Louisiana community (even if that community has been relocated to Texas or California). Zydeco music would not, however, be known beyond the confines of this community if it were not for another factor. That is, of course, the way that regional artforms interface with the commercial entertainment industry in the United States.

It is not difficult to understand how zydeco managed to survive the relocation of its audience from rural Louisiana to urban settings in Texas and California. People who settle in communities with recognizable group identifications will naturally preserve cultural heritage, even if only in a ceremonial way. A zydeco dance is, of course, a special kind of secular ceremony. Novelist Al Young described his experience of an evening at the Continental Zydeco Ballroom in his book *Things Ain't What They Used To Be* (1987):

> What the hell, I thought, and proceeded to shed my coat and tie right then and there. It didn't take long to get back to that state I had experienced while dancing to Clifton Chenier in California. Soon those feelings of being on the verge of turning infrared or blue seemed only a matter of temperature and gyration. What was that old line about everything being one percent inspiration and 99 percent perspiration? It felt good to be moving with all those kids and old folks and people my age, people who had obviously come here to forget about the rest of the week and who weren't much for conversation at all. (Young 93)

The initial exposure of a wider audience to zydeco music came from attention by folklorists such as Mack McCormick, the late British musicologist Mike Leadbitter, and Arhoolie Records producer Chris Strachwitz. "Strachwitz," wrote Arnold Shaw in *Honkers and Shouters: The Golden Years of Rhythm and Blues* (1978), "recognizes the blues as a minority art, perhaps revels in that fact, and has not in a decade of scrambling ever attempted to reach for majority acceptance" (257). Strachwitz, in other words, was content to record what his musicians wanted to play, to document their authentic style. Though uninterested in reaching the pop charts, Arhoolie nevertheless recorded ten Chenier albums—including a live dance at a parish hall in Richmond, California—thus making the music available to record collectors across the United States and in Europe. Strachwitz also issued a recording of older zydeco artists such as the duo of Armand and Alphonse "Bois Sec" Ardoin who first recorded for folklore field workers in Louisiana in the 1930s. This catalogue is currently being reissued in CD format so that the performances remain accessible to new listeners.

Through the efforts of the late Joseph Lomax, many of Houston's avant garde art crowd were introduced to zydeco in its local venues and acquired an enthusiasm for the music that lasted long beyond the season; and the New Orleans Jazz and Heritage Festival and Houston's Juneteenth Blues Festival exposed Chenier and other artists to huge audiences and mainstream media attention, as well. For the past seven years, in fact, the Juneteenth Blues Festival has devoted an entire day to zydeco performers. Local newspaper reporters seem to put out a touristy feature article every few months that send adventurous music lovers to seek out the authentic places where Lonnie Mitchell's name is like a secret password.

A number of trendy Houston restaurants and clubs such as Billy Blue's, Shakespeare Pub, and the Atchefalaya River Cafe, have joined the venerable Pe-Te's Cajun BBQ House and long-standing inner-city venues such as the Silver Slipper and the Continental Zydeco Ballroom in presenting excellent local zydeco bands such as Wilbert Thibodeaux, L. C. Donatto, Wilfred Chevis and the Texas Zydeco Band, Pierre and the Zydeco Dots, Willie Davis, and Little Brian Terry and the Zydeco Travelers—a young group who blend traditional "la-la" upbringing with a 1990s "hip-hop" image (Howard, "Cajun Country" 16). And, of course,

Lonnie Mitchell and the Zydeco Rockets can be heard at a couple of different places each week and weekend.

Beyond the ever expanding city limits of Houston, the signing of Buckwheat to a recording contract by the mammoth multinational Island Records label and the success of Rockin' Sidney's "Don't Mess With My Toot Toot" as a novelty tune on country & western radio stations around the country also brought wider recognition. Promoted by the indefatigable Houston record producer Huey P. Meaux, 'Toot Toot" even surfaced in a Spanish-language version widely distributed in South America.

Interestingly, the rise in popularity of recording and radio broadcast of music by artists such as Chenier, Rockin' Sidney, and Buckwheat parallels the decline of ethnic neighborhoods such as Houston's Frenchtown, and one is tempted to suppose that the commercial exploitation of the music denotes, in some inexplicable way, the disintegration of its community groundings. Commercial exploitation, by its very nature, means at the very least that artists perform at some distance from the community—both geographically and, often, aesthetically. But it is not wise to jump to conclusions.

At first sight, for example, it seems that Buckwheat's hit version of the standard "Hey, Good Lookin'"—which received extensive airplay on country music video programs—was a carefully calculated "crossover" ploy that would have delighted Arnold Shaw but might indicate Stanley Dural's abandonment of his black roots or, at least, his zydeco shoes. It is a fact, however, that such country & western standards have long been part of the repertoire of zydeco and even blues bands in East Texas; so much so that this kind of "crossover" might be considered an aspect of the region's demographics. Up to twenty years ago, there were large segments of the rural African-American population in Texas and Louisiana whose only access to radio was country music stations and, in the 1960s, a song such as Willie Nelson's "Funny (How Time Slips Away)" was marketed with enormous success by New Orleans-based Backbeat Records as pure rhythm & blues once it was performed by singer Joe Hinton. In some ways the cultural interaction of "black" and "white" musical forms resembles the relationship of zydeco and Cajun music. It is necessary to note, however, that the actual video images for Buckwheat's "Hey, Good Lookin'" demonstrated the usual "united colors of Benetton"-style ethnic integration that predominates on MTV more for marketing reasons than for social statement.

The new popularity of zydeco is, to use current show biz slang, phenomenal; club and concert venues for the music continue to increase in northeastern and midwestern cities such as Boston, New York, Toronto, Montreal, and Detroit. In Houston, a popular African-American dancehall such as JB's Entertainment Center continues its usual bookings of rhythm & blues masters such as Bobby Bland, Denise LaSalle, and Johnny Taylor. For the past five years, however, the opening acts for these shows have often been zydeco bands such as Jabo or Louislana-based BooZoo Chavis. Such billings are frequent enough to indicate that it is now an expected formula for the thirty-five-to-sixty-year-old audience JB's attracts. And the future of the music seems remarkably secure due to the presence of excellent young players such as twenty-three-year-old Bryan Terry, a native of Crosby, Texas, whose father can still be found checking on the band's equipment.

Zydeco, as Tony Russell said, is "vivacious"—which means "full of animation and spirit." As long as its community—or, more precisely, its sense of community—survives, the music will survive. And as long as its talented performers continue to expand its tradition and its audience, zydeco will continue to add to the richness of America's uniquely syncretic culture.

Bibliography

Fuerman, George. *Houston: The Once and Future City*. Garden City, New York: Doubleday, 1971.

Howard, Aaron. "Cajun Country." Houston *Public News* 28 September 1994: 14, 16.

___. "Zydeco Connection." Houston *Public News* 5 April 1995: 14.

Kaplan, David. "Houston's Creole Quarter." *Houston Post* 19 March 1989: F-1, F-4.

Lomax, Joseph F. "Zydeco—Must Live On!" *What's Going On (In Modern Texas Folklore)*. Ed. Francis Edward Abernethy. Publications of the Texas Folklore Society XL. Austin: Encino Press, 1976. 205–23.

Lopate, Philip. "Houston Hide-and-Seek." *Against Joie de Vivre*. New York: Poseidon Press, 1989. 210–33.

Minutaglio, Bill. "La-La Tonight!: Squeezin' and pleasin' on the zydeco church circuit." *Houston Press* 11 January 1990: 14–17.

Minton, John. "What is Texas Zydeco Music?" *Accordion Kings*. Concert program brochure published by Texas Folklife Resources, Inc. June 1990.

Mitchell, Lonnie. Interview. Houston, Texas. 24 June 1990.

Orlean, Susan. *Saturday Night*. New York: Fawcett Crest, 1991.

"A Portrait: The Continental Zydeco Ballroom." *Texas Folklife Resources Newsletter*. Spring 1989.

Richard, Zachary. *The Tonight Show*. NBC-TV. October 1990.

Russell, Tony. *Blacks, Whites and Blues*. New York: Stein and Day, 1970.

Shaw, Arnold. *Honkers and Shouters: The Golden Years of Rhythm and Blues*. New York: Collier Books, 1978.

Young, Al. "I'm the Zydeco Man." *Things Ain't What They Used To Be: Musical Memoirs*. Berkeley: Creative Arts, 1987. 91–94.

Anderson Moss. (Courtesy, Joseph F. Lomax)

Charlie Parker and Gene Ramey. (Courtesy, Duncan Schiedt Collection.)

From Bebop to Hard Bop and Beyond: The Texas Jazz Connection

By Dave Oliphant

In 1955, Harold Meehan, my orchestra teacher at South Park High School in Beaumont, proved the open sesame to many a wondrous unknown world, and in particular to the recorded one of bebop. Pictured on the covers of the albums Harold purchased with district funds were altoist Charlie "Bird" Parker and trumpeter John Birks "Dizzy" Gillespie, the two inventors of that challenging 1940s form of African-American music. Long before 1955, the year of Parker's death at age thirty-four, bebop had already established itself as required thinking for all avant-garde practitioners of jazz. But as an aspiring trumpet player, I immediately felt on hearing such music that in terms of theory and technique it was beyond anything I could ever hope to understand or perform.

Dizzy Gillespie's phenomenally fast runs and his stratospheric high notes were to me completely inconceivable. Not even trumpet star Harry James, who had grown up in Beaumont, came close to Dizzy's breath-taking, pyrotechnical brilliance. Harry's virtuosic performance of "Flight of the Bumble Bee" was a mere showpiece with nothing of bebop's ingenious improvisational artistry. Also, Parker and Gillespie's playing of their intricate "contrafacts"—that is, tunes entitled "Anthropology or

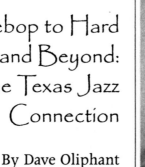

Ornithology" but based, as I would learn much later, on the pop songs "I Got Rhythm" and "How High the Moon"—was unlike anything James ever attempted in the late 1930s when he recorded with the Benny Goodman Orchestra or even in the 1940s and 1950s with his own big bands. All of this I could recognize even if I could not comprehend the differences between swing and bebop, could not know at that point the evolutionary developments that led to the emergence of the musical language designated as bebop.

What I never suspected in 1955 or for many years to come was the fundamental contribution made to this "new" music by Texans, including even Harry James, but more notably by a number of black musicians: Buster Smith, Gene Ramey, Budd Johnson, Charlie Christian, and Kenny Dorham, among many others. All of these jazz figures were alive and active in 1955, with the exception of Christian, who died in 1942 at age twenty-six. But the only figure I would meet in person was bassist Gene Ramey, who in the 1970s returned from New York to his hometown of Austin. In the early 1980s my son and I shook hands with Ramey after having viewed him on screen in *The Last of the Blue Devils*, a documentary film on that vital Southwestern territory band. Featured in this film are Buster Smith of Dallas and Eddie Durham of San Marcos, two of the Blue Devils's major stars. Both Smith and Gene Ramey had performed with Charlie Parker early in the Bird's career, and Ramey later recorded with such bebop greats as trumpeter Fats Navarro and baritonist Leo Parker.

In 1955 I knew none of this, and the closest thing to a living bebop musician I could hear in Beaumont, or anywhere in Texas so far as I was aware, was Harold Meehan, who played "legit" violin in the symphony but jazz alto sax when he could find jobs with local bands. Of course, my awareness of jazz activity in Beaumont was limited at the time by segregation. The black high schools may have produced many gifted musicians, but neither then nor since have I heard of black jazz players from Beaumont. I do recall that in 1958 at Lamar State, the city's College of Technology, there was a trumpeter—the first black musician I ever knew personally and the only one majoring in music—who could play in the style of Clifford Brown, the marvelous second-generation bebopper whose Pacific Jazz album from 1954 I had found in a neighborhood record shop. Unfortunately, this student musician was not a good sight reader and apparently gave up college when he failed to make his grades.

The question of which ability is preferable in jazz—reading or playing by ear—has always stirred up controversy among aficionados of the music. The great white cornetist, Bix Beiderbecke, was a poor reader for most of his life, yet few instrumentalists have ever matched the beauty of his sound or the inventiveness of his melodic improvisations. For some jazz enthusiasts, the further a band strays from group improvisation based on spontaneous rather than written music, the less genuine and inspiring the performance. But even black jazz musicians who could read "charts" were highly critical of those who were "illiterate." For some listeners, it is a combination of improvised and composed jazz that results in the finest work in this African-American form—the hyphenation itself a reminder that such music is something of a blend of aural African and written European traditions. In the case of bebop, a jazz musician like Budd Johnson of Dallas emphasized the necessity for having bebop themes notated because otherwise they were too difficult to perform. On the other hand, a jazz composer of the bebop era like the marvelous Thelonious Monk—whose music was recorded with the help of both Gene Ramey and trumpeter Kenny Dorham of Fairfield—would teach his band members a new tune by playing their parts on the piano before he would show them a written score. This would certainly have been the case with Monk's most treacherous composition, "Skippy," which he rarely recorded, the first time in 1952 with Dorham on trumpet.

When Harold Meehan moved to Beaumont in 1952, he brought with him a knowledge of bebop from firsthand hearings in his native St. Louis of Charlie Parker, trumpeter Miles Davis, and drummer Max Roach. In 1945, while serving in World War II, Harold had heard the Dizzy Gillespie big band in South Carolina at a time when the group would have included Kenny Dorham. In April 1946, Harold was discharged and returned to St. Louis where he studied violin at the city's Institute of Music and regularly listened to such bebop classics as "Groovin' High," "Koko," and "Ornithology" on a jukebox at Bal Tabern. On first hearing bebop, Harold had wondered why Gillespie played so many weird, dissonant notes, but by 1946 Harold was a convert to the new music. He would haunt the St. Louis night spots with other white musicians who dug bebop, especially Eddie Johnson, who could scat-sing Bird and Dizzy's most famous solos. Harold remembered Parker clowning on stage at the St. Louis Birdland, puffing through his fingers as if he were smoking pot. On one occasion, when Stan Kenton's Orchestra came to the city's Tune Town Ballroom, Harold spoke with bop trombonist Kai Winding, and during this same period, he also chatted with Max Roach, who told him that a bebop drummer could not be so metronomic in his playing because a bop ensemble weaves a little off the beat so the drummer must go with the band.

Although Harold arrived in Beaumont with a keen appreciation for bebop, he soon discovered there was little in the local music scene to encourage this kind of jazz. Most gigs were designed for businessmen dances or a type of polite society Muzak, not serious improvisation. While Harold tried to interest students like myself in bebop, he could not realistically expect us to be anything but intimidated by what we heard. And yet his early introduction of bebop made a lasting impression—at least on me—and led to a lifetime of listening pleasure. Eventually, this early experience with bebop stimulated my interest in the role of Texas musicians in the history of jazz. But only in the late 1980s was I struck by the revelation that Texans not only influenced the creation of bebop but affected all the major forms of jazz music, from ragtime (Scott Joplin of Texarkana), blues (Blind Lemon Jefferson of Wortham, Sippie Wallace of Houston, Lillian Glinn of Dallas), and boogie woogie (Hersal Thomas of Houston) to hot jazz, swing, and—following from bebop—hard bop and free or action jazz. Indeed, Texas musicians not only contributed to the evolutionary developments leading up to bebop but several participated in historic recordings that helped make this form of jazz one of the most profound expressions of African-American culture.

Prior to the classic bebop recordings Parker and Gillespie cut in 1945, these two jazz giants crossed paths with a number of Texans who played a crucial part in Bird's and Diz's early careers. In 1932, Parker first met Buster Smith, who would become his mentor on alto saxophone. Born in Alsdorf, south of Dallas, in 1904, Smith was self-taught on clarinet and alto saxophone, and also as a composer-arranger. Credited with some of the finest and most advanced big band arrangements of the 1930s, Buster collaborated with two other Texans, Eddie Durham and Oran "Hot Lips" Page of Dallas, in the writing of the Count Basie theme song, "One O'Clock Jump." Like many other Texas blues-based musicians, Buster got his start on the streets of the Deep Ellum section of East Dallas where guitarist-singers Blind Lemon Jefferson, Leadbelly, and T-Bone Walker entertained along Elm Street and Central Avenue. Buster began with the Voddie White Trio at the Tip Top Club on Central, performed with medicine shows, and by 1925 had been picked up by the Blue Devils out of Oklahoma City. In November 1929, Buster first recorded with the Blue Devils, and his alto chorus on "Squabblin'" has been heard by jazz critics Ross Russell and Gunther Schuller as a presaging of Charlie Parker's style and conception. The same fluid lines, which were new to saxophone performance at the time, the airy tone, and the floating, bluesy sound of Smith's chorus are all characteristic of Parker's approach to jazz alto.

Buster Smith's impact on the younger Parker came primarily through the fact that Charlie signed up in 1937 as a member of Buster's first band. During this formative period, Bird would share choruses with "The Professor," as Smith was called, and obviously emulated his leader's method and manner. One important effect of this experience with the Smith band would surely have been Parker's exposure to the leader's facility for setting riffs—short, repeated phrases against which soloists would improvise their own melodic lines. An outstanding example of contrasting riffs is found in "One O'Clock Jump," which, as noted above, is credited to Smith and his fellow Texans, Durham and Page. Such riffs became the basis of various bebop tunes, like Gillespie's classic "Salt Peanuts," a riff widely quoted and heard, for example, in "Bop Bounce," a 1948 recording by the Benny Carter Orchestra, which includes a trombone solo by Henry Coker of Dallas. Although riffs were utilized throughout the swing era, their origins in the blues are documented by the 1920s recordings by the Central Texas "King of the Country Blues,"

Blind Lemon Jefferson. Territory bands of the Southwest, which included many Texas sidemen, employed Lemon's blues practice of building improvisations over one or a series of memorable riffs. In part, bebop style also derives from riff-like figures, with such repeated patterns allowing for complex and imaginative flights that yet remain rooted in a folk-like phrase or chord progression.

Charlie Parker's meteoric rise at age nineteen was marked by an early mastery of his instrument through intense practice. One of the secrets to his amazing improvisational skill was his ability to play a tune in any of the twelve keys, whereas most players were limited to those with fewer flats and sharps, such as C or B flat major. According to Gene Ramey, who knew Parker in the early 1930s and toured with him in the Jay McShann Orchestra beginning in 1939, Parker was encouraged by the bassist to "jam" everyday, the two men working out together the relationships between notes and chords. McShann, a blues and boogie-woogie pianist, organized what is considered the last of the great Kansas City bands, following in the line of Bennie Moten and Count Basie. With Ramey on bass and Gus Johnson of Tyler on percussion, McShann and his rhythm section formed a firm foundation on which Charlie Parker developed his swinging, highly inventive melodic and rhythmic improvisations. Bird's first recordings, made with the McShann Orchestra in 1940, are astonishing displays of his technical and imaginative prowess, even though these performances are still basically in the swing tradition. But after some three years with McShann, Parker left for New York City, where he joined the Earl Hines Orchestra, taking the place of Texan Budd Johnson, who as the leader's straw boss had already hired Dizzy Gillespie for the Hines organization. It was at this time that Bird and Diz began to experiment with altered chords and to produce what bandleader Cab Calloway characterized snidely as Gillespie's "Chinese music."

Budd Johnson of Dallas has primarily been credited in the history of bebop for his role in organizing the first recording session for the new music held early in 1944. During this same year, Johnson was a member of the first organized small bebop combo, along with Dizzy Gillespie and Oscar Pettiford, which performed at New York's Onyx Club

ing with which Charlie invested his remarkably relaxed but driving rhythms.

After Charlie Parker had recorded extensively, first with Dizzy Gillespie and then with trumpeter Miles Davis, the altoist chose for the latter's replacement Texan Kenny Dorham. While the Bird's recordings made at this time are not quite on the same level with those featuring Diz and Miles, the leader found in Dorham a musician with a thorough understanding of the bebop language, which Kenny began to speak in his own lyrical style. Dorham had already made important recordings with beboppers Fats Navarro and Bud Powell before he joined Parker in 1948 for a two-year stint, but during his stay with the Bird, Kenny learned to match the master bar for bar. While engaging in bebop's penchant for quoting popular songs, Kenny also developed an approach that some have considered unique among jazz trumpeters, a combination of touching warmth and stabbing attack. In common with trombonist Henry Coker of Dallas and trumpeter Richard "Notes" Williams of Galveston, Dorham had studied at Wiley College in Marshall, but whereas Coker and Williams concentrated on music, Kenny majored in chemistry and physics, even though he also played in the college band. It would be interesting to know more about the Wiley program, which obviously prepared these musicians for making it with the leading beboppers in New York. Of course, neither Parker nor Gillespie was the product of a college education, so that bebop's complex artistry was never determined by academic credentials.

Of prime importance to all the beboppers must have been the black music traditions that were shared wherever the musicians were born or lived, made possible through radio and phonograph as well as by the hearing of bands on tour or of traveling with them as sidemen. Most musicians learned through imitation, teaching themselves by listening and applying what they heard to the playing of their respective instruments. What often made Texas jazzmen distinctive was their blues-riff background, and even Dizzy Gillespie remarked that he was not a bluesman in the same class with Lips Page, an early member of the Blue Devils and active in New York at jam sessions in the 1940s. Kenny Dorham also was deeply immersed in the Texas blues tradition, and this may account in large part for his role in the development away from bebop's more cerebral approach and toward the greater emotive style of what became known as hard bop. Dorham in fact was a founding member of one of the most influential hard bop ensembles, The Jazz Messengers, which began officially in 1954, headed up by drummer Art Blakey and pianist Horace Silver. This group emphasized getting across to its audience a greater emotionalism than was characteristic of bebop, even as the hard bop musicians based much of their thinking on bebop phraseology. The difference lay in the intensity of hard bop's almost religious revivalism, which was indicated by Blakey's remark that if an audience wasn't patting their feet and nodding their heads to the music, something was wrong, they weren't getting the message.

Ironically, perhaps, the finest example of Kenny Dorham's emotive hard bop approach is found on four tunes he recorded in January 1960 in Oslo, Norway, with an obviously inspiring Norwegian rhythm section. Included on a compact disc entitled *Kenny Dorham: New York 1953–1956 and Oslo 1960* are *Con Alma* by Dizzy Gillespie, *Lament* by J.J. Johnson, and *Short Story* and *Sky Blue* by Dorham. Kenny's playing on these four pieces offers something of a workshop in hard bop, a kind of master class in jazz trumpet. Also, these four tunes represent a type of mini-history of bop and hard bop, for the compositions by Gillespie and Johnson, the premier bop trumpeter and trombonist respectively, are interpreted by Dorham through his definitive hard bop styling.

Like Kenny Dorham, Richard Williams also participated in this post-bebop movement as a member of one of the foremost hard bop organizations, the Charles Mingus Jazz Workshop. Along with Williams, two other Texans formed part of the Mingus "Dynasty": tenor saxophonist Booker Ervin of Denison and altoist John Handy of Dallas, while a fourth Texan, altoist Leo Wright of Wichita Falls, also served briefly as a member of the Mingus Workshop. Shouting blues-derived performances rooted in black church traditions characterize the Mingus recordings on which Williams, Ervin, and Handy add fundamentally to the ecstatic religious feeling the leader sought and achieved with such fervid results. In the playing of Texas musicians, Mingus found exactly the kind of eloquent, heightened expression that hard bop aimed to create, even as it worked largely within bebop's technical and harmonic vocabulary.

By the end of the 1950s, hard bop had, for some, expended most of its dithyrambic energy and was wearing itself down in a sort of tired repetition of what was referred to as funk or soul music. Whether this was true or not, another movement was developing that would extend bebop one step further by eliminating chord progressions as the basis of improvisation. Denominated free or action jazz, this new phase of bebop was spearheaded by Ornette Coleman of Fort Worth, who began on alto but became a multi-instrumentalist and a composer of a more flexible type of blues-riff structure through which soloists ventured further into the frontier reaches of musical space. Sounding a bit like a version of rhythm and blues, jump bands, and even at times country and western all combined, with a touch of classical music thrown in for good measure, Coleman's brand of free—or what he would come to label "harmolodic"—jazz was greeted with open arms by the Third Stream, that is, jazz-classical composers like George Russell and Gunther Schuller, as well as Coleman's fellow Texan, Jimmy Giuffre of Dallas. Essentially, Ornette's free jazz of the early 1960s is still the most advanced stage of jazz—and bebop—in practice today, and yet even his album-long "Free Jazz" contains overlapping riffs so characteristic of early Texas blues.

Although it would be an oversimplification to suggest that Texans have always had such a major impact on the development of jazz as has Ornette Coleman, it is true, nonetheless, that black jazz musicians from Texas have made an enormous contribution to jazz history—along with a white trombonist like Jack Teagarden of Vernon who, deeply influenced by black blues singers, forecast in his own playing in the late 1920s the technical innovations of 1940s bebop. Undeniably, the Texas legacy to this African-American music is owing to the state's wealth of black folk culture that has formed the subsoil of enduring jazz compositions and performances by the state's native sons and daughters before, during, and after the "bebop revolution."

Biblio-Discography

Basie Rhythm. HEP Records, CD 1032, 1991. With Harry James, Eddie Durham, and tenorist Herschel Evans of Denton.

Bebop Revolution, The. Edited by Dave Oliphant. Austin: Harry Ransom Humanities Research Center, The University of Texas at Austin, 1994.

Benny Carter and His Orchestra Live Broadcasts 1939/1948. Jazz Hour Records, JH-1005. With Henry Coker.

Best of Thelonious Monk, The. Blue Note Records, CDP 7 95636 2.

Budd Johnson and the Four Brass Giants. Riverside Records, 343.

Charlie Christian—Guest Artist: Dizzy Gillespie and Thelonious Monk. Everest Records, FS-219.

Charlie Parker at The Roost. Savoy Records, SJL 1108, 1977. With Kenny Dorham.

Charlie Parker With Jay McShann and His Orchestra: Early Bird. Stash Records, ST-DC-542, 1991. With Gene Ramey and Gus Johnson.

Coleman Hawkins: Rainbow Mist. Delmark Records, DD-459, 1992. With Budd Johnson's Bu Dee Daht.

Jazz Messengers, The. Columbia Records, CL897.

Jazz Portraits. Blue Note Records, CDP7243. With Booker Ervin and John Handy.

Litweiler, John. *Ornette Coleman: A Harmolodic Life*. New York: William Morrow, 1992.

Mingus, Mingus, Mingus, Mingus, Mingus. Impulse Records, Mono A54. With Richard Williams, Booker Ervin, and John Handy.

New Grove Dictionary of Jazz, The. 2 vols. Edited by Barry Kernfeld. London: Macmillan, 1988.

Oliphant, Dave. *Texan Jazz*. Austin: University of Texas Press, 1996.

Owens, Thomas. *Bebop: The Music and Its Musicians*. New York: Oxford University Press, 1995.

Peretti, Burton W. *The Creation of Jazz: Music, Race, and Culture in Urban America*. Urbana: University of Illinois Press, 1992.

Russell, Ross. *Jazz Style in Kansas City and the Southwest*. Berkeley: University of California Press, 1971.

Schuller, Gunther. *Early Jazz*. New York: Oxford University Press, 1968.

___. *The Swing Era*. New York: Oxford University Press, 1989.

Left to right: Max Roach, Budd Johnson, Oscar Pettiford, George Wallington, and Dizzy Gillespie. Onyx Club, 52nd St., New York, 1944. (Courtesy, Duncan Schiedt Collection)

Charlie Parker in pin-stripe suit; Kenny Dorham beside him with trumpet; Max Roach on drums. (From the Ross Russell Collection, courtesy of the Harry Ransom Humanities Research Center, the University of Texas at Austin.)

Frank Green at the forge.
(Courtesy, Richard Allen Burns)

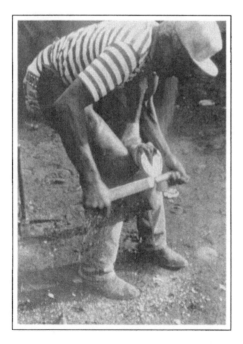

J. T. Ruffin dressing a horse's
hoof. (Courtesy, Richard Allen
Burns)

African-American Blacksmithing in East Texas

by Richard Allen Burns

Ninety years ago, the blacksmith was the pivotal craftsman of his community, and in Texas he could be found in nearly every town and at every crossroad. His importance is reflected in the fact that he is as much a part of the world of myths as of human society. In Africa he was seen as the master of the four elements—air, earth, fire and water. The Dogon, an African society of Mali, believe him capable of transforming himself at will into various animal and plant shapes. The blacksmith is an ambivalent character in West African folklore, bound to the living and the dead, and an intermediary between them. In Central Africa, the founders of the state were described in legend as blacksmith-kings; and in the Congo, the blacksmith still possesses authority that ranks him with chiefs, priests, and sorcerers (Balandier and Maquet 62–63). Such mythical powers are not ascribed to blacksmiths in Texas folklore, but the African-American blacksmith's social status in Texas today reveals parallels to the status afforded his forefathers before they crossed the Atlantic more than 150 years ago.

During the 1980s, while a student of folklore at the University of Texas at Austin, I developed a deep interest in African-American folklore, specifically as a result of having heard stories black craftsmen told as they continued a tradition of ironworking.[1] Such a tradition thrives throughout the cotton-producing South, a tradition embodied in the work of a father-and-son blacksmithing operation in a farming community near Liberty and in the work of a farrier in a community outside of Tyler. What links these East Texas black ironworkers with one another is their intense involvement in their communities, occupying a status similar to the role of a blacksmith in ante-bellum Texas.

Strategies for survival, based on knowledge of folkcrafts and skills, afforded many slaves and free blacks opportunities to continue traditions their predecessors taught them.[2] Moreover, the larger the repertoire of cultural items from which to draw, the more equipped a craftsman became to face the seemingly insurmountable problems of slavery. Such an ability to blend elements of one's parent culture with that of a new one, especially where traditional technology was involved, did not go unnoticed by community members who relied upon the blacksmith in the ante-bellum South. An imported blacksmith was held in high regard, and apprenticeships to master blacksmiths were encouraged by white owners. Evidence of this appears in a 1929 issue of *The Southern Workman*:

> From the owner's point of view, a slave with mechanical ability was worth more than an unskilled laborer . . . from the slave's point of view, such skill was likely to give him a larger measure of independence. Not infrequently he was hired out from his master to other planters; sometimes he was allowed to keep for himself a share of his earnings; in certain instances he was able to save money to buy his freedom. (Gregg 224)

The magazine article also conveys the importance of apprenticeships: "A Negro craftsman of known ability was altogether likely, therefore, to have a number of apprentices from his younger fellow-slaves" (Gregg 224).

The status of blacksmiths in Texas at the turn of the last century attracted the attention of W. E. B. Dubois, who publicized employment opportunities for black artisans: "Ours being an agricultural state, blacksmiths are in greater demand than perhaps any other tradesman" (1902:98). The blacksmith's ubiquitous presence in Texas must have depended on the recognition that his mechanical skills in some manner were the result of his efforts. Evaluating and describing the social conditions of black artisans in the United States, Dubois concluded in 1912: "The Negro blacksmith held absolute sway in his line, which included the many branches of forgery and other trades which are now classified under different heads from that of the regular blacksmith. The blacksmith in the days of slavery was expected to make any and everything wrought of iron."

Blacksmiths in ante-bellum Texas may have enjoyed a relatively high position on plantations, but their status and those of other black artisans did little to mitigate the horrors of slavery. His early nineteenth-century travels throughout the South led Frederik Law Olmsted to report in 1857 that, unlike other slaveholding states, "In Texas, the state of war in which slavery emerges, seems to continue in undertone to the present" (123). Indeed, some slaves revolted, and blacksmiths were particularly capable of subversive activities, such as making weapons for purposes of uprisings. Slaves and slaveholders alike respected the value of a talented blacksmith. Such value is obvious from advertisements appearing in nineteenth-century Texas newspapers. For example:

$25 REWARD

Will be given for the apprehension of my boy HENRY, who ran away from Port Lavaca about the 12th inst. Henry is a blacksmith by trade, about 30 or 35 years of age, and, when interrogated, will tell a very plausible story. He is acquainted along the road from this place to Lockhart, and he may attempt to go up that way, and then, by way of San Antonio, to Mexico. The above reward will be given, if lodged in jail, or for such information as will lead to his recovery. David Irwin per John Irwin. Lavaca, Nov. 28th, 1853 (Olmsted 508).

For descriptive information about slave craftsmen, their productions as well as their relative status on a plantation, one must examine not only travelogues of nineteenth-century writers, but also plantation records and slave narratives collected in the 1930s by WPA workers. In fact, one of the best historical sources that reflects the realities of slavery in Texas is the collection of slave narratives organized under the Federal Writer's Project of the Works Progress Administration. Though the principle task of the writers was to prepare a series of guides on each state, folklorist John Lomax encouraged organizers of the project to include interviews with former slaves as part of its endeavors (Tyler and Murphy viii). The importance of skilled craftspeople on a plantation emerges from these interviews, particularly with respect to a slave's ability to buy his freedom from income he received from his labors. Moreover, many of these testimonies contrast sharply with the popular attitudes Texans held that argued "our" slaves were not only well treated and happy, but were better cared for and happier than those in other states (Tyler and Murphy vi). Finally, with respect to the role of nineteenth-century black artisans, it is noteworthy that the value of African-American material culture soon becomes clear as you "listen" to the voices of the 1930s from those who experienced plantation life.

It is also important to note that the blacksmiths I discuss below reside in the eastern half of the state, so do not think of their work as part of a larger Southwest tradition which has been shaped primarily by the social histories of Anglos and Mexicans. East Texas more properly belongs to the plantation South, arguably an extension of Louisiana. Indeed, the heaviest concentration of blacks has always been in the eastern portion of the state, and this is still true today. The white planters moved on to West Texas, but their former slaves did not go with them.

As elsewhere in the South, only a minority of the white Texas families owned slaves, but the influence and prestige of these families were so far out of proportion to their numbers that there was never any doubt Texas was a slave state at the outbreak of the Civil War. Of the half million blacks who were free before the Civil War, the largest concentrations were along the Atlantic coast and in Louisiana. To combat political, economic, and social discrimination, many individuals, like William Goyens, sought a better life in the West (Treat 19). Goyens, a free black man from Louisiana and a blacksmith by trade, became an early example of the success that potentially awaited other black frontiersmen who came to Texas. Although the blacksmithing tradition is no longer pervasive in East Texas, a few black Texans still practice the art. Until 1983, two of these artisans owned and operated Ames Fix-it Shop—James Goudeau (now deceased) and his son, Pete.

Ames, Texas, approximately forty miles east of Houston, was James Goudeau's home since the 1930s. Until his death in 1983, James and Pete owned and operated Ames Fix-it Shop, a refurbished World War II canning factory housing a corn mill, a forge, a saw and tooth filing business. In another section of the building Pete fashioned iron grill work and built barbeque pits. James and Pete belonged to that class of rural blacksmiths who were once the pivotal craftsmen in their communities, serving as intermediaries whose job was to provide community members with the means for accomplishing their own work. Numerous stories James told in the 1980s about the work he did reveal an understanding of his central role in his community's livelihood, and his appreciation of the strong identity that his experience and competence as a blacksmith gave him.

But these stories also reveal another dimension of James' craft which was every bit as essential to the completion of a task as his technical ability: his social skill. James was an asset to his community not only because of his prowess in working with iron but also because of his facility for working with people, understanding them and making himself understood, convincing them of his reliability and trust. For example, when a customer once asked James to build a branding iron according to a design that James immediately recognized as impractical, he was at first reluctant but eventually agreed to a compromise:

> He [the customer] said, "I tell you what you do; just go ahead and build it anyway. If it don't work, I'll throw it away and let you build it like *you* wanna' build it." Two weeks time he was back [laughter]. "You sure know what you're talkin' about." I said, "I *know* I do. I build a million of them things, brandin' irons, you know." I used to build them things. I had a

book; I keep a record of 'em, see, and I had a big ol' wood door in my other buildin' I had on the corner, and there wasn't a place on that door that didn't have a brand on it. While it was hot, I stick it on that wood, see? That's right. I done some mysterious things. They were crazy, them brandin' irons [laughter]; they're crazy! Everybody got a different idea. I don't know.

James' recollection of the brand-burned door from his old shop sums up both his accomplishments as an individual and his role within his community. In one sense, it stands as a cumulative symbol of James and his life; the individual jobs, which, taken together, constituted his career as a blacksmith and provided him a social identity. Once James finished the branding irons and they left the shop, the brands became highly pragmatic symbols of another sort, used to identify and differentiate stock. The brand-covered door encompassed the entire community—the individual families and ranches that constitute social life in a rural Texas culture. These two levels of interpretation enjoyed a totally reciprocal relationship, since it was only through James and *his* work that the community could pursue and accomplish *theirs*, and vice-versa. The brand-burned door that James remembered from his old shop, or even the tool-covered walls and tables in his workplace, cast in high relief the web of day-to-day activities that bound James to his social world; they also revealed the importance of labor as a source of identity within this sphere.

Although there is a distinct tradition of highly ornamental iron work in African-American blacksmithing, a tradition which may or may not ultimately have African origins (*cf.* Thompson 122; Vlach, *Afro-American Tradition* 120), the Goudeaus neither imparted nor attached any conventional aesthetic dimensions to their work, emphasizing instead the purely utilitarian aspects of their products. But even though their work may not have revealed any of the overtly beautiful qualities we normally associate with the plastic arts, everything James and Pete created in the Ames Fix-it Shop remains embued with a highly refined aesthetic of practical social living. This dimension of blacksmithing, a dimension implicit in the purposes which motivate production, became explicit in the stories James told me as he described his work. Indeed, even when he described procedures for working iron, James often expressed them in terms of human interaction. In the following example, James describes the actual working of the metal itself, drawing an analogy between this process and the kind of ongoing dialogue which defined his relationship to others and to his world:

> It's just like . . . take a gun and hold it on a man and you can change his mind. You put that piece of iron in the fire and get it hot and you can do just what you want with it. . . . All you gotta' do is have it hot. You can twist it, you can bend it, curl it . . . you can do what you want with it. You can heat it, put it in water, and harden it. It's just like a bullit'll change any man's mind, and that heat'll change any kinda' iron. You gotta' get it hot to work with it. You can make anything you want. You can design it just any way you wanna' do it.

In 1980, when I first met James, after a few minutes of conversation I discovered how hard work and determination paid off in the pride and looks of a man. Over six feet tall, the slender eighty-one-year-old was an endorsement for hard work, his personality emanating good wit and wisdom. By that time, James had also received attention from various Texas newspapers, one which described him as a man who had "forged character for his family, for himself and hopefully in at least some who have had contact with him" (Pickett 3A).

Though the role of a blacksmith in East Texas must have changed as technological advances reached the rural areas, there still exist features that echo the communal importance the blacksmith had in folklore and history. The blacksmith has always played a key role in frontier societies, and Texas was no exception. The accelerated growth and change following the Civil War created an even greater demand for enterprising individuals, like the ex-slave Sylvester Wickcliffe, whose son later employed James Goudeau in the Liberty area. During the 1930s, Wickcliffe gave WPA collectors the following account:

After freedom I decide to learn a trade. I apprentice myself
to the blacksmith trade for clothes and board. I learn all I can in
three years and quit and open a shop on Bayou Torti. . . . I
charge two dollars for to shoe a horse all the way around. Then
I beat plows, build two-wheel buggy and hack. I made sweep
stocks and Garret and Cottman plow. That after the time of the
wood mould board. I made mine with metal.

I come to Texas in 1890, to Liberty and been right round
there and Ames for forty-seven year. I start me a gin and blacksmith shop when I first come. (Rawick 158–59)

James Goudeau was born in 1902 near Evergreen, Louisiana, a state
that, before the Civil War, had one of the highest concentrations of free
blacks of any state. One of those free souls was Charles Ray, James'
maternal grandfather, who distinguished himself as an educator as well
as a prosperous businessman and landowner, and who had a fully
equipped blacksmith and farrier operation on his property. During one
of my visits to his shop in Ames, James told me the following about life
on his grandfather's land in southwest Louisiana:

I lived in Louisiana until I was seventeen years old. Everybody had a shop. My grandfather on my mama's side . . . he
had a big ol' shop. He had them eight-wheel log wagons 'n' all
that stuff. He had sharecroppers . . . livin' on his place. And we
had a big ol' shop . . . two or three people workin' in that thing,
keepin' them wagons 'n' all that mess goin' . . . buggy wheels,
wagon wheels . . . just anything that had a wheel on it, he did it
there, see . . . made wagon axles 'n' all that stuff. . . . I was right
there in the midst of 'em. And I told you while ago [pointing to
his head], if you ain't got it there, you can forget it. Ain't that
right?

He [James' maternal grandfather] had men doin' all his work.
. . . He worked all his days just like he was . . . starved to death.
And he didn't have to work. He had a little ol' store called a
commissary, and he had a little ol' room in the back he used to

on 52nd Street. In addition, Johnson wrote arrangements for and soloed with the Billy Eckstine Orchestra, which also featured Parker and Gillespie and was part of the transition from swing to bebop. Johnson was an example of the type of Texas jazz musician who received important training as a youngster, in his case through lessons taken with local Dallas music teachers. His arrangements and compositions for the Earl Hines, Boyd Raeburn, and Billy Eckstine bands, among many others, were largely in the blues-based riff style, and for the first bebop recording date in 1944, Budd co-composed with pianist Clyde Hart the "hip" riff tune entitled "Bu Dee Daht." Later, in 1960, Johnson composed and arranged "Trinity River Bottom," a piece for himself on tenor sax accompanied by four trumpets. Of this composition named after his hometown river, Budd commented that the Trinity "has caused a lot of trouble and taken a lot of lives so I always associate it with people having a hard time. I therefore thought there ought to be a blues about it." As with so many other Texas jazz musicians, Budd Johnson's background was often reflected in his writing and playing—in particular a riff tradition deriving from the country blues—whether he was performing swing or bebop, or, in the early 1960s, the experimental orchestrations of Gil Evans.

Another Texas composer/arranger noted for his work in the blues-riff mode was Eddie Durham. One of the principal composer arrangers for the Bennie Moten, Count Basie, and Jimmie Lunceford orchestras, Durham helped give definition to the riff style prevalent in much of the swing era's dance music. Equally important was Eddie's influence as the first jazzman to record on an amplified guitar, which would encourage the career of Charlie Christian of Dallas, who became a major figure in the transition from swing to bebop. From Durham's father, who was Irish-Mexican (his mother black-Indian), Eddie learned the folk-music practice of filling a cigar-box fiddle with snake rattles. Later he would place a resonator with a tin pan inside his acoustic guitar in order to amplify the sound as bands became larger and louder. Eventually Durham found a commercial amplified guitar, with which in 1935 he recorded his own arrangement of "Hittin' the Bottle" with the Lunceford Orchestra.

One reaction to the elephantiasis of the big bands was bebop's return to the five-piece instrumentation of early jazz as represented by Louis Armstrong's Hot Five of 1925. But in 1936, even before bebop reduced the size of a normal jazz ensemble, trumpeter Carl "Tatti" Smith of Marshall was the nominal co-leader for a session of Jones-Smith, Inc., a quintet featuring tenorist Lester Young, whose first recordings on this date significantly influenced Charlie Parker. In 1938, Eddie Durham headed up another recording date with Young, and on this occasion Eddie's electric guitar choruses clearly look forward to the work of Charlie Christian as well as to the more intimate group improvisation of bebop. As an electric guitarist *par excellence,* Christian came into prominence through his work with the Benny Goodman Orchestra, but more importantly, he also took part in small-group jam sessions held at Minton's in Harlem where drummer Kenny Clarke and pianist Thelonious Monk began around 1940 to introduce the new rhythms and harmonies of bebop. Among the tunes with Christian, Clarke, and Monk, recorded on a home tape machine in 1941, was Eddie Durham's "Topsy," made popular by the Count Basie band but appropriately retitled by the Minton crew as "Swing to Bop."

Charlie Christian's approach to the guitar grew out of the southwestern tradition of riffed blues and single-string improvised melodies. Blind Lemon Jefferson had mastered the riffed blues combination of guitar and vocal, but Christian developed beyond this style in creating long, swinging lines that have often been compared to the "cool" manner of Lester Young. In many ways both of these players prefigure the coming of bebop—both lending innovative melodic phrasing to jazz, at the same time that they expanded the harmonic and rhythmic dimensions of the music. Christian exhibited the new altered chords, the asymmetrical patterns, and the off-beat accents that became the hallmark of bebop. Working within the blues-riff tradition, Christian reeled off his surprising, extended eighth-note lines that with their enriched progressions opened up the possibility for bebop's more inventive, wide-ranging explorations into musical time and space. In this way, too, Christian would influence several generations of jazz guitarists, although no other player has ever achieved the special southwestern blues-riff feel-

teach school. He had everything in the world that a man could wish for. He had two or three men in the shop all the time, and had four or five wagons runnin' all the time.

In his grandfather's shop and through close association with others at work in the store James began to acquire blacksmithing skills:

It's like the guy born with a silver spoon in his mouth. You've heard that story before, haven't ya? Well, I was born with a shop in my face, ya see what I mean? I just went and picked it up that way . . . nobody taught me. I just watched and when they turned their back I take over.

According to James, he learned the craft in the same day-to-day fashion in which he acquired French language skills in culturally diverse, turn-of-the-century Louisiana: "[J]ust like that broken French *we* knew, you know what I mean? . . . they talk to you in the language and they point their finger at it so you'll know what it means. . . . And it [blacksmithing] grows up that way, see?"

Also according to James, no course of instruction can develop the skills of a good blacksmith, only a natural aptitude and intuitive understanding of the craft combined with observation and, most importantly, involvement in the work process itself will yield results. Although James remembered watching a number of blacksmiths, he credited not one of them as his teacher in a traditional master-apprentice relationship. Instead, he prefers to think of himself as having developed his capabilities on his own: "That's the way it goes. If you don't have it up there, you can just throw it away, forget it. That book ain't going to teach ya. It'll show you a picture of it, but if you can't put it together, you in bad shape."

In 1918 James left Louisiana to go to work in the Gulf refinery in Port Arthur, Texas. On one of his trips between Port Arthur and Louisiana, he stopped at a store in Ames to get a drink of water, and when he subsequently learned that land was cheap in the area, he decided to buy some lots. The decision proved fortuitous. When the Depression struck, James lost his job and in 1935 moved his family to Ames, where he built a three-room shack on his land; three weeks later he went to work as a helper for Plato Wickcliffe in adjacent Liberty.

Plato was the son of Sylvester Wickcliffe, the ambitious ex-slave who moved to Liberty and opened a shop in 1890. James worked for Plato for nearly three years before another three years working as a mechanic for Chevrolet. Just prior to World War II, James felt confident enough to open his own shop: "I figure if I got sense enough to work for the guy [Plato] and can satisfy everybody, I don't see why I can't go in business for myself."

Although James conceded that Plato was a good blacksmith, he viewed himself as far superior to his former employer, particularly in dealing with the public. Plato's manner was abrupt and dismissing, in contrast to James' easy rapport. As a result, customers at Wickcliffe's shop would ask specifically for James. "Well, you have to live with the public 'n' I been livin' with 'em for years. And I know 'em, I know how to handle 'em. . . . If you know the do's 'n' the don't's of a thing then it's not hard to convince 'em."

After setting up shop on his own, James managed to get by. "When push comes to shove," he said, "I can push with the best of them." He raised four sons, teaching them blacksmithing, farming, and carpentry and he was as proud of their independence as he was of his own: "I don't ask them for nothing; they don't ask me for nothing." One son, Pete, was still living near Liberty where he was a supervisor for a local chemical company. While I was a graduate student in the Folklore Program at the University of Texas at Austin during the early 1980s, Pete had been coming to the shop, usually on Saturdays, when I would conduct most of my interviews with him and his father. I would frequently find him building barrel-style barbeque pits, burglar bars, or gates.

The experimental trial-and-error manner in which James and Pete developed their technical abilities is reflected in the ways they tackled individual jobs. Said James:

> You know, you can't just build things outta your mind, you
> know what I mean? You just go ahead, see? I'm going to do this

and design it and do it. You don't have to worry over it too long, see? . . . just go ahead and do it.

    [E]verything comes natural to me. . . . It just fell in my lap, ya see, and I just went ahead and did it. I design it in my mind . . . and go ahead and make it. . . .

Like his father, Pete emphasizes the processual and imaginative, as opposed to static and fixed nature of design and construction.

    See, you don't go by a blueprint. Ya just gotta use your imagination. . . . I design things at night when I sleep, when everybody else goes to bed at night . . . the next day, I wanna make somethin' it comes to me about two o'clock in the mornin.' . . . When I get up in the mornin', it's made.

This reflects the traditional nature of folk art and its transmission via informal means (Teske 35), as well as the mystical aura that has traditionally surrounded blacksmithing. Both Pete and James explained that their ideas for designs emerged during sleep; solutions to problems in design seemed to appear almost magically.

Pete certainly had a pragmatic approach to blacksmithing, always concerned with the practical purposes his product would fulfill. When I asked him what he thought of ornamental ironwork while showing him some photographs of decorative ironwork that appear in John Vlach's *The Afro-American Tradition in Decorative Arts*, Pete's response described his own orientation succinctly: "That ain't blacksmith work. . . . That's just one of those added attractions. Blacksmithing is all this crappy looking stuff around here . . . all them plows and all them saw blades. . . . *That's* the old blacksmith style." Pete not only commented on his own sense of aesthetics in his work, but expressed a communal aesthetic as well. Because this farming community's aesthetics emphasized utilitarian objects over decorative ones, James and Pete never had a demand for decorative work, and they placed little value in such ironwork.

Yet Pete did some work that his father considered "fancy," though Pete nevertheless stressed a utilitarian function in his products. Pete explained:

> I do all the fine work, repair stuff for farmers. . . . I made a gate for a guy . . . delivered to one of the big shots. I . . . designed it real neat, and then his name . . . his brand . . . was a circle, and then a "V." . . . he wanted that to go on that gate I made for him. It looks real good. He lives downtown in Liberty. He's a millionaire . . . I don't know why he fools with me. I do a lot for him . . . for people that's got plenty of money.

James Goudeau viewed his life and work as a continual change, and in the face of the adversity, he boasted, "When push comes to shove, I can shove just as hard as you can push." Moreover, he enthusiastically embraced hard work and perseverance, which he expressed in another of his favorite proverbial expressions: "One of these days when I get good enough, I'm gonna quit work. But a winner never quits, and a quitter never wins."

Though toward the end of his life James used a trip-hammer for extremely heavy work, as did other blacksmiths, he frequently used a twelve-pound shop hammer when he was younger. Said Pete during a visit I made in 1983, "He used a three-pound shop hammer . . . that's what he used to do all of his work for years, but now he don't use that anymore . . . well . . . he *used* it, but he uses a trip-hammer for most of it." In 1983, shortly before his death, James still looked strong. He once mused, "If you could beat that iron about a third of the time I beat on it, you'd be in pretty good shape."

The kind of iron James used for each job determined the kind of tool he used to shape it. Most of the tools were made of wrought iron, which was practically carbon free and contained impurities totaling no more than about 0.1 percent. Because so much of James' work was done on very hot metal, he had to use a variety of types of shop equipment and tools for shaping iron. And, according to James, "if you can't make the tools, you can't be a blacksmith." Among the tools that he used most often was a pair of tongs which he made about forty years ago. They are about twenty-four inches long and two inches wide at the lip and hold flat objects. "Yeah, you *got* to make your own tools to be a blacksmith," he declared. Other tools in his shop included punches, chisels, flatters (used to smooth out iron), various hammers and tongs, and of course, an anvil and forge.

Once when he made a branding iron for me, I asked him how long it took to get the coals hot. "That's the biggest problem . . . see, get it going and after that it goes on." Using paper to light the coal, James started the blower fan. "I use an electric blower. I used to pump one of them [bellows] when I was little boy. You see this thing right here [pointing to the blower fan] . . . that regulates the air." The unit was a rotary blower that contained a series of fans mounted on a wheel, similar in appearance to a portable hair dryer. The fire started up, but James complained about the kind of coal he was then using in his work. "It ain't worth nothin'! Too soft! No heat!" The temperature of the iron had to reach approximately 500° F before it was ready for shaping (Watson). Only an experienced ironworker can tell when iron should be removed from the fire.

Making a branding iron depicting my initials, R-A-B, James used mild steel 3/4 inches wide and 3/16 inches thick; each letter was made up of two sections. Rather than bending the letters on his anvil, James used a vise to hold each piece he would shape, and held a pair of tongs on the iron as he bent it. For the handle, James used a 3/8-inch-thick square stick of iron, about eighteen inches ling. It took him about thirty minutes to make the letters, heat the end of the iron stick, and with the tip of the iron on his anvil, shape the end into a ring with a one-inch diameter before cooling it in a bucket of water. "I made the 'R' and 'B' right quick, didn't I?" he boasted. As he shaped each letter, he simply used a cutting torch to break off the necessary amount for each letter from a stick of iron. "You gotta treat iron like you do a dog. Ya just can't go around *kickin'* it, you gotta *whip* it," he mused as he described the way he manipulated iron. He used an oxyacetylene torch, instead of old-time forge welding, to weld the sections of letters together.

I asked him how much skill goes into making branding irons. He said, "Ya gotta know what you're doin.' Just like pullin' a rabbit outta your hat." The pride James took in the speed and the skill with which he made the branding iron reminded me of something he said he used to tell Pete as he was growing up: "No matter how fast you work and how much you turn out, whenever you do a job, just give it a hundred percent." Similarly, James nurtured an attitude toward his work which he expressed in another saying he memorized for recitation in the third grade: "Once a task is begun, never leave it 'til it's done. Be thy labor great or small, do it well or not at all."

When a customer came to James for forge welding, a skill which James saw as the mark of a true blacksmith, it was not a matter of simply creating a bond of trust and understanding between himself and the customer. The following excerpt from an interview I conducted with him during one of my visits illustrates this:

> Customer said, "You a blacksmith?" I said, "Yeah." He said, "Well, I got a piece of iron out there that's four foot long, two inches too short. I want it fifty inches long, which would be . . . two more inches to add to four feet." He said, "I don't want to add it to the end, but I want it the same size all the way around when you get through with it."
>
> A blacksmith can do it, 'cause he splits it with a chisel . . . and then puts that piece of two-inch piece in the middle, then draw it out, see. It was two inches longer when I got through with it. Now that's when you can tell if a guy's a blacksmith or not.

Flexibility is a desirable quality in both iron and people, although it always requires a measure of work to achieve such a condition. The appropriate agent for inducing flexibility in iron is fire; in people, sociability; and James was an artist in both. Not only did he listen to and communicate with customers to exchange necessary information, but he also entertained them with stories—"just crackin' jokes" he called it—nearly all day long while working in the shop. The following preacher joke commented not only on his relationships with customers but on the kind of bumbling naiveté some visitors displayed regarding the blacksmith's trade:

> Well, the mornin' that preacher came in the shop . . . he was standin' around the anvil . . . and . . . the blacksmith was makin' horseshoes, see. And . . . there was several of 'em standin' around there. . . . Every time he finished one he'd throw it on the ground. . . . The preacher stooped down and grabbed one of the horseshoes, turned loose right quick, and he [the blacksmith] says, "What's a matter Reverend?" [The reverend] says, "I got a fast way of testin' horseshoes!" I guess it was, it was hot. Pick it up and turn it loose in a hurry. . . . That's one of them lies you know they tell. . . . *You* know. . . . [laughs]

All of these elements—his practical orientation and strong work ethic, his knowledgeability, imagination, and experience, his ability to communicate and socialize—made James a master smith whose services were truly valued and appreciated by his customers. While the Goudeaus tended to emphasize design and a communal sense of aesthetics in their work, other black ironworkers I interviewed, especially farriers, dealt more with animals and cattle, such as J. T. Ruffin of the Jones Valley Community near Tyler. Both Ruffin and the Goudeaus stand out in their communities not so much by overt Africanisms that exist in their work as by the communal aesthetics which guide their senses of innovation and improvisation, truly a part of black cultural traditions. Though Ruffin's status as a skilled ironworker is related to the cattle industry, for which he does not find it necessary to mentally design iron shapes crafted at the forge the following day (like the Goudeaus), he does have a gift for responding to animals in a manner that community members fully recognize and appreciate.

While an intern conducting folklore research for the Institute of Texan Cultures in the summer of 1989, I accompanied John Minton and Terry McDevett (both with the Institute at that time) to Shelby County, near where John and Terry had attended Stephen F. Austin State University in Nacogdoches. John and I interviewed some long-time residents of Shelby County, including a practicing black midwife and an eighty-three-year-old retired songster. During that time I also met sixty-four-year-old John T. Ruffin at his house in Jones Valley.

He told me he was an ex-Marine and had learned to shoe horses through a white Navy buddy of his while they were in the service. The next morning he not only shod a horse but he also dressed the wounds of one who was injured during a storm and whose owner was advised by a friend that if J. T. couldn't save him, nobody could.

Additionally, the owner told J. T. if he could save him, the horse was his. After J. T. shod his favorite horse (a quarter horse he called "Peanut," named after Jimmy Carter), he brought the injured horse out to dress its wound and to trim its mane and hooves. I watched, as did the horse's previous owner, who had dropped by to see how her $3500 lost investment was doing. Using one microphone, I left my Nakamichi 550 on "record" during the entire time I was there.

I asked Mr. Ruffin how he would describe his work: "Well, I'm a farrier, that's a horseshoer . . . and I catch cattle . . . out on the road and shoe horses . . . mess with small animals' n' things. . . . The main thing I like is just animals, any kinda animals." It was evident that both J. T. and his wife, Mary, took great pleasure in showing off their livestock. It was near feeding time and Mary Ruffin, J. T.'s wife, invited me to take photographs of their various breeds of animals in the corral out back. Among the animals I photographed was a cross between a goat and a deer, which Mary called a "go-daddy." As she fed the horses, J. T. continued:

> Most the kids up in town call this place a zoo 'cause I got these coons 'n' these dogs 'n' ducks 'n' things out here. But I just enjoy them 'n' they enjoy talkin' to people. . . . I ain't specialize in nothin' but shoein', horseshoein'. I love to shoe horses. . . . I tell everybody that I prefer to die with the horses myself. . . .

J. T.'s way with animals was similar to that of a white farrier's I had interviewed a few days before in nearby Ben Wheeler. The blacksmith in Ben Wheeler, one William Tillary, had told me about a time he and a buddy once shod 365 head of mules in Louisiana. Tillary said, "Yeah . . . a man could get killed on some of them ol' mules. They're pretty stubborn . . . you gotta get 'is 'tention." Like other blacksmiths I had interviewed in the area, J. T.'s mechanical know-how was fused with a tough mental outlook. Just as Tillary knew how to handle mules when he used to shoe them, J. T. knew horses:

> When I get holt of a mean horse, I don't think 'bout beatin' him up, I think bout beatin' him to the draw at what he's doin'. . . . If he's a mean horse don't be mean unlessen you let 'im be mean. But, it's good to be kind to a horse . . . and not beat 'im up all the time and best not to *love* 'im all the time. I don't b'lieve in feedin' a horse carrots 'n' sugar 'n' all that stuff, because he's s'posed to be fed and . . . when I go out 'n' tell 'im "whoa," I want 'im to stop. If he don't I'm s'posed to train 'im how to stop 'n' then if he don't stop then me 'n' him get into it. Uh, I shoe 'em 'n' train 'em, train 'em obedience trainin' . . . break 'em to ride.

He had gained his knowledge of horses informally at a very early age from his grandmother: "[M]y grandmother was Indian and . . . she didn't believe in nothin' but farmin'. And she learned . . . stuff about these horses." There were no vets back then; consequently, J. T. learned some folk remedies for ailing horses. He described a method his grandmother had taught him for treating a sick horse:

> I noticed one time we had some horses . . . got in the barn eatin' 'em a buncha' peas. She had us stand them horses in the creek. And they got all-right, and ever since then I've been standin' 'em in the creek. I wasn't but 'bout twelve or thirteen years old . . . she used to have us to trim their feet and carry them to the creek, stand 'em in there. . . . I been doin' that ever since. . . . Oh they got better medicine now. . . . I seen her take blue stone . . . and put it on horses' legs. Lime, they take that

flesh in it, put this sack a' lime on it. That lime would eat that flesh off. . . .

He told me he hated to tell youngsters about this method "'cause they think, 'Oh, he's just an old fogey.'" Yet, J. T. admits that it is not too good to do "*everything* the old way, but some o' the things the old way'll work." I asked him to give me an example, and he told me the following:

Yeah . . . like grandmother 'n' them had us doin' that—now you can talk to the vet, he'll tell ya' "aw, give 'im some bute[3] or somethin'." Well, it's all-right to give 'im bute to keep down pain, but . . . grandmother'd say, "Take the horse off of feed 'n' put 'im on hay, stand 'im in water." But now they'll tell ya', "Take 'em off of so much protein and give 'em some bute."

His common sense approach to treating an ailing horse is matched by his approach to shoeing horses, which became obvious to me as he told the following story about what happens when a horse is shod improperly:

Put a bar-plate on it. I *hope* a man put a bar-plate shoe on one too; cut his foot down in the quick 'n' get that shoe on 'im, I say. "He gonna die." [Customer said] "No. he's gonna make it." I hauled 'im off, 'cause I hauled these dead ones off, I told 'im. "Yeah, he's gonna die." I said, "Any time that you cut your fingernail past the part that's out from the quick, it's gonna hurt. And you cut it deep enough, you gonna get in bad trouble." And that's what happened to this horse; he died. . . . And so, another lady heard about it 'n' she had a bar-plate she put on *her* horse. She had me come out 'n' look at it 'n' says "What do you think about it?" Say "I tell you what, your horse is gonna die." She says, "The man didn't say he was gonna die." I said, "*I* say he's gonna die." The next time I saw her, she said, "I had to put 'im down." I say "I know it." I can't go against him [the customer's veterinarian], 'cause they went to school. . . .

When he was very young, J. T. received his education informally from his grandmother, and then later through the Marine Corps: "I was raised up with step-daddies. . . . I had two [or] three of 'em. . . . I caught the devil [from] them step-daddies in the Marine Corps, but it made a man out of me." I asked how he first got started shoeing horses, and he gave me the following account:

> I had a friend . . . in the Navy 'n' I was in the Marines—we got to be friends overseas . . . when he came back, well, we talked about animals all the time 'n' when I come back, why he knew that I was comin' back. He invited me over 'n' so there was calf-ropin'—he got out before I did—and I could rope pretty good before I went but . . . I never was able to own a horse . . . but in the neighborhood where we lived back before I went into the service, there was some white fellas that lived there and was about my age and they had horses and I was sittin' on the fence 'n' watch 'em all the time. . . . After I went down there for so long, why they let me rope on their horses. And I got to where I could catch good. They learned me how to rope 'n' I could . . . beat them ropin'. And so we'd go to showin'—you know, things wasn't like that now—they'd let me rope at the show but I'd have to rope . . . after the show. And they told me "Them boys don't need you."
>
> You know, a lot of people do things because . . . the company they keep. Now as long as *we* was together, we was just like that, we was good buddies. If we went to get a drink of water, we'd drink outta' the same thing. But, when they had company, he wasn't like that. And they told me at the ropin', say, "They gonna letcha rope tonight," say, "so you can rope after we rope," say, "but I tell ya what," say "we goin' stay here with it, because you got our horse 'n' you gonna stay here with it. Ain't one thing we want you to do is catch that sucker." So I caught . . . and his mother told me, say "Well," say "I tell you one thing," say "you caught that calf as good as anybody." Say, "Now you keep catchin' and people'll stay here 'n' watch." And I done that for *years* or so.

Me 'n' Bill got to workin' together 'n' his daddy was a horseshoer. I'd hold the horses while he'd shoe 'em. And . . . his
daddy told me one day, says, "John, who trimmed this horse?"
I said, "I did." He said, "You can trim that good," said "You can
shoe." And I've been doin' it ever since. It meant a lot to me. . . .

Such a display of technique and bravery finally brought J. T. the
recognition he deserved, but only after he suffered a great deal of humiliation from those he called "the white fellas." Even friend Bill found
it difficult to rise above his cohorts' unfair treatment of J. T., something
J. T. quickly excused as simply the result of the company his friend
kept. J. T. did not allow such pettiness to discourage him from watching, learning, and eventually participating in rodeo events. His desire
and persistence in acquiring the skills of a horseshoer eventually paid
off. As he put it, "It meant a lot to me." The discipline he learned while
in the Marines and his ability to succeed socially in such an oppressive
environment gave him a solid background which would serve him well
as he learned horseshoeing from Bill's father.

J. T. was not going to settle for a lowly job working for unfair em-
ployees: "The good Lord know I needed to do somethin' outside steve-
dore all my life . . . it's hard workin' all my life 'n' [for a] bad boss man."
His pride and confidence in his work as a horseshoer, as his own boss,
became even more explicit when he declared: "You don't have to worry
about no money if you're a horseshoer. You can shoe a horse anywhere.
You can shoe a horse *any*where. I can leave here and go to *your* home and
I can . . . stop down the road and shoe a horse."

The tools of his business have changed over the years, and he has
adjusted his work accordingly: "You don't have to have the forge 'n'
everything with ya. They got the shoes set up [pre-fabricated] and all
that stuff . . . that's the best deal that ever happened to *me*. . . . You
know that's the best thing that *ever* happened to me." J. T. showed me
some of the pre-fabricated shoes which he had been buying for the past
thirty years. Each shoe was shaped and sized according to the type of
horse that was to be shod. He then declared: "But now I tell ya, I go out
there 'n' get that horse [Peanut] and shoe 'im for ya, and we'll shoe 'im
right here, and I'll use the anvil and everything."

J. T.'s early love for animals and his eagerness to learn horseshoeing are qualities that young members of the Jones Valley Community seem to lack, according to J. T. However, he was quick to add: "If I knew a kid . . . twelve or thirteen years old, want to learn how to shoe horses, I could learn 'im free of charge. But I couldn't pay 'im for it while he was learnin'. But, I learn 'im what *I* know about it." The knowledge he would pass on to such a helper would be ample reward enough. J. T. places great value on hard work and a desire to learn. A story J. T. told me about a hammer he received from another horseshoer over forty years ago further illustrates this point. The hammer symbolizes the relationship between master and apprentice, holding a value that money cannot measure:

> But now I been usin' this hammer here with this same handle in it for about . . . forty-four years. And there was a man walked up 'n' asked me would I sell the hammer 'n' I said, "No, man." I said, "But I tell you what I'll do. If you find me a kid that wants to shoe horses, and when I get to where I don't . . . I *give* 'im all that stuff that was give to me." [J. T. holds up a few tools he is using while shoeing "Peanut."] This little ol' box . . . I'd give it to a kid that wanted to shoe a horse when I quit. . . . But now I'm not gonna' *sell* it. Oh, he wanted me to sell it. "Oh no, man, you don't have enough money to buy that." [The man responded] "Well, I got quite a bit." I say, "I don't care, you just don't have enough to buy *that*."

J. T. was not talking about passing his tools on to somebody who had been trained at a horseshoeing school, but somebody who knows animals as well as how to shoe, something you cannot learn in a formal setting:

> Them people that would go to horseshoein' schools . . . knows all the nerves 'n' everything 'n' . . . but now . . . I rode horses and I know how a saddle horse should be shod and a workin' quarter horse . . . and a walkin' horse. I know you gotta

weigh him 'n' all that stuff, and a racehorse . . . I gotta guage to feed a racehorse 'n' get him all set to weight . . . if you set the shoe right and set your nail right . . . and keep the horse level, why you can shoe it. But now the main thing about horseshoein', you can't be scared o' animals. If you scared you gonna get in trouble. . . . When a horse walks up to you and smells of you, he's checkin' you. . . . If you scared of 'im, he know it, he'll try ya too.

Not only does J. T. know the ways of horses and the kinds of shoes suitable for particular types of horses, but he knows people as well. His foreman, a Mr. Dupree, could attest to that. As soon as he arrived for work, J. T. sent him to get some Cut 'n Heel, a medication he would later spray liberally on the wound of a horse he had recently acquired. Jackie Ungerecht, whose daughter once owned C. T. (the injured horse), had arrived about the same time as Mr. Dupree. A few months earlier, according to Mrs. Ungerecht, a strong wind sent a guy-line ripping through the horse's stall, cutting the valuable horse's hind leg to the quick. A local veterinarian recommended that Jackie "put the horse down" (put it to sleep). A friend she telephoned "just for moral support," reminded Jackie

> "John T. has always loved that horse." He'd been wanting to buy it and had said, "Mrs. Ungerecht, when you gonna sell this horse?" I said, "Well John I can't *do* it 'cause that's *Julie's* horse." So she said, "Why don't you call John and see if he can *save* the horse. And if he can save it, give it to 'im." That's what we did, so this is John's horse now. I just came to see it.

Jackie Ungerecht knew her daughter's horse was in the very best of hands. As she watched J. T. unwrap the bandaged area, she declared, "He's apparently doin' real well. The horse keeps running away [laughs]." Walking up to C. T., she whispered, "He's a lucky boy, isn't he?"

J. T. is quite actively involved with community members, particularly kids. He built a covered wagon in which he hauls around the local black children. "Juneteenth, they have a parade here for 'em, and I have that wagon in it [and in] the Rose Parade here." Additionally, J. T. has been involved in other festive occasions. The following further illustrates his commitment to participating in worthwhile events, as well as what community members expect of him:

> I left from here and rode to Houston—horseback. Now we're plannin' on leavin' *this* year about the seventh of February. . . . That's a long ride 'n' it be cold, but I can take it. A lotta people don't wanna do it but . . . *I'll* go. I rode *this* horse to Houston. First year I rode to Houston, when he was a *three*-year-old I rode 'im. . . . We rode for *cancer* research, sickle-cell . . . some kinda' *blood* cancer. And . . . we rode for Skoal Tobacco Company. . . . I was the oldest guy on the ride. And they gave me a pair o' chaps . . . but . . . I gotta' stop down the road you know 'n' shoe a few horses . . . when we got ready to camp out. *I* had a good time, but . . . I was the oldest guy on the ride 'n' Earl Campbell, he was the big wheel of it. We started from up at his ranch right up there. . . . And man, we had a good time the night before . . . he wanted me on it, *shoot!* . . . Man, he said he just couldn't have it without *me*. And I been goin' ever since . . . but, we woke up one mornin' it was twelve . . . degrees!

Freezing temperatures during his trek to Houston were no obstacle to a man who seems to thrive on adverse conditions and can improvise when called upon. His stories, such as the one above, revealed to me another dimension of his craft which is as every bit as essential to the completion of a task as his technical ability: his social skills. He, like other African-American blacksmiths I have interviewed, is an asset to his community not only because of his knowledge of horseshoeing but also because of his ability to work with people, to understand them, to make himself understood, and to gain their trust. Local resident and football hero, Earl Campbell, as the above excerpt attests, could not have traveled on horseback to Houston without him! J. T. Ruffin therefore understood his central role in his community's livelihood and appreciated the strong identity that his experience as a craftsman had given him, a theme which also became apparent in interviews with other blacksmiths I have met.

The traditions of self-sufficiency and creativity embodied in crafted items and artworks represent older ways of thought that continue to live on today. Like the Goudeaus, there were other black ironworkers whom I interviewed during the 1980s, some who were continuing to perform in the manner of their forebears. Also, like James, they were octagenerians. Frank Green proudly displayed his smithing talents at Brenham's Mayfest in 1981 when I interviewed him; however, Jake Zephyr had long since retired in Washington County, but nevertheless sat in his dilapidated shop a few hundred yards from his house, reminiscing about bygone days while fearful of a newly emerging prison farm near his house. He, like the others, missed the strong ties he once had with the community.

Blacksmithing is a living tradition that has been in existence among cultures world-wide for more than ten thousand years. When turning to the historical distribution of a traditional technology throughout the world, we are dealing with a phenomenon that can diffuse freely between individuals, and we are obliged to investigate such materials, forms, and the diffusion of various cultural traits. We now know there is a long heritage of smithing in Africa, which was brought to the United States through slavery. Even mythical powers associated with blacksmiths in African folklore may have influenced the African-American's status in the Old South, since a mystique surrounding the black ironworker's ability seems to linger.

The interrelationship of an artisan with his community, an accounting of the role blacksmiths have played in Texas communities, and the life and times of the few blacksmiths I have discussed here should bear witness to the importance of black craftsmen in Texas. Moreover, I did not identify overt connections to Africa their artifacts display, but rather explained the work they do in terms of the behavior surrounding blacksmithing, which perhaps reinforces their African affinities after all.

Notes

1. I wish to thank John Vlach, from whom I took my first graduate courses in folklore at the University of Texas and who first inspired me to pursue fieldwork on black ironworkers in East Texas. I would also like to express my gratitude to John Minton, José Limón, Kay Turner, M. Jane Young, and Marcia Burns for ideas they generously offered after they read earlier drafts of my master's report, "Afro-American Blacksmithing in East Texas," which forms the basis of this paper. For their critical comments and suggestions regarding earlier drafts of this article, I also thank Pat Mullen and Alan Govenar.

2. Until the mid-twentieth century, most scholars, except for such notable exceptions as W. E. B. Dubois and Melville Herskovits, assumed that slavery wiped out all of the fundamental aspects of traditional African cultures (Levine 4). Robert Ferris Thompson later persuasively argued that because much of the slave trade came into Louisiana from the Congo, there is a wealth of continuities in the Deep South derived from this Congo-Angola section of Africa (122). More recently, the debate over the search for African origins has appeared in Daniel J. Crowley's edited collection of articles, *African Folklore in the New World*, and Joseph E. Holloway's *Africanisms in American Culture*. Particularly noteworthy is Beverly J. Robinson's "Africanisms and the Study of Folklore" in Holloway's book. I would like to thank Pat Mullen for bringing this last article to my attention.

3. A generic term that refers to any form of phenylbutazone, a non-harmonal, anti-inflammatory type of medication used by veterinarians on injured horses to reduce pain.

Bibliography

Balandier, Georges and Jacques Maquet. Trans. Lady (Mariska Caroline) Peck, Bettina Wadia, and Peninah Neimark. *Dictionary of Black African Civilization*. New York: Leon Amiel, 1974.

Banta, Bob. "Bastrop craftsman gives bit of discarded metal a new life." *Austin American-Statesman* 6 October 1980: B2.

Burns, Richard Allen. "Afro-American Blacksmithing in East Texas." Master's report. University of Texas at Austin, 1984.

Crowley, Daniel J., ed. *African Folklore in the New World*. Austin: University of Texas Press, 1977.

Dubois, W. E. B. *The Negro Artisan*. Atlanta University Publication No. 7. Atlanta: Atlanta University Press, 1902.

___. *The Negro American Artisan*. Atlanta University Publication No. 17. Atlanta: Atlanta University Press, 1912.

Goudeau, James and Pete. Personal interviews in Ames, Texas. 15 November, 6 December 1980; 19 March, 16 April, 2 September 1983.

Goudeau, Pete. Personal interview in Ames, Texas. 14 July 1992.

Gregg, James E. "Industrial Training for the Negro." *Southern Workman* 58 (1929): 223–31.

Green, Frank. Personal Interview at Brenham, Texas during Mayfest. 10 May 1981.

Herskovits, Melville J. *The Myth of the Negro Past*. 1941. Rpt. ed., Boston: Beacon Press, 1956.

Holloway, Joseph E., ed. *Africanisms in American Culture*. Bloomington: Indiana University Press, 1990.

Levine, Lawrence. *Black Culture and Black Consciousness: Afro-American Folk Thought From Slavery to Freedom*. New York: Oxford University Press, 1977.

Livingston, Jane. *Black Folk Art in America: 1930–1980*. Oxford, Mississippi: The University Press of Mississippi, 1982.

Olmsted, Frederick Law. *A Journey Through Texas: Or, a Saddle Trip on the Southwestern Frontier*. New York, 1857; Barker State History Series No. 2. Austin: University of Texas Press, 1978.

Pickett, Betty. "Goudeau Forges Horseshoes and Character 'When Push Comes to Shove.'" *Liberty Vindicator* [Liberty, Texas] 25 October 1979: 3A.

Rawick, George P., comp. *The American Slave: A Composite Autobiography*. Vol. 5, pt. 4. Westport, Ct., 1972.

Robinson, Beverly J. "Africanisms and the Study of Folklore." *Africanisms in American Culture*. Ed. Joseph E. Holloway. Bloomington: Indiana University Press, 1990. 211–24.

Ruffin, John T. Personal interview in Tyler, Texas Archives, University of Texas Institute of Texan Cultures at San Antonio. 2 August 1989. Cat. no. RB89-5-1:1, 2:2.

Smith, Cyril Stanley. "On the Nature of Iron." *Made of Iron*. Houston: University of St. Thomas Art Department, 1966. 29–42.

Teske, Robert. "What is Folk Art: An Opinion on the Controversy." *El Palecio: Magazine of Museums of Mexico* 88 (1983): 34–38.

Thompson, Robert Ferris. "African Influences on the Art of the United States." *Black Studies in the University*. Eds. Armstead Robinson, Craig Foster, and Donald Ogilvie. New Haven: Yale University Press, 1969. 122–70.

Tillary, William. Personal interview. Archives, University of Texas Institute of Texan Cultures at San Antonio. 21 July 1989. Cat. no. RB89-3-1:1

Treat, Victor. "William Goyens: Free Negro Entrepreneur." *Black Leaders: Texans For Their Times*. Eds. Alwyn Barr and Robert Calvert. Austin: Texas State Historical Association, 1981. 19–48.

Tyler, Ronnie C. and Lawrence R. Murphy, eds. *The Slave Narratives of Texas*. Austin: The Encino Press, 1974.

Vaughn, James H. "∂hkyagu as Artists in Marghi Society." *The Traditional Artist in African Societies*. Ed. Warren L. d'Azevedo. Bloomington: Indiana University Press, 1973. 162–93.

Vlach, John Michael. *The Afro-American Tradition in Decorative Arts*. Cleveland: The Cleveland Museum of Art, 1978.

___. "Arrival and Survival: Maintenance of Afro-American Tradition in Folk Art and Craft." *Perspectives on American Folk Art*. Eds. Ian Quimby and Scott Swank. New York: Norton, 1980. 177–217.

___. "Afro-American Folk Crafts in Ninteenth Century Texas." *Western Folklore* 40 (1981): 149–61.

___. *Charleston Blacksmith: The Work of Philip Simmons*. Athens: The University of Georgia Press, 1981.

Watson, Aldren. *The Village Blacksmith*. New York: Thomas Y. Crowell, 1968.

"What is Amerian Folk Art?: A Symposium." *Antiques* 57 (1950): 355–62.

Zephyr, Jake. Personal interview at Zephyr's shop in Washington, Texas. 23 November 1980.

Tony Lott of Corpus Christi. (Courtesy, Documentary Arts, Inc., Dallas)

Vincent Jacobs, Circle 6 Ranch in Raywood, Texas. (Courtesy, Documentary Arts, Inc., Dallas)

Musical Traditions of Twentieth-Century African-American Cowboys

by Alan Govenar

Photo by Kaleta Doolin

While the importance of African-Americans in Texas ranching before and after the Civil War has been recognized, the musical traditions of the cowboys themselves have remained virtually undocumented. John Lomax in his book *Adventures of a Ballad Hunter* recalled that African-American ranch hands were more reluctant to sing for him, but that "two or three Negro cowboys sang lustily" when he got them away from the crowd (46). Unfortunately, Lomax does not discuss the songs that these cowboys performed, although he does describe his encounter with another black cowboy, whom he learned about from a German saloonkeeper in San Antonio, Texas, in 1908. "He directed me to another drink dispenser, a Negro, who ran a place down near the Southern Pacific depot out on a scrubby mesquite grove," Lomax writes, explaining that the man had been a trail cook for years and apparently knew a "world of cowboy songs" (61). Lomax, however, only recounts one of his songs, "Home on the Range," which he recorded and later concluded, after the music was "set down" and "touched up here and there, has since won a high place as a typical Western folk tune." Regrettably, Lomax was somewhat ethnocentric in his approach to collect-

▼

ing cowboy songs and seemed to neglect those tunes that didn't fit his preconceived notions, formulated from his knowledge of Anglo-American balladry and published sheet music.

Moses Asch and Alan Lomax in *The Leadbelly Songbook* include two cowboy songs that Leadbelly recalled from his days working on farms and ranches in East Texas: "Come Along All You Cowboys" and "Cow Cow Yicky Yicky Yea" (Asch). However, Asch and Lomax do not explore the natural context in which these songs were originally performed, or how they related to other songs in Leadbelly's repertory.

From contemporary oral accounts and anecdotal evidence, it appears that although black cowboys did sing some Anglo-American folk songs for collectors, their musical traditions among themselves were somewhat different than among their white counterparts. According to Alfred Johnson, who worked as a ranch hand in the 1920s and 30s, black cowboys sang blues and church songs rather than what are thought of as "cowboy songs."

Johnson was born in 1913 in Cedar Creek, Texas, the son of Frank and Pearl Lee Johnson, who were sharecroppers on a farm and ranch owned by a man only remembered as "Mr. Yost." Johnson's memories of his childhood are sketchy, though he says that he often felt unwanted and that around the age of fifteen, he went to work on another of Mr. Yost's ranches near Manchaca in Bastrop County. "They give me to them," he says. "They'd feed me, you know, shoe me and clothe me. And I did horseback riding, taking care of the cattle, herding the cattle, and farming. Everybody sang the blues in them days. Black cowboys sang blues. They didn't sing cowboy songs. They sang them blues and some church songs. All through this country now, if you go down there, and if you hear them singing, they're singing the blues."

Johnson learned about music by listening and watching. "All of my peoples," he says, "played some. My daddy was a fiddler and he played blues on the fiddle. My uncle, named Will Johnson, played guitar all the time. I couldn't get to play too much, because I wasn't over twelve or thirteen years old. That's when they gave me the nickname 'Snuff' because I started using snuff around that time. Well, they'd let me pick up the guitar every once in a while. And I'd be paying attention to what my uncle was doing, how he was playing. And I would get to play a little bit. And then it would probably be a week or two weeks before I could get a chance to pick up another one. But I kept at it in my mind what he was doing and I wanted to be a guitar picker and play like the way he did. He stayed down there at Cedar Creek, and we'd always go to the country ball, because he'd always have one.

> Those country balls were good. The people weren't like they are now. People would associate with one another. Maybe they'd have a country ball over to this place, maybe they have a country ball over to that place. It'd be just a house. That was every Friday and Saturday night. They'd have fiddle, guitar, and then we didn't have no drums. They'd get out there and slow drag, you know, and dance. They wouldn't get out there hopping and jumping and picking and kicking. They wouldn't do that. They just slow dance, mile-long slow dance. And we'd go because it was within walking distance. They would play country music, blues, just like I play now. Oh, Lord, they'd have some of all kinds. "Blues in the Bottle," "Goin' Downtown," "Black Gal." It was sorta like Mance Lipscomb.
> I didn't know Mance Lipscomb personally. I knew of him a few times. I got to see him a few times. And then he would be playing. He mostly went on horseback or in the wagon. I guess I was about fourteen or fifteen. He was well known all around Cedar Creek. He was well known all the way through Bastrop, Elgin, Taylor, La Grange. He was from Navasota in Grimes County. Cedar Creek's in Bastrop County, seven miles out of Bastrop.

The influence of Mance Lipscomb is apparent in Johnson's playing, especially in his use of a strong thumb on the bass string, almost like the drum in a dance tune. About this, Johnson says, "That's right, when I be playing, I carry my bass with me. You can't find too many guitar pickers who can play and carry a bass."

In addition to playing a distinctive style of what might be called "black cowboy" blues at house parties and country balls, Johnson has also performed in his church. "It'd be with the sermon," Johnson says. "I get up there and play while the people are singing and I play along with them."

Many of the songs Johnson performs are remembered in bits and pieces and combine traditional lyrics with those he improvises as he goes along. He sings with a deep, almost moaning tone, accompanying himself on guitar and sometimes humming. "While you're humming," he smiles, "it gives you the thoughts of what verses to place in with your singing." Overall, Johnson's memory of his songs is inexact. His versions of "Hey, Little Girl" and "The Good Book Told Me," for example, are essentially guitar instrumentals that incorporate humming with the repetition of what seems to be a truncated lyric of a longer song that might have been forgotten or never learned. When asked about these, he says that "blues" of this kind were sung by people at leisure and at work. "They sang the blues when they were sitting or walking, sometimes when they were herding cattle or riding down the road. The blues comes from worries, and to sing the blues gives relief."

In some respects, American music specialist Kip Lornell suggests, Johnson's performance style is reminiscent of the black southern banjo/song/string band tradition that "could be found throughout the south, but especially in the southeastern United States during the teens and 1920s, and perhaps even earlier." Moreover, many of the lyrics in Johnson's blues or blues-like songs, such as in "Good Morning Blues," consist of recompositions of familiar tunes.

Johnson's religious singing is largely indicative of the post gospel camp meeting era. Such well-known gospel hymns as "Old Time Religion" and "Going Back to Jesus" typify the songs of the period from roughly the 1870s to the early part of the twentieth century. In addition to gospel hymns, Johnson draws upon the earlier African-American spiritual tradition.

In many ways, Johnson's style of performance typifies the repertory of the African-American cowboy songsters of his generation. However, within Texas, there are some regional variations. Tony Lott, born in 1905 on bottom land near the San Antonio River in Southeast Texas, recalled that his father often sang while he worked and that the lyrics were often spiritual in nature.

"My dad used to sing 'Time Has Made a Change' when we were little. He used to sing that song and we'd walk right behind him. And he'd sing that song when riding on a horse or watching them cows. Another one was 'The Word of God Is Right, Hallelujah to His Name.' He'd sing that song when he was working in the field. We were picking cotton."

When asked about blues, Lott replied that his parents were "church going people" and that they didn't sing secular songs, although he did remember one tune called "Angelina." "It was an old song," he said. "I don't know where he (my dad) got that from, and all I know is part of it":

Miss Angelina, I sure love you, I sure love you
There's no other one so good and true, so good and true
Miss Angelina, oh, my black baby's you
She's a daisy, run me crazy
Miss Angelina, oh, my black baby's you.

Cowboys, Lott maintained, didn't do much singing while they were herding cattle. "They did a little hoop and hollering—we'd do that at night when we'd be cutting out yearlings from the herd. And the boys had to keep them yearlings from going back. That's when we'd be hollering, something like that."

At night, however, Lott said, "We had to calm the herd. Well, we'd sing 'Whoo-oo-oo, doggie, whoo-oo-oo, doggie. We'd sing the same verse over and over. That would calm them down. And then, sometimes, we'd have to hoop and holler to get them going again."

Given the relatively flat terrain of the coastal plains region where Lott worked, "calming the herd" was a fairly common practice at night on the range. Sudden and loud noises, like a gun shot or thunder and lightning, might cause the herd to stampede. In southeast Texas, in the area between Beaumont and Houston, the land was marshy and overgrown and consequently, driving cattle was considerably more difficult.

Elton Laday, whose father owned a 50-acre ranch in Cheeks, Texas (near Beaumont), said, "I wasn't too much of a singer, but I used to holler and squall, 'Yeeeea, Yeeeea, hurry cattle, hurry, hurry,' and they'd just come on. They start walking up. And sometimes we had to go behind them and pop the whip. You know what I mean, just sling a whip, and then we'd drive them out of these marshes and stuff. And if they got bogged down, you'd have to squall and jump off your horse and keep your horse from kicking you. But we'd manage to get far enough away. We had long reins and held onto them, and drag on out, and the horse and them cattle would come across."

Often, by dusk, Laday recalled, the cattle were "tired out" and rarely ever had to be calmed. "They didn't get agitated. When you finally got them together, they'd all stay together. You had to ride around them on your horse a little bit. That was about it. You'd have to keep them from riding away in the bottom of the marshes. So, you'd throw a few squalls, and them old cows were pretty well-trained. They knew when you got to squalling, they'd come on out."

Laday was born in 1920 in Ville Platte, Louisiana, but moved with his family to Texas, near Beaumont, when he was two years old. He grew up baling hay and working as a cowhand on trail drives for the family-owned ranches in the area. Each year, Laday remembered, about fifteen cowboys drove approximately 300 to 400 head of cattle from Cottonwood, where the herd fed on native grass during the spring and summer months, across the intercoastal canal to Port Bolivar, where they were able to feed on salt grass from October to March or April, when they were brought back.

In southeast Texas, there was a greater concentration of black-owned ranches, some of which were started by freed slaves after the Civil War. Others were acquired by families, like the Ladays, who migrated from southwestern Louisiana, and were slowly able to buy acreage.

A. J. Walker, born in 1930 in Opelousas, Louisiana, moved with his parents to Raywood, Texas, east of Houston. His father, Tom Walker, was a rodeo promoter who, after several years of work as a cowhand, was able to purchase forty acres near Raywood in 1941. There, he established the Circle 6 Ranch and began hosting his own rodeos. Today, A. J. Walker continues to operate the ranch with the help of his sons, raising his own livestock, and training and breaking horses. From March to October, Walker promotes rodeos on a monthly basis at his ranch. He coordinates his efforts with the other members of the Anahuac Saltgrass Cowboy Association, who also organize ranch rodeos. The Anahuac Saltgrass Cowboy Association is principally comprised of African-Americans and currently has about four hundred members.

In addition to promoting ranch rodeos, A. J. Walker organizes zydeco dances, which attract a cross-section of the African-American community in the region, especially those who have mixed French and Creole ancestry. Walker said that some of the working cowboys he knew as a child spoke and sang in French, although English has now become the principal language. French, however, is preserved among the zydeco bands, most of which travel from southwestern Louisiana, performing at the Circle 6 Ranch, as well as at clubs and dance halls in the small towns between Beaumont and Houston.

Vincent Jacobs, born in 1932 to parents of mixed Indian and African ancestry in Huffman, Texas, has worked as both a ranch and rodeo cowboy, but has also performed as a singer in rhythm and blues bands. Growing up, Jacobs remembered hearing the older cowboys singing blues and church songs, but his personal interest in music derived more from what he heard on radio and in movies.

"When I was a boy," Jacobs said, "I used to go to them old Westerns at the movie theaters in Crosby and Barrett Station. The theater in Barrett Station was owned by a black man, James Thomas, but the one in Crosby was segregated. If you were black, you had sit up in the balcony. And I never saw any black cowboys in them movies, but I did see Gene Autry and Tex Ritter. The black folks were doing the washing, the cooking, and working out in the fields."

Jacobs, however, was unaware of the "Negro singing westerns" produced in the late 1930s when he was a child. The first of these was *Harlem on the Prairie* (1937) produced and directed by Jed Buell and starring Herbert Jeffrey. Jeffrey, who was originally from Detroit, used the stage name Herb Jeffries and got his start as a singer for Earl Hines and his big band in 1933. After touring with Hines, he became a vocalist for the Duke Ellington Orchestra, and by the time he started making westerns, he was well-known as a singing emcee.

Harlem on the Prairie was a genre film and despite its billing as the "first all-colored" western musical, the plot and music were not distinctively African-American. It included such songs as "Old Folks at Home" and "Romance in the Rain" that were performed with a jazzy sentimentality, common in the popular music of the day. Nonetheless, *Harlem on the Prairie* was relatively successful and inspired Richard C. Kahn, another white Hollywood producer, director and writer to make three other black westerns featuring Herb Jeffries: *Bronze Buckaroo* (1937), *Harlem Rides the Range* (1939) and *Two Gun Man from Harlem* (1939). In sum, these movies, film historian Thomas Cripps maintains, "suffered from a reluctance to explore the realities of black life on the frontier. Instead they chose to mirror the most gimmicky white musical horse operas" (Cribbs 336–37; Sampson).

Distribution for black musical westerns was limited to black theaters around the country, most of which were concentrated in urban areas. Consequently, these films were barely accessible to African-Americans like Vincent Jacobs, who lived in a rural ranching community. As a ranch hand, Jacobs recalled hearing the old black cowboys humming some of the songs he heard in the movies, but they rarely sang the lyrics. "They'd hum songs like 'Back in the Saddle Again' and 'Home on the Range,' but they hardly ever seemed to want to sing the words."

In response to the apparent lack of a distinctive repertory of black cowboy songs, Jacobs wrote one of his own, adapting the tune from "Ghost Riders in the Sky"[1] and creating his own lyrics.

> An old black cowboy riding along one dark and windy day
> He rides along the devil herd as they ride on their way
> If you want to ride forever, riding in the sky
> Ride along, black cowboy, ride
> The horse was shining black with sweat as they ride on their way
> They've been riding at them for a month

They haven't caught them yet
If you want to ride forever, riding in the sky
Ride along, black cowboy, ride
Yippee, yi-o
Yippee, yi-ay
Ride along, black cowgirl, ride

Jacobs wrote the song when he was nine or ten years old, and has continued to sing it upon request for his fellow cowboys. "Sometimes," Jacobs said, "we'll be just sitting around, taking a break, in between events at the rodeo, or maybe after, when we get together to party or dance." For a brief period, during the 1960s and 1970s, Jacobs played an organ and was a singer in Pete Mayes' rhythm and blues band. Mayes' uncle Manuel River, owned a dance hall in Double Bayou, Texas, which was frequented by cowboys and African-Americans in general in the region.

At the Double Bayou Dance Hall, Rivers presented not only rhythm and blues, but zydeco bands as well. According to Cleveland Walters, who has worked as a cowboy with Jacobs over the years, "They didn't call the French music zydeco in the old days. They called it 'La-la,' and usually they'd have an accordion and a rub board [*frottoir*] or sometimes just a fiddle and a rub board."

Walters, who was born in 1925 in Liberty, Texas, said that his father was a dance fiddler and that his brother played accordion, but that he preferred the harmonica. "I was raised up on the farm and we didn't have much of anything. And at Christmas, we got an apple, an orange, and a choice of either a cap pistol or a ten-cent harmonica, and I always picked the harmonica."

Like Jacobs, Walters's early influences were the Western movies that he saw on Saturday afternoons when he was growing up. "I liked Tex Ritter and I'd try to figure out the songs on the harmonica, songs like 'Riding old pink and leading old ball, Old Ball ain't good for nothing at all, Yippee, Ti Yi Yay, Yippee, Yippee, Yippee, Yay'."

In addition to the popular songs he heard in Westerns, Walters also plays some traditional blues and zydeco tunes, as well as a traditional "train song," which, he said, he altered to make it his own: "I took the song "Freight Train Boogie" and renamed it "Crawfish Train," adding some of my own words:

Crawfish train goes all around
Crawfish train goes town to town
Crawfish train goes all around
Crawfish train goes town to town
Crawfish train is moving on down the line
Crawfish train goes all around
Crawfish train goes town to town

In this song, the harmonica mimics the sound of the train as it "goes up and down and all around, bringing the crawfish from Louisiana to Texas." Overall, Walters repertory on the harmonica is essentially traditional and is reflective of the musical styles popularized through ranch dances and other community gatherings.

Given the mobile, and sometimes transient, lifestyle of cowboys, the harmonica was a relatively easy instrument to carry and consequently, as Walters reported, was fairly common. Clearly, however, the musical repertory of African-American cowboys in Texas varied from ranch to ranch, and often reflected not only the cultural backgrounds of the cowboys themselves, but the taste of their ranch bosses. Tony Lott said that "Mr. Welder [of the Welder Ranch] liked to hear us sing Christian songs. And if we wanted to sing anything else, we had to do it when he wasn't around." E. J. Garza, who worked with Lott on the O'Connor ranch, concurred with this view, but added that African-American cowboys were also influenced by the Mexican *vaqueros*.

Garza was born in 1918 on the McFaddin Ranch in Victoria County. His mother was black and his father was Mexican. On the ranch, Garza said, many of the working cowboys were bilingual and had mixed racial ancestry. As a young man, Garza was known among his peers as the "singing cowboy." He played guitar, and like his contemporaries, performed the songs popularized by Tex Ritter and Roy Rogers, but his repertory also included "Allá en el Rancho Grande," popularized by the bilingual sheet music and the Mexican movie of the same name and other songs in the *ranchera* tunes.[2]

In sum, the musical traditions of black cowboys in Texas are clearly varied, embodying not only the values of African-American culture at large, but the cross-pollination of musical styles—itself a result of the migratory patterns of blacks—as well as the impact of the recording industry and mass media commercialization. Not only is the black population of Texas less concentrated than that of other states in the South, but "black cowboy" music in Texas also evolved in proximity to other important musical traditions: the rural Anglo, the Cajun and Creole, and the Hispanic.

Notes

1. "Ghost Riders in the Sky" was copyrighted by the Edmond H. Morris Company in 1949 with words and music by Stan Jones. The song was introduced by Burl Ives and was also a hit Victor recording by Vaughn Monroe. Gene Autry sang the song in the movie "Riders in the Sky" and the song was revived in 1966 as "Ghost Riders in the Sky" by the Baja Marimba Band.

2. John Lomax in *American Ballads and Folk Songs* (New York: MacMillan 1934) identifies Silvano R. Ramos as the composer of "Allá en el Rancho Grande," with an Edward B. Marks publisher's copyright of 1927. Cataloged sheet music at University of Texas, however, lists Emilio D. Uranga as composer and J. Del Moral as lyricist for a 1934 New York bilingual edition published by . . . E. B. Marks. For more information on the musical traditions of Mexican *vaqueros*, see "14 Traditional Songs from Texas" transcribed by Gustavo Duran, Music Series, No. 4, April 1942.

Bibliography

Asche, Moses, and Alan Lomax, eds. *The Leadbelly Songbook*. New York: Oak Publications, 1962.

Cribbs, Thomas. *Slow Fade to Black: The Negro in American Film, 1900–1942*. New York: Oxford University Press, 1977.

Jacobs, Vincent. Personal interviews. 3 March 1993, 11 and 23 November 1994, and 20 May 1994.

Johnson, Alfred. Personal interviews. 1 and 12 December 1992, and 15 March 1994.

Laday, Elton. Personal interview. 14 March 1993.

Lomax, John A. *Adventures of a Ballad Hunter*. New York: MacMillan, 1947.

Lorness, Kip. Personal interview. 16 March 1994.

Lott, Tony. Personal interview. 21 July 1994.

Sampson, Henry T. *Blacks in Black and White: A Source Book on Black Films*. Metuchen, New Jersey: The Scarecrow Press, 1977.

Walters, Cleveland. Personal interviews. 27 April 1994 and 22 November 1994.

Elton Laday, Circle 6 Ranch in Raywood, Texas. (Courtesy, Documentary Arts, Inc., Dallas)

E. J. Garza of Goliad. (Courtesy, Documentary Arts, Inc., Dallas)

"John Biggers." Photo by Earlie Hudnall, Jr.

John Biggers—Artist:
Traditional Folkways
of the Black
Community

by Alvia J. Wardlaw

When John Biggers arrived in Houston in 1949 to teach art at the newly established Texas State University for Negroes, now Texas Southern University, he lost no time in establishing himself as an artist who would draw upon the traditional folkways of the black community for his inspiration. From his own background of Gastonia, North Carolina, and from his training from Viktor Lowenfeld, Biggers had come to value the beauty of "plain folk," and this was a tradition that he would pass on to generations of students. His mural commissions for black institutions such as the Eliza Johnson Home for the Aged, the Blue Triangle YWCA in Houston, the George Washington Carver High School in Morris County, Texas, as well as his collaboration on two books with folklorist J. Mason Brewer, prepared him in significant ways for his travel to Africa in 1957.

In Houston, John Biggers had come to the attention of Susan McAshan, who had seen an exhibition of his work at Hester House, a community center in the city's Fifth Ward, during the summer of 1949. Mrs. McAshan had recommended to the college president Dr. R. O'Hare Lanier that he interview the young artist for the position of chairman

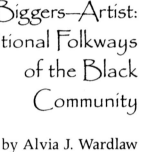

of the art department at the school, which was renamed Texas Southern University in 1951. Mrs. McAshan's family, especially her father, Will Clayton, had been instrumental in the development of an administrative structure and plan for TSU, and she had the ear of the newly appointed president. As a patron of the arts in Houston, and as a member of one of the city's most prominent families, Susan McAshan would become a long-time ally of John Biggers and the TSU art department. Dr. Lanier, himself a graduate of Hampton, already knew and admired Biggers' work, and he was eager to hire him, as well as Joseph Mack, another Hampton graduate, for TSU. Lanier envisioned creating a "museum of Negro culture" for the university. He felt assured that Biggers and Mack would share his philosophy of the importance of the arts, especially with regard to black cultural heritage.

Biggers brought with him a deep understanding of folk culture which had been part of his early life growing up as the youngest of seven children in Gastonia, North Carolina. Raised in a household where his parents Paul and Cora Biggers insisted upon cooperative involvement from all their children in the running of the household, John Biggers had witnessed firsthand all of the traditional African-American crafts which were practiced in his home. His mother, grandmother, and aunts quilted on a regular basis, and these were times when he and his sisters and brothers would gather to hear many stories told by the adults. In the author's interview with John Biggers on November 24, 1986, the artist discusses how he enjoyed listening to the adults during these pleasant evenings as a child:

> At evening reading time at fireside, the background behind the circle, around the fire, we'd be with the quilts. Yeah the quilts would be stretched in the back behind us—we were in a semicircle around the fire. There behind us were the women quilting. So you felt the color and the warmth of the cotton and the wood. You felt all of this around you while the people still read, people told stories. There was such a wonderful quality of family and community.

Paul Biggers, his father, was a teacher and a preacher who had learned to make shoes as a young boy on the plantation where he grew up. He had a shoe shop in the corner of the yard and the children had their own garden where they grew food for the animals as well as treats like popcorn for themselves. Paul Biggers also knew how to make chair backs and bottoms from willow strips, and like the other men in Gastonia could make wheels for wagons which they in turn took to the black-smith to have covered in iron rims. Paul Biggers also had a beautiful voice, and he and neighbors would sometimes go from house to house singing "rounds." This kind of creative self-reliance defined Biggers' childhood and he would draw from it frequently during his later years as an artist.

Perhaps Biggers' earliest experiences in creating art came during his childhood summers in Gastonia, when John and his brother would build a replica of the town in which they lived. As described in *Black Art in Houston*, the task took practically the entire summer:

> When a warming spring sun began heating his small world after a cold winter, he and an older brother, Joe, would crawl under their house, and in cool shade, devote hours to modeling various objects from the cohesive earth on which the dwelling stood. A favorite and recurring enterprise was the reproduction in miniature of the town in which they lived. After two or three months a tiny Gastonia would appear, completed to an accurate scale, with streets and buildings (including two seven-story "skyscrapers"), houses with lawns of moss, streams of real water, and even a sprinkling of mules and horse-drawn wagons.

Very early in his life John Biggers saw man connected to nature in an unending cycle. One watched the moon to understand when to set out plants. One observed what plants were available nearby for teas, home remedies, and natural food supplements. Certain activities—planting, slaughtering of livestock, canning and quilting—were determined by the seasons. The elements—earth, air, fire, and water—became part of the definition of one's daily routine. Even as a small child Biggers became acutely aware of the power of these elements.

Personifying this connection to the earth around her was John Biggers' maternal grandmother, Elizabeth Finger Whitworth, or Grandma Lizzie. A woman of immense strength and independence, her proud spirit always amazed young John. In her nineties, when Biggers was a young boy, Grandma Lizzie lived alone on her small farm near the mountain. She not only used the plow on her land, she could use a shotgun as well as any man in the area. She had her routine which consisted of reading her Bible, taking an occasional sip, and smoking her corncob pipe. There was a creek near her house where her grandchildren would play. There was a snake in the spring which Grandma Lizzie referred to as "her" snake and she would warn the children not to disturb it as they played. Grandma Lizzie became one of the archetypes of Biggers' later work and was his inspiration for the figures of Harriet Tubman and Sojourner Truth in the Blue Triangle YWCA mural *The Contribution of Negro Women to American Life and Education.*

After the death of his father in 1937, John Biggers and his brother Joseph attended Lincoln Academy in nearby King's Mountain. It was at Lincoln that Biggers began to draw seriously in his spare time. As a scholarship student, Biggers worked as a fireman on campus. In this position, he was responsible for providing heat for all of the buildings, much as he had done in his own home in Gastonia. In his spare time, after tending to the boilers in all the classroom buildings, Biggers would sit in an armchair in the boiler room and begin to pore over old copies of the *New York Times Book Review* which were kept to help start the fires. Biggers remembers these images well and describes them as strong, black-and-white engravings which he would copy in the same fashion that he and his brothers in Gastonia had copied the drawings from the Bible for their neighbors.

It was also at Lincoln Academy that John Biggers began first to consider the role of African culture as a part of his African-American heritage. At the time that John Biggers was a student at Lincoln Academy, Dr. Henry C. McDowell was principal of the school. His positive interpretation of African culture, having spent over twenty years in

West Africa, had a lasting impact on Biggers. This was Biggers' first occasion, outside of a black church setting, to hear of the complexity of civilization in Africa. Young Biggers had heard many sermons about the rich heritage of Egypt, Kush, and Ethiopia, but this was the first time that he had learned directly from an adult who had lived many years in Africa. Dr. McDowell's years in Liberia made him a proponent of Pan-African thought and led him to bring a number of West African students to study at Lincoln. Dr. McDowell wanted his students to have a sense of the richness of African history that he had become aware of while living there. African students enrolled at Lincoln became Biggers' first contact with individuals born in Africa. Such experiences prepared him well for the intense cultural education that he was soon to receive at Hampton Institute.

When he arrived at Hampton and began to study with the great art educator Viktor Lowenfeld, Biggers immediately drew upon his early experience. Lowenfeld, an Austrian Jew who had been forced to leave his homeland during the cataclysm of World War II, brought to his teaching an awareness of ethnic struggle which served as a parallel to the experiences of his African-American students. He encouraged them to look not towards the work of European modernists for their inspiration but to the spirited genre paintings of Peter Breughel, and to the simple yet monumental compositions of Jean Francois Millet for parallels to their own experiences of having grown up on the land, often working it with their parents. The southern landscape, the small hamlets and towns from which many of them traveled to Hampton became their focal points. Underscoring this art was also Lowenfeld's emphasis upon understanding the true spiritual genius that was at the essence of African art. For the first time Biggers was exposed to collections of art and artifacts created by ancient people in central Africa. In coming to appreciate over time the profound beauty of these works, Biggers began to regard his own African-American culture as a rich and under-explored source of American culture.

By the time Biggers had arrived in Texas he had already created a body of work which dealt with the black family—including his first painting *Crossing the Bridge*, the *Sharecropper* mural, and *Gleaners*. The work which Mrs. McAshan had seen at Hester House, *The Baptismal*, was one of many that Biggers had created which depicted the African-American's abiding connection to the land—be it spiritual or for survival, the connection was always there. As the artist once stated about his life in Gastonia:

> We were literally an earth people. It was not unusual for our sitting parlors back home to have floors of smooth, naked earth. We swept the yard around our little clapboard house so clean that an admirer would say, "You could eat off of it." We sat on the earth, cooked on the earth, danced on the earth, and when a summer sun's heat had made our house unbearable for the night, we slept on the earth (Biggers, *Black Art* 16).

The first few years of establishing an art department for Texas Southern were characterized by constant frustration, which had to be countered with continuous innovation. As was often the case in higher education, the arts were given low priority in the allocation of funding. Equipment was practically nonexistent, and the faculty had to make do with inadequate facilities. This meant teaching painting in classrooms without sinks, and teaching drawing without paper or crayons. Often the faculty had to procure materials for themselves and their students, once embarking on a five-hour drive to San Antonio in a truck to dig clay for Professor Carroll Simms's sculpture and ceramics classes (Biggers, *Black Art* 30, 31). Despite these hardships the art department established itself in a small building, the "Quonset hut," where studio and art history classes were held. The first classes were primarily filled with women studying for their teacher certification. The art department rapidly developed a reputation for training excellent art teachers.

One of the most important events to occur in the first decades of the Texas Southern art department was its hosting of the annual meeting of the National Conference of Artists (NCA) in 1965. Organized in 1959, the NCA was the first professional group of black artists to exist on a national scale. Hosting the NCA meeting signaled the department's arrival as a new and vocal component of the black art world, and was a momentous professional milestone for Biggers, Simms, and Mack. Although he had already attracted the attention of the region's mainstream museums, recognition within his own community was for Biggers the true validation of his work as an artist and educator.

Viktor Lowenfeld and Alain Locke attended the conference. Locke, who was still teaching at Howard University, spoke on the importance of cultural heritage, and Lowenfeld delivered the keynote address on art education. Houston had never before witnessed such a prestigious gathering of black artists and educators. Student displays of art, together with performances by music and voice students, demonstrated the success of the school's program. Very evident in the display of artwork was the philosophy that Biggers had acquired at Hampton and brought to Texas Southern: students should be encouraged to draw upon their African-American cultural heritage rather than look to European history for inspiration.

The treatment of commonplace aspects of black southern life as artistic subject matter was confusing even to many black viewers, who criticized Biggers for encouraging his students to create "depressing" art instead of pleasant still lifes or gentle landscapes. Although this criticism continued for many years, it did not deter the TSU art faculty from their pursuit of African-American cultural awareness. The 1950s were years of immensely painful self-consciousness for blacks, many of whom felt that they had to prove themselves to society at large. The discussion of whether African-American artists should exclusively portray the black experience was not limited to Houston. This dilemma was as old as the Harlem Renaissance and lives on today.

The other aspect of innovation which Biggers brought with him from Hampton was the concept of the student mural as public art. Viktor Lowenfeld regularly had his students create murals on the campus of Hampton Institute as their expression of feelings about the war and growing up in the South. At the same time students were creating murals on campus, Charles White had come to Hampton as a Rosenwald Fellow to create his work *The Contributions of the Negro to American Democracy*. Thus Biggers came to Houston with the idea that murals could be used as expressions of public education, and he instituted a program in which each art graduate at Texas Southern created a mural on campus which was a reflection of his or her cultural experience.

John Biggers found Texas to be much like his home of Gastonia with the exception of geography. The warmth and folkways of its people were quite the same. Many of Biggers' students came from rural parts of East Texas and their parents were still working the land. In the fifties these students had direct knowledge of dealing with crops and live-stock and depending upon the skills of one another for their livelihood.

It is important to note that the first murals completed by John Biggers in Houston were his mural series *Negro Folkways*, in which he examines the traditional activities of the black family. Created after Biggers spent time with the residents of Eliza Johnson Home for the Aged, who told him of their lives growing up on farms in rural Texas, the mural is as much about the early life of Biggers as it is about the life of the older residents at the nursing home. The three panels which were hung in the day room of the home represent various aspects of daily life of the black community. First, in the Piney Woods of East Texas, a congregation bap-tizes its members in the river while nearby men fell the trees in the forest to be used in the lumber industry. In the second panel, in the interior of a home, a group of women quilt while one stirs a pot over an open hearth. Children lie sleeping below on a rag rug, while nearby a circle of men play instruments to entertain the group. A groaning board of food lines the walls. The scene is one that is humble and rich in fellowship. In a third segment, families load produce on wagons to be taken to the market while a group on a wagon goes fishing. These genre scenes formed a basis for Biggers' later interpretations of black life.

Commissioned by Mr. and Mrs. C. A. Dupree, owner of the Eliza Johnson Home for the Aged, this multi-scene work represents one of several which would be commissioned by members of the black com-munity for its own institutions. In their entirety, the Eliza Johnson murals represent an epic depiction of the cycle of the seasons coupled with those values held steadfast by the African-American South. That Biggers found continuity between Texas and North Carolina indicates how strong were aspects of the expressions of the African diaspora. The scenes of harvesting, quilting, logging, and fishing evoked familiar memories in the men and women who lived at the home, many of whom had grown up in rural East Texas.

Biggers' work had come to the attention also of the Reverend Fred T. Lee, whose late wife, Dora, had been active in the Blue Triangle YWCA, which served the black women of Houston's Third Ward. Reverend Lee wanted a portrait of his wife to hang in the YWCA building in her memory. Biggers, however, convinced Lee that a mural depicting the history of black women in America would be a much greater tribute. He created *The Contribution of Negro Women to American Life and Education* (1952–1953), a monumental statement of the struggles and achievements of black people as evidenced through their women. The mural was painted during an era in which black history was virtually ignored in public-school textbooks. Many of the women of the Blue Triangle YWCA were teachers, and they often supplemented their history lessons with information about black heroes and heroines.

Biggers' boldly conceived mural, which features such pioneering women as Harriet Tubman and Sojourner Truth, was so powerful that it made some of the refined ladies of the YWCA uncomfortable. The mural's larger-than-life figures told the story of a difficult history, and for many of the women it was too painful to accept. *Black Art in Houston* recounts an incident that occurred during the painting of the mural:

> One morning several middle-aged women gathered around the ladder on which Biggers was working. At that time he was engaged in a monumental depiction of Harriet Tubman, giving her powerful hands and feet to fit the title, "General Moses." One woman, obviously the group's leader, spoke up in a high, trembling voice. She told Biggers he must stop the painting. "Why?" he asked.
>
> The spokeswoman replied that the images of the slaves and especially of Harriet Tubman disgraced Negro womanhood. "Come down, young man. Get down from the wall and stop the flagrant disrespect immediately," she said. "We will have to have the space covered with some lovely pea-green color." Biggers

stopped work for a week or so until YWCA officials convinced the group that the depiction of black women had value (62).

For Biggers, however, *The Contribution of Negro Women* was the watershed work that saw the transformation of his earlier depictions of black men and women into heroic images of struggle and survival. The mural established the foundation for all of his images of black women and their communities that Biggers would create during the next forty years.

In preparing for the mural, Biggers had conducted extensive research into the history of black women in American society. Viktor Lowenfeld was so impressed that he suggested to Biggers that the project was worthy of a doctoral dissertation. Biggers' research and written presentation of the mural made his first major academic statement on the uncelebrated role of black women in American life, and earned his Ph.D. in education at Pennsylvania State University. The documentation of the mural project leaves no doubt that Biggers saw the work as a means by which African-Americans could better understand their own history and folklore. Biggers intended his mural to inform and inspire its viewers, just as the frescoes of Raphael, Michelangelo, and Leonardo had enlightened a largely illiterate audience in Renaissance Italy.

The community of Morris County commissioned Biggers to execute a mural depicting the founding of the high school for black kids in the area. Entitled *The History of Negro Education*, this work depicts as its central character, Mr. Gray, the principal whose efforts enabled the community to have its own school. The drawing style of Biggers is naturalistic and imbues purely natural expression upon the faces of the members of the community. Recalling again his childhood in Gastonia and especially the times when he accompanied his father to the small three-room rural school where he was principal, Biggers discusses the community which created the high school:

> In a center panel the Carver High principal, P. Y. Gray, and his assistant, a homemaking teacher, instruct students in quilting, weaving, cooking, preserving, farming, and animal hus-

bandry as well as in reading, writing and arithmetic. In the background can be seen frame additions representative of an interim period of growth and consolidation. Symbolic of the area's industry that gave support to the education vision are a railroad, oil storage tanks, warehouse, and smokestacks. These represent also a deliberate attempt compositionally to balance and contrast rural earthiness with community industrialization. (Interview)

It is this same ability that will allow him to depict the psychological content of African expressions when he travels to West Africa. In this mural all of the natural activities of the community—quilting, painting, planting gardens, saving money bit by little bit—are captured, just as he had depicted them in the Eliza Johnson sketches. For Biggers, it was critical that one see how the people lived during their everyday existence. He was not interested in formal poses or artificial backgrounds; he wanted the natural surroundings and activities of the people to be an extension of themselves.

In the *Web of Life* created for the Science Building at Texas Southern University, Biggers again considers the folkways of the community as they relate to the cycle of life itself, as represented in the passing of the seasons. In the center of the mural, dominated by a mother and child, the mother seems like the womb of the earth itself, while all around nature expands and expresses itself.

One of Biggers' most important collaborations at this time was with Vivian Ayers, a poet whom he had known in North Carolina, and then one of the few serious creative writers working in Houston. Biggers made a series of pencil drawings for Ayers's masterpiece "Hawk" which was nominated for a Pulitzer Prize in poetry. He later said that this experience had introduced him to the power of mythology. The hawk in the poem is, in its efforts to fly, an allegory of man's creative spirit. Biggers' drawings for "Hawk," geometric and abstract in form, demonstrate his ability to convey the energy of the universe. For Biggers and Ayers, the collaboration, which lasted several months, represented the spirit of a young, exciting creative Houston. The courage and determination of these two black artists to break new ground was extraordinary. Ayers recalls with delight their staying up until 4:00 A.M., matching words with imagery. Their art elevated them beyond the boundaries of segregation into a new arena of creativity.

Another notable collaboration occurred in 1956 between Biggers and the Texas folklorist J. Mason Brewer. Brewer collected many of the traditional folk tales found in East Texas. Like Biggers, he was ahead of his time in comprehending the importance to American society of southern black material culture. For a collection of folk tales, Brewer had created a feisty old woman named Aunt Dicy, whose earthy wisdom and spirited personality made her someone to reckon with. Aunt Dicy was a composite of all of the women that Brewer had interviewed and become acquainted with during his research. Biggers' drawings for Brewer's book *Aunt Dicy Tales* evoked the female archetypes in his own community. In his illustration of Aunt Dicy at the polls, Biggers shows her casting her vote while reviewing the political scene. He also created a terra-cotta sculpture of Aunt Dicy. Biggers' collaboration with Brewer continued through the illustration of Brewers's anthology *Dog Ghosts and other Texas Negro Folk Tales* in 1958.

During the 1960s, John and Hazel Biggers traveled to Mexico together with Dr. and Mrs. F. B. McWilliams, where they spent time with Elizabeth Catlett and her second husband Francisco "Pancho" Mora. Biggers was finally able to view firsthand the murals of Rivera, one of his favorite artists. He also saw works by Orozco and Siqueros, but it was Rivera's interpretation of Mexican peasant life that most impressed the artist. Like Hale Woodruff, who had also traveled to Mexico to study, Biggers was particularly interested in Rivera's use of color and his inclusion of the human body as an architectural element in his compositions.

For Biggers, seeing Rivera's work and its relationship to the artist's Mexican homeland affirmed and underscored his need to continue the art program at Texas Southern University. He believed that students from small rural towns in Texas, Louisiana, Arkansas, and Mississippi should use art as a means of expressing their own cultural heritage.

Later, in his travels to West Africa, Biggers would come to see the direct relationship between African and African-American folk culture.

John Biggers worked in Texas for over forty years before moving back to his homeplace in Gastonia, North Carolina. That was in 1989, and in 1995, he is still moving, but now between homes in Gastonia and Houston. His artistic spirit thrives. In addition to his painting, he is sculpting and sketching and building a forge and foundry. The Museum of Fine Arts, Houston, honored John Biggers and his art with an exhibition—*The Art of John Biggers: View from the Upper Room*—which showed from April through October in 1995, before it went on a national tour. *The Art of John Biggers* captures the human spirit and condition of African-Americans—of all people—with sensitivity and wisdom. It is well that he dwells among us.

Bibliography

Biggers, John, Carroll Simms, and John Edward Weems. *Black Art in Houston: The Texas Southern University Experience*. College Station and London: Texas A&M Press, 1978.

___. Interview by author. Houston. 24 November 1986.

Texas folklorist J. Mason Brewer (1896–1975). (Courtesy, James W. Byrd)

The African-
American Folktale
and J. Mason
Brewer

by Lorenzo Thomas

The African-American folktale is, wrote folklorist J. Mason Brewer (1896–1975), "definitely in the mainstream of American tradition." The actual place of African-American expressive forms in that tradition has, however, been viewed in varying ways. The folktales that have been accepted as popular literature in the versions of Joel Chandler Harris have also been carefully analyzed by academic critics of differing persuasions.

The African-American folktale has often been cherished for its quaintness—its presumed depiction of a simple-minded and unthreatening rusticana. But such an "affectionate" niche also has a less pleasant aspect. Thirty years after the end of slavery a correspondent to *Atlantic Monthly* characterized blacks as "a people hardly a century out of barbarism" and described their dialect as "grotesque," "shadows cast by words from fairly educated lips into the minds of almost totally ignorant people." Rather than colorful regionalism or metaphoric ingenuity, this writer saw black folk expression as a racially deficient grasp of English. "It is little wonder," he wrote, "that this language of ours assumes in these startled brains most fanciful shapes" ("Word Shadows" 254–55).

▼

In other circles the tales have been prized as examples of subversive commentary—the chosen weapon of a weak but spiritually unvanquished race. Yet even this view has often been unwittingly condescending.

Brewer, an African-American Texan, understood the normative function of these folktales and the importance of the form as both presentational and representational performance. The African-American folktale, as collected by Brewer, is an important form of communal and oral historiography.

Brewer's collections, especially *Dog Ghosts and Other Texas Negro Folk Tales* (1958) and *The Word On the Brazos* (1953), are quite remarkable in the political implications of the tales he chose to record, repeat, and to some extent, refashion. In effect, Brewer uses the tales—in the very spirit of their originators—to comment on racial relations. Brewer viewed these tales as an essentially African form of oral historical commentary, a record of the African-American's "reactions to the incidents and pressures in his environment" (*American Negro Folklore* ix). For almost half a century he devoted himself to celebrating this legacy.

Brewer was uniquely qualified for this mission. "The strong family from which he came," wrote biographer James W. Byrd, "is a microcosm of the history of Texas." Born in Goliad in 1896, John Mason Brewer was the son of a cowboy who later became a barber and storekeeper, and both of his grandfathers had been what he called "wagoners," hauling supplies between Victoria and far-flung frontier settlements. "It was from the lips of these three that I heard, as a child, fascinating and dramatic stories of early life in Texas," he wrote. "From them stemmed the resolution that some day I would collect and record some of the Texas Negro's folk tales" (*Word* v). At the age of twenty he graduated from Wiley College in Marshall, Texas, and became a school teacher in Fort Worth. Later he served as professor of English at Austin's Huston-Tillotson College and elsewhere, earned a master's degree in folklore under the direction of Stith Thompson at Indiana University, and published a number of books.

We should carefully establish the contextual framework wherein an African-American scholar views folkore as history.

A curious notion of the historical value of folklore was presented early in this century by G. L. Gomme, who subscribed to the Spencerian evolutionary idea that European *märchen* were records of "the period before written history had begun" (46). Betraying the self-congratulatory ethnocentrism of his day, Gomme says, "The modern savage is better off. . . . He has an outside historian in the traveller and the anthropologist of modern days. The savage who was ancestor to our own people had no such means of becoming known to history" (82–83).

Gomme's black contemporaries in the United States held a somewhat different view of the historical utility of their own folk heritage. For Fisk University's John Wesley Work, the spirituals form "a reliable account of our people's past. It tells of their suffering and how they bore them . . . it tells the stuff of which the Negro is made. With this as a source of fact and inspiration, the author is conscious of a power enabling him to present effectively the cause of his people before the bar of humanity" (118).

Work's comments, however, express an investment in the idea of the "outside historian" that even now can create confusion. "The folk are not historians," writes Lawrence W. Levine in *Black Culture and Black Consciousness* (1977), "they are simultaneously the products and creators of a culture, and that culture includes a collective memory" (389). A few pages later, Levine chastises scholars for ignoring the "vibrant and central body of black thought" that is found in African-American folklore. Somewhat ahistorically, he writes:

> The concept of Negro history was not invented by modern educators. Black men and women dwelt upon their past and filled their lore with stories of slaves who, regardless of their condition, retained a sense of dignity and group pride. (397)

In fact, the concept of Negro history as a necessary part of an American elementary curriculum can be credited to the work of modern African-American educators led by Carter G. Woodson. And the importance of folklore to formal history in the African-American context is crucial precisely because American society (and academia) has so strenuously attempted to prevent black people from "becoming known to history."

Explaining the necessity of heavy reliance on oral history interviews rather than documents in writing his dissertation, historian George
C. Wright was unequivocal: "Simply stated, blacks have been either
ignored by scholars of Kentucky history or, on the few occasions when
Afro-Americans are mentioned, not taken seriously by them" (75).
Wright discovered that the same problem extended from standard history texts to city directories and even census materials (77). It goes
without saying that the situation is not unique to the state of Kentucky.

Most important, of course, is the idea that folklore allows the African-American "Everyman" to speak for himself.

The historical focus of folk tales belongs to the teller as much as to
any period detail that can be discerned. Richard M. Dorson has noted
that both Zora Neale Hurston and Brewer "gave some literary gloss to
tales [they collected] and neither provided the comparative notes that
identify traditional narrative" (14). Both Hurston and Brewer, however,
are clearly able to transmit an "insider's perspective" that has eluded
most other collectors. Hurston's novelistic method of presenting her
methodological notes in dramatized scenes with her narrators makes
her, in fact, a character in *Mules and Men* (1935). Brewer, from the first,
offers an unstated Afrocentric focus that is woven into the narratives
and, one suspects, not always by his own transcribing hand.

It is interesting to compare these collectors. Hurston, for example,
includes a well known tale as a passing comment. Sitting around waiting for their foreman to arrive with job assignments, Hurston's Eatonville,
Florida, informants become restless:

> "Must be something terrible when white folks get slow
> about putting us to work."
> "Yeah," says Good Black. "You know back in slavery Ole
> Massa was out in de field sort of lookin' things over, when a
> shower of rain come up. The field hands was glad it rained so
> they could knock off for a while. So one slave named John says:
> "More rain, more rest."
> "Ole Massa says, 'What's dat you say?'
> "John says, 'More rain, more grass.'" (68)

Brewer recorded the same story in Texas in his 1932 essay "Juneteenth." His set-up for the joke is pointed toward slave resistance rather than laziness:

> One day in August it had showered all day long on the Burleson plantation so that it was impossible to pick any more cotton that day. Isaiah and Jasper, on occasions like this, were always sent out to the large woodshed to saw and split wood, and always they got to talking about how they might obtain freedom, or how to do less work, or something else in which both were interested. They also usually took time to dance a jig every now and then, using their hands to clap for the music.
>
> On this particular day the topic of conversation was the weather. There was not anything that the slaves considered more fortunate during the harvest season than a good hard rain. Isaiah, not knowing that the master was on the other side of the woodshed feeding the hogs, said, "Jaspah, Ah sho' is glad hit rained. Mo' rain, mo' res'."
>
> The master, overhearing the remark, stepped around the corner of the woodshed into view and said, "What did you say, Jasper?"
>
> "Ah sez, Massah, Ah sez," answered Jasper, "dat de mo' hit rain de mo' de grass grow." (23)

Editor J. Frank Dobie, longtime Secretary of the Texas Folklore Society, could not help noting:

> This was a favorite story in our family—initiated by my father, as I recall—in Live Oak County, Texas, on those rare and expansive days when it rained. As our story went, the master during a rain took some of his darkies into a crib to shuck corn. (That was what the Mexicans about our place often did on a rainy day.) Presently the master heard a darkey say (to be spoken very rapidly), "Mo' rain, mo' res'."
>
> "What's that, you rascal?" the master asked.
>
> "Ah said, Massa, mo' rain, mo' grass." (23n)

It should be carefully added that Dobie's use of the word "darkies" is a recollection of his father's way of telling the story; in his own writing Dobie tended to avoid the term "colored" and preferred the word "Negro"—with a capital letter N.

The political subtext in Brewer's transcription of this tale is evident also in his understanding of a historical change that differentiates contemporary African-American folktales from the animal fables that are so firmly rooted in African oral tradition. "As a slave," wrote Brewer in "Old-Time Negro Proverbs" (1933) "so far as his life was reflected in song and proverbs, the Negro's primary interest seems to have been in God and religion" (101). Since the Reconstruction era, however, "the earlier concerns have been replaced by . . . 'reality thinking,' i.e., the Negro's folk narratives today concern his hopes, his problems, his worldly observation, and his struggle to gain respectable citizenship for himself'" (Byrd, *J. Mason Brewer: Negro Folklorist* 40).

Today, most commentators agree with Daryl Cumber Dance that African-American folktales are entertaining but that "political, psychological, and sociological meanings . . . lie beneath the humor" (xvii; Dorson 18). It is clear from Brewer's earliest work that he had a firm grasp of this fact.

One of Brewer's greatest contributions to the field of American folklore was his recognition that the animal fables made famous by Joel Chandler Harris's Uncle Remus books in the 1880s were a form that had been superseded. "After freedom came," Brewer wrote, "the Negro weaver of tales supplanted Brer Rabbit with 'John,' the trickster hero of the southern plantation. Like Brer Rabbit, John always comes out victorious in his contests with his 'boss-man'" (ANF 28). When he doesn't win, his failures are at least instructive, and the sly—and spry—old trickster even makes an appearance in Little Richard Penniman's 1956 rock-'n'-roll hit song "Long Tall Sally." Brewer made his first collections of John tales in 1932 and 1933 and, writes James W. Byrd, "made the non-animal tales known and accepted—even those that, like some of the 'blues,' are frank and direct in their social criticism and protest" (37).

The most wonderful of Brewer's works is a little book called *Aunt Dicy Tales*. Privately printed in an edition of 400 copies, the book appeared in 1956. Unlike other collections, there is a kind of framing mechanism here beginning with Aunt Dicy's meeting the mailman, a situation that in earlier days was the stage for a well-told tale, and ending with "Aunt Dicy at the Heavenly Gates" after her death. The chapters are not mere stenographic transcriptions of interviews but well-crafted narratives with a continuity that links them. Ostensibly a series of tales about Aunt Dicy's outrageous and unfortunate habit of "dipping snuff," these stories are really a portrait of a family and a record of its progress.

"I looked at it as folklore," says John Biggers, "though it is partly original because it is Brewer's interpretation of the material." Biggers, the extraordinary painter and teacher, illustrated the volume. "He taught at Texas Southern University [in Houston] in the summers," Biggers recalled of his collaboration with Brewer. "I knew of *The Word* as soon as I got to Texas and folklore was something I was interested in. He would tell me the story and the rest of it and then I'd show him the drawings to see if I had captured the image he had in mind." Their collaboration continued in preparing *Dog Ghosts* for publication by the University of Texas Press.

"Aunt Dicy and Booker T. Washington's Speech" [which is also reprinted in *American Negro Folklore*] exemplifies Brewer's theme. The story begins just after Emancipation Day. "Many of the plantation owners bargained with their former slaves and made contracts with them to pay them a certain sum of money for every acre of cotton they chopped. But there were a few of the freed Negroes who refused to work for the prices offered them for chopping cotton. Among those who would not accept the wages . . . were Uncle June and Aunt Dicy" (ADT 15–16). They moved to another county and, after sixteen years of sharecropping, saved enough to buy their own farm and send their daughters to Prairie View College. Uncle June and Aunt Dicy, "being lonesome, travelled quite a bit attending public lectures, camp meetings and revivals in nearby towns." One of these events is a memorable visit by "The Great Educator" from Tuskeegee.

On his September 1911 Texas tour organized by the state's chapter of the Negro Business League, Booker T. Washington emphasized his goal of "winning the respect of the white race" by encouraging local community leaders, as he said in his Houston speech, "in the direction of helping the Negro in Texas to get homes, become farmers, save their money and lead useful lives" (Harlan XI, 325). Washington's appearance at Austin's Wooldridge Park on September 30 was attended by 5,000 people and, if we are to believe J. Mason Brewer, Uncle June and Aunt Dicy were among the throng. As Brewer tells it:

> The subject of Mr. Washington's address was "Great Americans and Their Contribution." He mentioned George Washington, and his contribution to the country; Abraham Lincoln, and his contribution to the country; Benjamin Franklin, and his contribution to the country; Jefferson Davis, and his contribution to the country; Sam Houston, and his contribution to the country; Thomas Edison, and his contribution to the country; John D. Rockefeller, and his contribution to the country; Frederick Douglass, and his contribution to the country, and many others.
>
> After Mr. Washington had finished his speech, the crowd, Uncle June among them, applauded so much that the great Booker T. Washington had to take several bows. But Aunt Dicy did not join in the hand clapping. So Uncle June turned to her and said, "Dicy, how come you are not clapping for Mr. Washington like everybody. Didn't you enjoy his speech?"
>
> "Humph! No, I didn't," replied Aunt Dicy, "He ain't said nothing about Levi Garrett—*he* wasn't nobody's fool!" (ADT 55)

Levi Garrett, of course, is the name of the manufacturer of Aunt Dicy's favorite brand of snuff.

J. Frank Dobie's friend Roy Bedichek found Aunt Dicy's response admirable because "to take a stand for good and sufficient reasons and to maintain it against the mass—or herd—opinion, indicates that quality of character we call the 'courage of nonconformity,' itself a sign of spiritual strength." In a comment that would have easily been deciphered in those days of vigorous McCarthyism, Bedichek added:

> The "courage of one's convictions" is the basis, also, of the virtue of loyalty, so highly prized in its proper forms—i.e., unadulterated with self-interest—because it is so exceedingly rare. (ADT x)

J. Mason Brewer's own political viewpoint is clearly transmitted in the story's details. Spiritual and intellectual development, thrift, appreciation and acquisition of material comfort, formal education, progress and hard work are shown to be the values supported and esteemed in the African-American community. Still that doesn't mean that you have to buy everything Booker T. Washington—or anyone else—has to say.

Aunt Dicy Tales, though written more as a book for young adults than an academic reliquary, may be the most fully realized expression of Brewer's method and purpose. Brewer viewed these folktales as stories that "reflect accurately social problems and attitudes." They are the verbal evidence of "reality thinking." Although his *American Negro Folklore* (1968) is well known and still much read, there hasn't been much attention devoted to Brewer since his death in 1975. His work, however, was important and remains both delightful and instructive. Unlike those who bemoan the passing of an unelectrified era, Brewer declared: "Negro folklore is definitely in the mainstream of American tradition, but rich strata of Negro folk phenomena still remain undiscovered" (ANF ix).

Dog Ghosts includes a tale that pokes fun at several targets at once, including folklorists. Told to Brewer in 1954 by George Holman in Travis County, Texas, the tale recalls Unkuh Green Williams "pacin' up and down the platform" at the Illinois and Gulf Northern depot:

> . . . a ole cullud woman comed up to 'im an' say, "Mistuh, when do de nex' train leave for Taylor?" Unkuh Green tell her dat de nex' train leave for Taylor at 6:09. De ole cullud woman say "Thank you Suh," but she walks rat on ovuh to whar a

white man was stannin' on de platform an' say, "Mistuh, what time do de nex' train leave for Taylor?" De white man tell her jes' lack Unkuh Green done tol' her, dat de nex' train leave for Taylor at 6:09.

'Well, if'n dat don' beat de ban'," 'low Unkuh Green; "she done ast me dat same questshun 'fo' she ast hit to you; dat's de way hit is wid some people—day hab to git evuhthing dey gits in black an' white!" (34)

For those of us who treasure the skepticism of "mother wit," and those who don't believe everything we hear, and for those who have never had the chance to hear the marvelous old tales firsthand, John Mason Brewer got them down in black and white. His unsurpassed collections of folktales from central and east Texas are not rehearsals of "survival motions" during slavery days but, if read properly, vibrant depictions of the "reality thinking" employed by an African-American community strategically fashioning its own identity in the first two decades of the twentieth century.

Works Consulted

Brewer, J. Mason. *American Negro Folklore*. Chicago: Quadrangle Books, 1968.

___. *Aunt Dicy Tales: Snuff-Dipping Tales of the Texas Negro*. Illustrated by John T. Biggers. Austin: Privately printed, 1956.

___. *Dog Ghosts and Other Texas Negro Folk Tales*. Austin: University of Texas Press, 1958.

___, ed. *Heralding Dawn: An Anthology of Negro Poets in Texas*. Dallas: Privately printed, 1936.

___. "John Tales." *Mexican Border Ballads and Other Lore*. Ed. Mody C. Boatright. Austin: Texas Folklore Society, 1946. 81–104.

___. "Juneteenth." *Tone the Bell Easy*. Ed. J. Frank Dobie. Austin: Texas Folk-Lore Society, 1932. 9–54.

___. "Old-Time Negro Proverbs." *Spur-of-the-Cock*. Ed. J. Frank Dobie. Austin: Texas Folk-Lore Society, 1933. 101–106.

___. *The Word On the Brazos*. Austin: The University of Texas Press, 1953.

Byrd, James W. "In Memory of John Mason Brewer (1896–1975)." *CLA Journal* 18 (June 1975): 578–81.

___. *J. Mason Brewer: Negro Folklorist*. Southwestern Writers Series, No. 12. Austin: Steck-Vaughn Company, 1967.

Dance, Daryl Cumber. *Shuckin' and Jivin': Folklore from Contemporary Black Americans*. Bloomington: Indiana University Press, 1978.

Dobie, J. Frank. "A Word On *The Word*." *The Word On The Brazos*. By J. Mason Brewer. Austin: University of Texas Press, 1953. vii–xii.

Dorson, Richard M. *American Negro Folktales*. Greenwich, Connecticut: Fawcett, 1967.

Emmons, Martha. *Deep Like the Rivers: Stories of My Negro Friends*. Austin: Encino Press, 1969.

Fisher, Miles Mark. *Negro Slave Songs of the United States*. 1953. New York: Russell and Russell, 1968.

Gomme, George Laurence. *Folklore as an Historical Science*. 1908. Detroit: Singing Tree Press, 1968.

Harlan, Louis R. and others, eds. *The Booker T. Washington Papers*. 13 vols. Urbana: University of Illinois Press, 1981.

Hemenway, Robert E. "Introduction." *Mules and Men*. By Zora Neale Hurston. Bloomington: Indiana University Press, 1978.

Hurston, Zora Neale. *Mules and Men*. 1935. New York: Harper and Row/Perennial Library, 1990.

La Pin, Deirdre. "Narrative as Precedent in Yoruba Oral Tradition." *Oral Traditional Literature: A Festschrift for Albert Bates Lord.* Ed. John Miles Foley. Columbus, Ohio: Slavica Publishers, 1981. 347–73.

Levine, Lawrence W. *Black Culture and Black Consciousness: Afro-American Folk Thought from Slavery to Freedom.* New York: Oxford University Press, 1977.

Sapper, Neil Gary. "A Survey of the History of the Black People in Texas, 1930–1954." Unpublished dissertation. Lubbock: Texas Tech University, 1972.

Turner, Darwin T. "J. Mason Brewer: Vignettes." *CLA Journal* 18 (June 1975): 570–77.

Vansina, Jan. *Oral Tradition As History.* Madison: University of Wisconsin Press, 1985.

"Word Shadows (1891)." *The Negro and his Folklore in Nineteenth Century Periodicals.* Ed. Bruce Jackson. Austin: University of Texas Press, 1967. 254–56.

Work, John Wesley. *Folk Song of the American Negro.* 1915. New York: Negro Universities Press, 1969.

Wright, George C. "Oral History and the Search for the Black Past in Kentucky." *Oral History Review* 10 (1982): 73–92.

J. Mason Brewer telling a story.

Juneteenth Parade, Dallas, 1947. Photo by Alex Moore. (Courtesy, Documentary Arts, Inc.)

Juneteenth Parade, Houston, 1976. Photo by Benny Joseph. (Courtesy, Documentary Arts, Inc.)

Juneteenth: A Red Spot Day on the Texas Calendar

by William H. Wiggins, Jr.

Juneteenth, Texas's Emancipation celebration, is the southwestern version of a series of regional African-American celebrations which commemorate the abolition of slavery in America. Like its fellow Emancipation celebrations, Juneteenth began to wane during the post-World War II era of integration; but, unlike its other siblings, Juneteenth celebrants of the 1970s were able to recapture the zeal of their emancipated ancestors and initiate a successful political lobbying campaign which culminated in their freedom celebration being accorded official holiday status by the Texas State Legislature in 1979. Despite repeated similar efforts by their fellow Emancipation celebrants in other states, none of these other celebrations have achieved such official state recognition.

Historically speaking, the first of these African-American freedom celebrations was held on January 1, 1808 to commemorate the legal ending of the foreign slave trade in America; and the last celebration was initiated on February 1, 1940 to honor the ratification of the Thirteenth Amendment. During this one-hundred-and-thirty-two year period, at least fifteen separate Emancipation celebrations emerged. Though they all share the common theme of human freedom, they were

▼

fashioned by differing historical circumstances. In addition to the two above mentioned celebrations, three other celebrations trace their origins back to the issuance of some state or federal edicts of freedom. The celebration dates and the events they commemorate are: July 4, 1827, the termination of slavery in the state of New York; August 1, 1834, the abolition of English slavery in the West Indies; and April 16, 1862, the passage of legislation ending slavery in the District of Columbia.

The origins of seven of these celebrations are not as easily explained. Just as many of their first slave celebrants had no known birth dates, so these celebrations have no certain year of birth. And, by the same token, just as the parentage of most slaves was undocumented, the historical circumstances which bore these celebrations are not known. Their lineage cannot be traced back to some historical act; their celebrants find justification for celebrating by simply saying that on some past May 5th, 8th, 20th, 22nd, 28th, 29th or August 4th and 8th, their ancestors heard that they were free.

Four regional celebrations began with the issuance of varied proclamations of Emancipation. On May 9, 1862, General David Hunter, Commander of the Department of the South, issued an order freeing all the slaves in South Carolina, Georgia, and Florida; on September 22, 1862, President Abraham Lincoln issued his "preliminary proclamation" which gave the seceding states one hundred days to abandon their pro-slavery position; on January 1, 1863, President Lincoln issued his historic Emancipation Proclamation and set in motion the hallowed "Day of Days" celebrations; and on June 19, 1865, General Gordon Granger landed at Galveston, Texas, and read the following General Order Number 3 from the balcony of the Ashton Villa:

> The people of Texas are informed in accordance with a Proclamation from the Executive of the United States, all slaves are free. This involves an absolute equality of rights of property between masters and slaves, and the connection heretofore existing between them becomes that between employer and free laborer. The freedmen are advised to remain at their present homes and work for wages. They are informed that they will

not be allowed to collect at military posts, and that they will not be supported in idleness, either there or elsewhere. (Wiggins, "From Galveston" 62)

General Granger's pronouncement set in motion a series of spontaneous freedom celebrations in east Texas, western Louisiana, southwestern Arkansas, and southeastern Oklahoma. Not surprisingly, one of the more popular legends associated with the start of Juneteenth celebrations has a strong Union Army motif, like the following one that Haywood Hygh told me:

My eighty-six-year-old father swears it is the truth; that an ex-Union [Negro] soldier rode a mule given him by Abraham Lincoln, yessuh, all the way to that section of the country. And when he got to Oklahoma, he informed the slaves that they were free. From there he went to Arkansas and Texas. It was on the nineteenth of June when he arrived in Oklahoma. My father swears it, and he says if his father was still alive, he would do same swearing without batting his eye. Many of the old-timers are with him one hundred percent. (Wiggins, "Juneteenth: They Closed the Town Up" 42)

Juneteenth's Sunday best dress code for its myriad rituals of rodeos, baseball games, barbecue and fried fish dinners, dances, and church programs was one of the most popular rituals used by the early celebrants to symbolize their new social status as free men and women. One informant summed up these sentiments well when he told me: "The 19th of June was just a second Christmas . . . everything . . . is especially set aside for that day. Even bought your new shoes, your new clothes, and dressed up." (Wiggins, "They Closed the Town Up" 43) White clothing merchants advertised early and often in such black Texas weekly newspapers as *The Houston Informer* in the hopes of cashing in on this Juneteenth clothes-buying spree. In 1926 Lander's ran the following advertisement which was aimed at attracting male celebrants to his store.

You don't need all cash to be dressed up this Juneteenth. Come to Landers Company and select the suit you want and only one-fourth down and the balance as you are paid. Use Landers Company Easy Budget Buying Plan—DRESS UP AS YOU SHOULD BE FOR JUNETEENTH. ("Dress Up Juneteenth" n.p.)

A decade later Foley Brothers ran this advertisement which was designed to catch the eye of Houston's female celebrants:

June 19th is the one time of the year when everyone must be dressed up. [My italics] We have striven to make this possible for the women in securing hundreds of dresses which we are offering at the very small price of five dollars. You may choose from a beautiful assortment of silk frocks in bright colors, patterns and combinations. They come in styles that every woman will like and a wide assortment of sizes. Very specially priced for Friday's selling. ("Dresses Special" n.p.)

A 1933 Franklin's department store advertised: "EXTRA SPECIAL! 2000 Pairs New Summer Shoes Are Here For The 'Big Celebration' On Juneteenth." And its millinery department promised "the best hat values in town" insuring that their customers would: "Be among the best dressed on 'JUNETEENTH'" ("Specials for Emancipation Day" 3). For those celebrants who couldn't afford to purchase new clothing, a cleaning company placed an ad in a 1940 edition of this Houston weekly reminding them they could still "Dress Up For Juneteenth [by] Send[ing] Your Suits and Dresses To Ineeda Laundry & Cleaning Co. For Sanitone Cleaning." ("Dress up for Juneteenth" 8)

"Eating high on the hog" was another universal Juneteenth ritual. Juneteenth picnic tables and baskets were a cornucopia of traditionally prepared dishes of meat, breads, vegetables, drinks, and desserts. Unlike their slave ancestors, emancipated Juneteenth celebrants could eat as much as they wanted; hunger did not dine at Juneteenth picnics. One celebrant recalled that her hometown Juneteenth committee served several hundred free picnic dinners featuring such traditional African-

American dishes as "barbecue chicken and ribs, potato salad, baked beans, mustard and collard greens, cornbread and red 'soda' water." She continued:

> The dinner was free. *And you got all you want to eat.* [My italics] You know how they used to bring those long, long tables, they had rows and rows of long, long tables and then they had waitresses. The young men usually served as waiters and the young ladies served as the waitresses. . . . And the ladies were grouped locally in a circle. And they would go down and . . . they'd have these trays, these big, large trays, and set the tables. And when they got the tables set they would call the people to dinner. And when the crew had eaten, they would close the gates and they would call others who would be in the line waiting. No part of the dinners was sold, but they did buy whatever cold drinks, ice cream that sort of thing. (Wiggins, "Juneteenth: A Freedom Celebration" 8)

In the east Texas town of Anderson, which is located in Grimes County, an old corn and cotton growing area of east central Texas, these free Juneteenth meals were served by the organizers of the celebration, who raised the money by sponsoring horse races, basketball games, and hayrides and by charging members of the organization $7 a year to cover the cost of meat and other purchases. One of the organization officials explained that they stopped accepting donations from their white neighbors because: "We figured we should be men who could hold up our own place. . . . We accepted help at first, but we got to the place where we didn't want to ask them. We wanted to do it ourselves, not just depend on others for help. I enjoy it, seeing my race get out and do for itself" (Watriss 83–84). Houston food store managers followed the lead of the clothing merchants and placed Juneteenth ads in *The Houston Informer*, too. In 1929, the three Henke & Pilot, Inc. stores ran this Juneteenth ad:

Upon the occasion of the one day in the year which means so much to them and theirs, this store expresses the wish that all of you will have a wonderful "Juneteenth."

We are very appreciative of your patronage and business during the past year, and shall endeavor to merit and enjoy even a larger share during the next year.

Remember that our three stores can supply all your food wants for your celebration, picnic or outing—yes, even for that "Juneteenth" dinner at home. ("Juneteenth" 5)

Weingarten's placed an ad some nine years later which read: "Celebrate June 19 With Weingarten's WATERMELONS. Those Big Red Ripe Guaranteed Melons Special For Friday—Saturday—and Monday" (*Informer* 18 June 1938, 4). And, on the same page, Mrs. Baird's Bakery ran this special Juneteenth ad:

For Emancipation Day Parties and Picnics . . . [serve] MRS. BAIRD'S BREAD. Mrs. Baird's bread, baked in the South's newest, most modern bread plant, tastes better because it's made right by Mrs. Baird's special slow-baking process. It's just the thing for sandwiches, and it goes mighty fine with barbecue. . . . When planning your Emancipation Day picnics and parties, don't forget to ask your grocer for Mrs. Baird's Bread . . . you'll like it better.

Some of these holiday feasts were enjoyed after a train excursion ride to either visit friends and family or to make a freedom pilgrimage to Galveston, Texas, where General Granger read his historical freedom decree. The June 16, 1928, edition of *The Houston Informer* carried three Juneteenth railroad excursion ads. The Santa Fe's ad read: "75 Minutes To Galveston. $1 Round Trip Sunday. Seaside Special Leaves Union Station 1:25 P.M. Arrives [in] Galveston 2:40 P.M. Morning Flyer leaves 8:05 A.M. Returning leave Galveston 8:25 P.M." In 1926 the Missouri Pacific Lines offered a $3 round trip excursion that would allow its customers to celebrate "Emancipation Day at Brazoria." The Southern

Pacific's "Juneteenth Excursions" ad urged its readers to: "Go somewhere for a real outing or visit with friends on this holiday occasion." A Brenham celebrant recalled how effective these ads were in attracting Juneteenth excursions for the railroad companies.

> The excursions from various places such as Beaumont where many of them, you might say, had gone down there to the Government Depot down at Beaumont. And we had . . . Spec Allen, to be exact, [who] would bring the excursion out of Beaumont to Brenham. He's a former Brenhamite. Dan Lewis out of . . . Galveston, Texas on the Santa Fe. He used to bring a bunch, a train or two up here and . . . Abner Carrol . . . used to bring the excursion down from Austin, quite a few Brenhamites used to live in Austin. (Secrett)

Between 1936 and 1951 the Texas State Fair, which is held in Dallas, became a popular excursion destination for Juneteenth celebrants. The 1936 Juneteenth celebration attracted an estimated 150,000 to 200,000 celebrants to Dallas to celebrate the State of Texas's Centennial and the seventy-fifth anniversary of Emancipation. This celebration featured a gigantic parade, a "Negro Hall of Culture" wing of the Centennial, and an integrated track meet at the Cotton Bowl which featured Ralph Metcalf, the 1936 Olympian Gold Medal Winner and teammate of Jesse Owens (Wiggins, "From Galveston" 62). The 1951 "Juneteenth Jamboree" attracted a crowd of 70,000 celebrants who spent $150,000 at the Fair riding the amusement rides, snacking at the food booths, and attending shows featuring nationally known African-American entertainers ("Juneteenth: Texas carries on" 27).

Ads announcing that Bill "Bojangles" Robinson, the "World's Greatest Tap Dancer," would headline Dallas's 1937 Juneteenth appeared in *The Houston Informer* with the call to: "Be in Dallas June 'Teenth." The ad, which featured a full figure caricature of the famous dancer, read in part: "Yeah Man, What a Show! EMANCIPATION DAY CELEBRATION! June 19. Pan American Exposition. Dallas. In Person. Admission Free. Bill 'Bojangles' Robinson." And the day's schedule of events:

PROGRAM For the Day!

Grounds Open 10:00 A.M.

1:30 P.M.—(1) Free Show and Tap Dance Contest judged by Bill Robinson; (2) Emancipation Day Address; (3) Fashion Parade, Bathing Girl Review, Baby Doll Parade. On the Patio [of the] Texas State Building.

8:00 P.M.—Band Shell: BIG FREE SHOW featuring "Bojangles" and entertainers.

9:00 P.M.—CABARET DANCE [at the] LIVE STOCK ARENA." ("Emancipation Day Celebration!" 2)

More often than not, these Juneteenth cabaret dances ended in violence. According to one report: "In the old days Juneteenth fights gave officers much trouble. One year [a] white Dallas newspaper reported the 'quietest celebration in years . . . only two men were killed.'" ("Juneteenth: Texas carries on" 28) Unfortunately, this type of random violence was not limited to big city celebrations like Dallas. It also occurred at Juneteenth dances held in small towns like Muskogee, Oklahoma. One celebrant wrote me a personal letter describing the heavy drinking and random violence that regularly occurred at her hometown's Juneteenth dances:

The non-church folks celebrated with a dance and "supper" in an area near the Arkansas River. I believe the area was called "Shady Rest."

These celebrations were held at night (The Sat. night nearest June 19th, and they had "bottle lights" (kerosene in pop bottles—no, I believe it was coal-oil. . . .)

The [alcoholic] beverages [included] "bootleg" whiskey in fruit-jars, and "Homebrew"; it was called "Sister-get-you-ready!"

Unfortunately, June 20th found our community buzzing with gossip. "Who got stabbed with an ice-pick?" or news of someone having cut someone else with a straight edge razor or knife known as a *Dallas Special.*" [My italics] (Riggins)

But Juneteenth celebrations were much more than Saturday night jollifications. A Brenham, Texas, celebrant told me that Juneteenth began as a quiet and safe religious service of thanksgiving that evolved later into a louder and dangerous affair:

> It started in church. The 19th of June celebrations really started as a camp meeting, church meeting. They prayed and sang and stuff like that. And it developed into a goodtime thing, you know. . . . It was just a thanksgiving. . . . It was really for the Negro. It was a method of thanksgiving as it started out. That's how they started out. Now this ballgame and this dancing and this stuff came later. But the original 19th of June was a thanksgiving for having been freed, so that's the history of it, the 19th of June. (Hogan)

The reading of President Lincoln's Emancipation Proclamation and an official proclamation from the Governor of the state of Texas were two important rituals used by Juneteenth celebrants to foster this spirit of religious "thanksgiving" in their celebrations. Hence, although a baseball game and dance were held at Houston's Emancipation Park during the 1938 Juneteenth celebration, the following proclamation of Governor J. V. Allred, which was published on the front page of the June 4 edition of *The Houston Informer*, was also publicly read during the Emancipation program:

> TO ALL TO WHOM THESE PRESENTS SHALL COME:
> Whereas, the Negroes in the State of Texas observe June 19 as the official day for the celebration of Emancipation from slavery; and
> Whereas, June 19, 1865, was the date when General Robert [sic] S. Granger, who had command of the Military District of Texas, issued a proclamation notifying the Negroes of Texas that they were free; and
> Whereas, since that time, Texas Negroes have observed this day with suitable holiday ceremony, except during such years

when the day comes on a Sunday; when the Governor of the State is asked to proclaim the following day as the holiday for State observance by Negroes; and

Whereas, June 19, 1938, this year falls on Sunday;

NOW, THEREFORE, I, JAMES V. ALLRED, Governor of the State of Texas, do set aside and proclaim the day of June 20, 1938, as the date for observance of

EMANCIPATION DAY

in Texas, and do urge all members of the Negro race in Texas to observe the day in a manner appropriate to its importance to them.

IN TESTIMONY WHEREOF, I have hereunto signed my name officially and caused the Seal of State to be impressed hereon at Austin, this 25th day of May, A. D. 1938.

J. V. Allred

Governor of Texas

Thirty-four years later two African-American State Representatives, Curtis Graves of Houston, some of whose relatives may have read Governor Allred's 1938 Juneteenth proclamation in the *Informer*, and Wesley Zan Holmes of Dallas, some of whose relatives may have seen Bill "Bojangles" Robinson perform at the 1937 June 'Teenth held at the Dallas Fair Grounds, persuaded their fellow Representatives of the 62nd Texas Legislature to adopt unanimously their House Resolution 23 which honored the social, political, and economic contributions of Texas's black citizens to the State and recognized the cultural and historical significance of June 19th to the State. The resolution that Representatives Holmes and Graves authored sounded much like Governor Allred's proclamation in style and substance:

Whereas, On June 19, 1865, Major General Gordon Granger, representing the United States Government, landed at Galveston and issued a general order from the President of the United States and declared that all slaves were free; and

Whereas, On June 19, 1865, Black people in Texas rejoiced in joining fellow Blacks across the nation who were freed January 1, 1865; and

Whereas, From that day, which is fully six and one-half months after the Emancipation Proclamation of President Abraham Lincoln came into force, Black people in Texas were recognized to be an integral part of our state's social, political, and economic structure; and

Whereas, The Black people in the State of Texas continue to make increasing contributions to the development and culture of the State of Texas; and

Whereas, Blacks serve in many high offices and capacities in Texas, including the State Legislature, where they have made distinctive contributions to the legislative process and in the service of all their constituency; now, therefore, be it

Resolved, That the House of Representatives of the 62nd Legislature, Third Called Session, honor the Black people of Texas for their contributions to the state; and, be it further

Resolved, That the House of Representatives recognize "Juneteenth" as an annual holiday of significance to all Texans and, particularly, to the Blacks of Texas, for whom this date symbolizes freedom from slavery.

Seven years later, on February 12, 1979, Representative Al Edwards of Houston filed House Bill 1016, which was designed to change the status of June 19 to that of a legal state holiday, with the chief clerk's office of the Texas State Legislature. Representative Edwards's HB 1016, which, like Governor Allred's proclamation, designated June 19 as "Emancipation Day in Texas," was sponsored by Senator Chet Brooks of Pasadena. It took four months for the bill to wend its way through the 66th Texas Legislature and make Juneteenth the Lone Star State's fourteenth official state holiday. The bill that Governor William Clements signed into law on June 7, 1979, read as follows:

AN ACT

relating to a declaration of Emancipation Day in Texas as a legal holiday.

BE IT ENACTED BY THE LEGISLATURE OF THE STATE OF TEXAS:

SECTION 1. Article 4591, Revised Civil Statues of Texas, 1925, as amended, is amended to read as follows:

Art. 4591. ENUMERATION. The first day of January, the 19th day of January, the third Monday in February, the second day of March, the 21st day of April, the last Monday in May, the 19th day of June, the fourth day of July, the 27th day of August, the first Monday in September, the second Monday in October, the 11th day of November, the fourth Thursday in November, and the 25th day of December, of each year, and every day on which an election is held throughout the state, are declared legal holidays, on which all public offices of the state may be closed and shall be considered and treated as Sunday for all purposes regarding the presenting for the payment or acceptance and of protesting for and giving notice of the dishonor of bills of exchange, bank checks and promissory notes placed by the law upon the footing of bills of exchange. The nineteenth day of January shall be known as "Confederate Heroes Day" in honor of Jefferson Davis, Robert E. Lee and other Confederate heroes. *The 19th day of June is designated "Emancipation Day in Texas" in honor of the emancipation of the slaves in Texas on June 19, 1865.*

After the bill was adopted, Representative Edwards commended the Texas Legislature for passing such an important historical bill.

By passing my House Bill 1016, the legislature was not just engaging in politics. The members were not just throwing a cheap bone to their black constituents. *The legislature was giving official recognition to a uniquely Texas holiday that has been celebrated for 115 years.* [My italics] These celebrations commemorate an event that was good for all of Texas and indeed the whole nation. Slavery was a burden on the entire society. Its existence paralyzed politics for decades. Slavery dehumanized slave and master alike. It is right that we joyfully celebrate the demise of the "Peculiar Institution" with picnics, music, conferences, and thanksgiving to God.

I want you to know that it would be impossible for me to let this session come to an end without calling to your attention the fact that the 66th Legislature has made one of the greatest accomplishments in the history of Texas and the nation in helping me to make June 19 a state holiday in Texas. There have been a great number of what I, and I am sure you, considered to be bad bills, but I want all of you to know that you can always be proud of the fact that you were actually a part of and were responsible for another great historical landmark in Texas. *I also want you to know that Texas is the first and only state in the nation to make this date a state holiday. I am sure that other states will try to follow our leadership.* [My italics]

In the spirit of rough and tumble Texas politics, all of Representative Edwards's colleagues did not agree with his glowing appraisal of HB 1016. Ironically, the most vociferous of Representative Edwards's critics was a fellow black representative, Clay Smothers of Dallas. Before the ink was dry on Governor Clements's signing of HB 1016, Representative Smothers, a conservative Democrat, held his own press conference and lambasted the governor's ceremonial signing of the bill, Edwards's political leadership and his bill. Representative Smothers dismissed the bill's signing ceremony with these harsh words:

I fail to understand, and I will not accept the premise that ceremoniously grinning and busting watermelons on the Capital grounds will have anything to do with reducing the burdensome crime rate in our communities, providing attention to the poor and delivering our people from the slavery of ignorance.

Turning his invective next to Representative Edwards, Representative Smothers added:

> While Rep. Edwards proudly witnesses the signing of this worthless piece of legislation, his small (legislative) district contributes to some 30 percent of the murders in the city of Houston, 28 percent of the aggravated assaults, an unknown but sizable percent of burglaries and robberies. Over 50 percent of the victims of these crimes are black.

And he concluded with this dismissal of HB 1016: "Rep. Edwards is stopping the wheels of government for a day to celebrate a lie (because the Emancipation Proclamation was issued on Jan. 1, 1863)" (Fly).

Although Representative Edwards, acting like a seasoned pol, chose not to respond to Representative Smothers's tirade, a Dallas newspaper columnist applauded the bill's passage. Bryan Woolley of the *Dallas Times-Herald* disagreed sharply with Representative Smothers's assessment of HB 1016:

> The Honorable Smothers' opinions notwithstanding, the signing was an historically significant occasion.
>
> After all, it was a predominately white legislature that passed Rep. Edwards' bill, and June 19, 1865, isn't a happy date in the historical memory of white Texans. In addition to emancipating the slaves, the landing of Gen. Granger at Galveston also began the occupation of Texas by enemy troops and that long, bitter, humiliating time known as Reconstruction.
>
> When the former Rebels regained control of their own destiny, it didn't take them long to declare the birthdays of two non-Texans—Robert E. Lee (Jan. 19) and Jefferson Davis (June 3)—official state holidays. . . .
>
> It's a sign of maturity, I think, that Texas is ready to give "equal billing" to the other side of its Southern heritage, to acknowledge that Juneteenth was an event significant to all

Texans, not just black ones, and that whites should share in the joy and pleasure with which black citizens have always celebrated the day.

Thanks to the annual prayers and parades of the first generation of freed black Texans and the proclamations and politics of the second generation of formally educated black Texans, Juneteenth is now one of fourteen official Texas holidays. Representative Edwards and the other elected members of the 66th Texas Legislature were finally able to take decisive political action upon the widely held folk belief expressed by a Juneteenth celebrant seven years before the passage of HB 1016:

They [white Texans] owe the 19th of June to us, in a way of speaking. I don't care what they might say that it's a nasty spot, but it isn't. It's true, it really did happen. They really did have slaves. They did do that. And since they celebrate their day for they freedom, then they ought to give the colored man a day for his freedom. It should be a red spot on the calendar and really took aside for. (Darby)

Bibliography

62nd Texas Legislature, 3rd Called Session. HSR 23—Adopted (Honoring the Black people of Texas and recognizing "Juneteenth" as an annual holiday of significance). Austin, 1972.

66th Texas Legislature. House Bill 1016. "An Act relating to a declaration of Emancipation Day in Texas as a legal holiday." Austin, 1979.

"75 Minutes to Galveston" and "Juneteenth Excursions." *The Houston Informer*. 16 June 1928.

"Celebrate June 19 With Weingarten's WATERMELONS." *The Houston Informer*. 18 June 1938.

Darby, Paul. Personal interview. 14 November 1972.

"Dress Up for Juneteenth." *The Houston Informer*. 15 June 1940.

"Dress Up Juneteenth." *The Houston Informer*. 19 June 1926.

"Dresses Special for June 19th." *The Houston Informer*. 19 June 1936.

Edwards, Al, Representative of Houston. Address to the 66th Texas Legislature. 25 May 1979.

"Emancipation Day at Brazoria." *The Houston Informer*. 19 June 1926.

"Emancipation Day Celebration!" *The Houston Informer*. 16 June 1937.

Fly, Richard. "Juneteenth holiday bill signed into law." *The Houston Chronicle*. 14 June 1979.

"For Emancipation Day Parties and Picnics . . . Mrs. Baird's Bread." *The Houston Informer*. 18 June 1938.

Hogan, Booker T. Washington. Personal interview. 15 November 1972.

"Juneteenth: Texas carries on tradition of emancipation holiday with amusement park celebrations." *Ebony* (June 1951).

"Juneteenth." *The Houston Informer*. 15 June 1929.

"Proclamation by the Governor of Texas." *The Houston Informer*. 4 June 1938.

Riggins, Elva S. Letter to the author. 11 April 1972.

Secrett, Rupert. Personal interview. 15 November 1972.

"Specials For Emancipation Day." *The Houston Informer*. 17 June 1933.

Watriss, Wendy. "Celebrate Freedom: Juneteenth." *Southern Exposure*, Vol. V, No. 1 (1977).

Wiggins, William H., Jr. "From Galveston to Washington: Charting Juneteenth's Freedom Trail." *Jubilation!: African-American Celebrations in the Southeast*. Eds. William H. Wiggins, Jr., and Douglas DeNatale. Columbia: The University of South Carolina Press, 1993.

___. "Juneteenth: A Freedom Celebration of Southwestern Blacks." *Juneteenth: Celebrating Emancipation*. Eds. Robert D. Selim and Niani Kilkenny. Washington: Smithsonian Institution Press, 1985.

___. "Juneteenth: 'They Closed the Town Up, Man!'" *American Visions*. May/June 1986.

Woolley, Bryan. "Juneteenth, Texas and Clay Smothers." *The Dallas Times-Herald*. 17 June 1979.

Juneteenth Parade, Nacogdoches. Photos by Dave Rossman.

Sam "Lightnin'" Hopkins. Photo by Benny Joseph, Houston, 1972. (Courtesy, Documentary Arts, Inc.)

Lightnin' Hopkins: Blues Bard of the Third Ward

by John Wheat

They held Lightnin's memorial service on a winter evening in 1982. A long line of mourners—most of them black, some of them white—stretched around the block from the funeral home in the heart of Houston's Third Ward, as family, friends, neighbors, and fellow musicians came to pay their last respects. Some of the white musicians who had jammed with Lightnin' attracted the attention of the media who descended on the neighborhood to cover the event. But after Lightnin' was laid to rest, and all the celebrities, cameras, and reporters had gone, the people of his precinct were left with their own memories of an extraordinary performer who had given voice to their experience. Lightnin' Hopkins was their singer, their storyteller, their poet. Though many outsiders could appreciate his music on some level, the full depth of "the blues according to Lightnin' Hopkins"[1] emerges only when understood as an expression of African-American experience created first and foremost for a black audience. There has always been a special quality to growing up black in America, and that experience lies at the heart of the blues.

Lightnin' Hopkins was a complex character. His personal life was a mess; his musical career often a shambles. He was justly praised for his inventive genius and equally justly denounced (by record companies) for ignoring contracts and recording for other labels. Everyone who dealt with Lightnin' has a different story to tell. The following narrative draws heavily from the views of David Benson,[2] who knew Hopkins intimately as his road manager for ten years. Benson is an articulate and energetic young African-American from Georgia who represents that generation of Southern blacks whose coming of age spanned the period of struggle for black empowerment in the 1960s. Raised in both the juke joint and the church (his father was a minister) and tempered by college and travel, Benson was able to understand Lightnin's generation and its culture and to relate them to the broader context of American life in which he and Lightnin' moved. His background and special relationship with Lightnin' Hopkins make Benson an ideal interpreter of his life and music to a general audience.

Though he lived much of his life in Houston, Lightnin' Hopkins was one of the last great country, or "downhome," blues masters. Born into a musical family in the small farming community of Centerville in 1912, Sam "Lightnin'" Hopkins grew up in the early blues tradition of Blind Lemon Jefferson and Alger "Texas" Alexander. Their music reflected the world of black East Texas, a world of racism, poverty, and lynchings, but also of family and community cohesion, religion, and cultural vitality. It was music of hope, despair, lust, melancholy, and joy characteristic of the blues, whose roots extended far back into black experience.

Blues was a cultural response to black disfranchisement in the South in the late nineteenth century. Flowing out of the same bedrock of black experience as the spiritual, blues music was a secular, materialist expression of identity and survival—a response to the burden of being nominally "free"—in a racist society. The music emerged from the rural black working class, drawing its form and content from slave and labor songs, spirituals, and African-American balladry. If gospel music stressed resignation, spirituality, and heavenly reward, the blues sang instead of resistance, carnality, and the search for a better life. More than just lamenting being mistreated and feeling bad, they often implied a remedy as well. One of the central themes to emerge in the blues was mobility. Metaphors of movement—trains, highways, freedom, opportunity, escape—resonated deeply among black people traditionally tied to the land and living in a world tightly circumscribed both geographically and socially by the dominant white society.

The lone, rambling bluesman[3] himself personified this mobility. The itinerant blues minstrel became a communal bard, building his reputation on the strength and validity of his individual performance. The country bluesman became the protagonist—and sometimes the victim—in his own stories and commentaries derived from personal experience in surroundings familiar to his listeners. The solitary performer, unencumbered by the demands of other instruments, could also give free reign to individual expression, extending and playing with the music to suit the moment and theme. Thus did the country bluesman become a new voice of black experience by the turn of the twentieth century, as potent in his realm on a Saturday night as was the preacher in the pulpit on a Sunday morning.[4]

Lightnin' Hopkins embodied this blues tradition, although he likely would dismiss this entire discussion of blues origins, meanings, and forms as irrelevant. David Benson explains this view in the following terms:

> Even that interpretation is to the blues what grammar is to language. The blues preceded that interpretation. . . . Lightnin' didn't play in meter. . . . He always said: "Blues is a feeling." The meter had to be staggered in order to get the effect. [Strict tuning and meter] that's grammar. Language was already there with its communicative possibilities and influences . . . prior to us starting to analyze it. And that's what he [Lightnin'] would look at. He would say there's too much talking about it, there's too much looking into what it means, and who these bluesmen are . . . and the music is nothing but a feeling. The blues is more the people who are experiencing it than the people who are playing it.[5]

Benson emphasizes that although Lightnin' was well grounded in musical meter and structure, he chose to stretch his phrases and rhythms to suit his own style. Benson expands further on the role of intuition and atmosphere in approaching the blues:

> [Blues] in a juke joint setting is more of a feeling than a format. [I was reading someone recently who argued that] there are no ideas outside of language. I don't know if I quite agreed with that or not. There are nuances of feeling and emotion that are not expressible in language. . . . If we talk about love, the word "love" demeans the emotion. Because it can't even begin to approach the phenomenon. It's the same with the blues in terms of the feeling. I grew up in juke joints where "white lightning" liquor was served in quart jars, and everybody knew what was going down, and you listened to the jukebox or somebody was playing. And it had a completely different aura to it. . . . It made you have a certain feeling. . . . And that juke joint in the little town in Georgia that I came up in was across the street from a church. People went into the church and got that feeling. When they sang hymns my uncle, who was a Methodist minister, would say, "Slow, common, or fast meter." So you'd sing the same hymn those three different ways depending on how they felt that day in church. . . . [Singing blues] had nothing to do with getting it over in those 12 bars. You want it to have that expressive nature.

Leaving Centerville as a boy, Lightnin' ranged over East Texas and other parts of the South, sometimes working with his cousin, Texas Alexander, in the small towns of Crockett, Grapeland, Palestine, Oakwood, and Buffalo. In years of roaming the area from the 1920s to the 1940s, Lightnin' built his repertoire, honed his musical skills, and lived many of those experiences that he later transformed into song. When he sang about chain gangs, he could relate his own 200-day stint on a Houston County chain gang:

> I had lots of trouble when I was young. Kinda mean. . . . Some places I'd be where we'd have a few fights. One of them cause

me to go to the road . . . ole boys say to the county road—
bridge gang. . . . Working out on the road gang—it ain't no easy
thing, I tell ya. Every evenin' when you come in they would
chain you, they'd lock you with a chain around your leg. . . .
Two hundred days in that was a long time. Got away from there
by singin' the blues.[6]

Similarly, Hopkins, an inveterate crapshooter and card player, was
stabbed in a gambling dispute in Houston shortly before he was to enter the army during World War II. Lightnin's blues commentary on the
experience reflected his sly wit, as he sang of lying in his hospital bed
thinking about all those soldiers going overseas and "all the women
stayin' here with me."

Lightnin's blues sang straight from the heart about prison, about
violence, about loneliness, about the joys and misfortunes of love, and
literally any other theme that might be on his mind. His years on the
road, at clubs, fish fries, and house parties had taught him how to "rock
the house" and get the people dancing, but Lightnin' could also be
melancholy and introspective. In either mood, he sang to his audience
about his and their own lives in telling images and masterful under-
stated guitar work.

As rural blacks began to move to the cities during and after World
War II, Lightnin' Hopkins became an important transitional figure in
the migration of Texas downhome blues to urban settings. His story
paralleled the experiences of other country bluesmen—Muddy Waters,
Howlin' Wolf, John Lee Hooker—who had come from sharecropping
families but latched onto music as their ticket out of drudgery. Imitating the bluesmen who passed through, they garnered a local reputation
before moving to the big city in search of opportunity. Finding work in
the rough bar and club atmosphere of urban ghettos, they learned to
amplify their sound in order to be heard over noisy crowds.[7] Lightnin'
Hopkins and his contemporaries became the blues spokesmen for rural
blacks, as well as for those who had migrated to the city yet still retained their country ways. David Benson saw a special chemistry at
work between Lightnin' and his audience on many occasions:

People could identify with him; they would have that "ah-hah" experience. . . . Intellectually, the "ah-hah" experience is the mental orgasm; . . . it's one of the best feelings a human being can have. It's that point of learning, of realization. And in music, if it's something in your everyday experience that you identify with, and you get to the club that night and are having a good time, and you can identify with it and see it, it's an "ah-hah" experience that creates, even heightens, that good time. And that's what Lightnin' was looking for.

When he wasn't "rocking the room," Lightnin' would underscore his songs with light, Texas-style guitar work, marked by single-line picking and delicate arpeggios:

There were lots of technically better guitar players, but he could make something so simple in terms of a quarter-note run, it would have such a feeling to it that you couldn't take any technical ability and replace that by any means. . . . He had a very clean pick that didn't have a lot of riffs and extra showmanship. It was very clean and only pertinent to what he was trying to get done. . . . It was a total song. . . . Everything had a meaning, a place . . .

Lightnin' came to Houston seeking opportunity. At the end of World War II in 1945, the thirty-three-year-old Hopkins had yet to make a recording. That chance came in 1946 when Aladdin Records in Los Angeles, one of many smaller labels tapping the blues market at that time, contracted with Hopkins and a pianist named "Thunder" Smith for a series of singles.[8] After his start with Aladdin, Hopkins cut a number of singles with Bill Quinn's Gold Star Records in Houston, 1947–1949, and made many recordings on independent labels in Texas and elsewhere in the late 1940s and early 1950s. Like most blues recordings made up to the end of the 1950s, these songs were created for a black audience. Because Hopkins' recording and performance career—and those of many other blues performers—took major excursions into white society beginning in the late 1950s, these earlier recordings more accurately reflect the blues as music of the black community.[9] Though less polished in performance and technical quality than some of the later recordings, they project a raw, rough-edged vitality that lies closer to the marrow of Hopkins' musical origins.

Those early sessions include some of Lightnin's best known creations. "Short-Haired Woman" (1947) was one of many satirical commentaries on black fashion and troublesome women drawn straight from Lightnin's surroundings. Complaining about waking up to find "rats" [hair pieces] on his pillow, he says he doesn't want a woman "whose hair's shorter than mine." Another song in the same vein was "Give Me Back That Wig" (1951), ". . . let your doggone head go bald." "Coffee Blues" (1950) reflects a more serious theme of domestic strife from the perspective of a child who overhears his parents fighting over "Papa's staying out late." "Lonesome Home" (1947) casts the singer as the victim suffering loneliness, but with the wry twist that he has been abandoned by both his wife and his girl friend!

Hopkins laid on plenty of sexual imagery in such openly carnal blues as "Miss Loretta" (1948), with "sugar mamas galore," and "Mama's Baby Child" (1948), with its confession/boast that "some women have made mama's baby wild." Lightnin' is the victim of a no-good woman again in "Highway Blues" (1953), where his girl friend makes off with everything he had. Lightnin' returned to that theme years later in "Big Black Cadillac Blues," in which a lady friend took off in his car when he stopped at a store in the Third Ward.

Lightnin' sang of the darker sides of black life in blues about prison and about white oppression. His "Groesbeck Blues" (1947) evokes a penitentiary theme long popular with Texas bluesmen, with its graphic images of back-breaking labor under the relentless sun, the urge to escape tempered only by the feared bloodhound "Rattler." Lightnin's version of "Tom Moore's Farm" (1947) is a variant of a ballad well known in Grimes County, where the Moores, the major white landowners, have ruled over the local black workers with a ruthless hand.[10] This blues ballad evokes all the evils of white racism in rural East Texas, a world that Lightnin' and many of his listeners tried to escape by moving to

Houston. Yet, Lightnin' always had a nostalgic urge to go back to his country roots and family (which he did from time to time), as reflected in such blues as "Picture on the Wall" and "Goin' Back to Talk to Mama" (both 1947).

Lightnin's classic blues ranged over the entire span of his experience and imagination. He could evoke human frailties in dramatic situations, as in "Mr. Charlie," where a young boy tries to stammer out the warning that the local lumber mill is burning down, or through the startling imagery suggested by "Did You Ever See a One-Eyed Woman Cry?" His "Mojo Hand" blues tapped a deep reservoir of folk beliefs among southern blacks, with its quest for magical remedies to ward off evil and misfortune. Here the blues did not merely imply a remedy to the singer's predicament but actually prescribed one in fundamentally African-American terms. "Trouble in Mind," a Hopkins favorite though he did not write it, expressed a more diffuse optimism that "the sun's gonna shine on my back door some day." Hopkins also adapted other material as he heard songs that suited his style, such as Ray Charles' "What I Say" and other 1960s soul band hits. Lightnin's songs were never static in form or content. Though he recorded his classics many times over, and his lyrics were set in print, these were just samples. There was no definitive version of any of his songs. Each performance was a unique event, dependent on the context: the setting, the moment, and Lightnin's state of mind.

Hopkins' gift for improvised verse and intimate communication with his listeners grew directly out of his African-American culture. David Benson identifies black versifying as a basic form of expression running from blues lyrics through the "Dirty Dozens" and the "Signifying Monkey" to today's rap:

> That whole history of rhyme is a history that was in every poolroom in black America. I knew guys who would come into a poolroom, and everything they say would rhyme for hours. And take a deck of cards and shuffle them and go through that deck of cards and tell a story, and every card would rhyme with the previous one. . . . But it wasn't anything that was relatively

new, it was throughout black America in terms of that kind of song making. . . . And Lightnin' was particularly good at putting it into that [blues] form and mirroring everyday life . . .

Lightnin' was not different from his listeners; he was just so much better at improvised verse than anyone else. And like all his neighbors in the Third Ward, Benson relates, he spoke a special form of black English in private:

Black folks have changed, in terms of black English, a guttural language into a tonal language. So instead of saying "Look at that woman go there," you'd say "[not renderable in print]." And they can talk to each other without you hearing them. Because we get so attuned to hearing that guttural English that you don't hear the nuances in between the words. And Lightnin' could literally sit in a room and talk to me without any of you hearing him . . . playing the rhythms of the room in terms of what he would say. You would think it was maybe just him making a sound or noise . . . and he'd actually be making a point. . . . And he would sit in a room with you, put his arm next to you, and we'd carry on a whole conversation, and nobody would ever realize that we were talking.

True to his country blues origins, Lightnin' often preferred to play alone. This was due partly to ego and partly to the need to give free reign to his musical expression, but Lightnin' always made clear that he was in charge. As Benson tells it,

Finger picking blues, carrying your own bass, is a very important part of being a street musician especially. Lightnin' would run 'em off the stage. He was willing to let anybody who said they could play anything. If you had hubris enough to say "I can play," then you can get up there and show me something. We'll get down. But if you get up there and you can't keep up, and you can't do what you claim you can do and there's nothing to you, he'll ask you to get off the stage. . . . He'd look at you, and he'd start talking about you, and maybe he'd talk about your mama, whatever. There were no holds barred in that situation. You either could do it or you couldn't. . . . But nobody ever played the blues as good as Lightnin'—to Lightnin' . . . "Nobody's better than me, my product's the one that everybody should listen to, 'cause I am the interpreter of the world." . . . He didn't need anybody else. Everybody else was there just mainly for decoration.

Drummer Robert Murphy, who played with Pete Mayes and the Texas House Rockers, shares details of his experiences backing up Lightnin' in the early 1960s:

You got used to listening for little things that would let you know that he was going to change at this point. . . . Because he might sing something, and then make some sort of little pause or something that would let you know he was fixin' to change to that next chord pattern. It was just a matter of listening and learning. . . . If you're going "Boom da, boom-da" and you hear it coming, and you knew you had to, instead of hitting, you'd just wait another beat and then hit it. Do something to make up that lost time, or that gained time. When I first came to Houston, I played with a lot of people who played like that. And all of the old blues players I knew did the same thing.

When Lightnin' got ready to play, the band usually knew what to do. They would automatically get up and get off the stage all but me. . . . But not all night, every night. I remember in the summer of 1961, when we were on the road—right on the border of Texas, Oklahoma, and Louisiana—where they sold that white lightnin' whiskey—some nights we'd jam, we'd go all night. And the next night we'd be somewhere different, we'd play a little while, and he would just turn around and tell the people, "Well, folks, I don't know. I don't think me and this drummer are gonna make it." I wouldn't say a word. I'd just get up and go on back stage. He'd want to play by himself. . . .[11]

Whether playing solo or jamming with other musicians, Lightnin' was always stretching in new directions. David Benson evaluates his music in that context:

The ability to innovate is the mark of whether you can belong to the club or not. If you are the churchhouse pianist, that's all good for the church, but when you come out of the church, can you do fours [trade four-bar solos]? He took great pride in the fact that he could do that, and would sometimes talk about people who couldn't do it as well. And he would say, "Aw, hell, ain't nothin' there."

The main issue was, who envisioned the sound, the original sound? And the innovations. Usually the innovations are not as technically developed as in later times, when that particular paradigm in music is accepted. So if you look at somebody like Leadbelly or "Texas" Alexander, it's a very different sound . . . from someone who came along later in that same form and had heard a lot of people. But can you hear that sound first? Had you ever heard Jimi Hendrix's sound prior to Jimi Hendrix? . . . So the technical abilities were not as important as being able to hear something that hadn't been heard before. . . . Just like there is a zeitgeist, a spirit of the times, there's a sound of the times. And those who came up with it are the ones we have to see as being really creative and innovative because anybody can come along later—Eric Clapton—and redo it. He [Clapton] is a great technician, but he didn't hear those sounds first; he heard those sounds through somebody else.

For all his musical talent and personality on the stage, Lightnin' Hopkins had a vulnerable side. His life as a rambling bluesman had been a hard and lonely one. His personal life was unsettled and his professional career wandered from one problem to another. As his later career took him into clubs, festivals, and tours far beyond the black wards of Houston, Lightnin' would assume the persona of the bluesman. Yet, according to David Benson, "he ached to get back to the comforting environs of familiarity. He wanted to be among regular folks."

Hopkins felt at home in the Third Ward. Settling there after World War II, he spent the rest of his life in its surprisingly country-like environment of pastured lots and one- and two-story frame stores and shotgun houses lying just across the freeway from the city's downtown skyscrapers. In the early days, Lightnin' was a street musician, working the city buses between the black wards:

> I used to ride buses—yeah, free. They'd see me goin' down the street with my git-tar. They'd say "Hurry on, boy! Jump on there! Let's go." I'd jump up there, ring down on that git-tar there, make me a little piece of change between Dowling Street and West Dallas and back. I did that for years . . . lots of fun at that time.[12]

Hopkins was a fixture of street life. When he wasn't holding court in his apartment, Benson tells us, he would hang out in his car at his favorite corner off Dowling Street. The car was Lightnin's turf:

> He didn't allow people to touch his car; he didn't allow people to come up on the back of his car. He didn't allow people to sit in his car, for sure. There were just certain rules. He'd see 'em and yell at 'em and that kind of thing. Everybody was up to something, you saw everybody from the drug dealers to gamblers. Then he'd have a thing where for years he'd go play "pittypat"[13] all night Friday night. And they'd play for money. He just had those kinds of patterns.

But Lightnin's world began to change in significant ways in the 1960s. The building of Houston's freeway system, for example, restricted his freedom of movement. Lightnin' would not drive on freeways.

He lost his ability to get around Houston . . . because it disoriented him in terms of going from one section of town to another. Lightnin' couldn't take the freeway from the Third Ward to the Fifth Ward, he had to go the old routes streetwise; and when you started changing those he sometimes couldn't make the connection. He couldn't go out to Sunnyside to his rental house. The area had changed so much. . . . [The roads] had changed so much, the boulevards didn't look the same, the sign-posts aren't the same. So your whole world becomes alienated from you just by modernization. And so he became trapped virtually in that Third Ward community he lived in. Now he could still go to the Fifth Ward by the old routes, and sometimes . . . the trip for him from the Third Ward to the Fifth Ward was virtually a trip to Centerville. And he didn't want to do that by himself.

Lightnin' also witnessed the gradual decline of the Third Ward community in his later years. A combination of city neglect, "urban renewal," and desegregation was dissipating the traditional cohesion of the neighborhood, sapping its economic energy and even its physical structure. Benson describes the change:

Our communities now are nothing but figments of their original selves, and there was such a life on the streets . . . and an intensity of that life that has disappeared from his [Lightnin's] world. Those places just aren't there anymore. It's just urban renewal, just decay. When people went to Wolf's on Dowling to buy clothing, which is also a pawn shop, too, they don't go to Wolf's anymore, they go to the Galleria. In those days, Wolf's was the only alternative. You couldn't afford Foley's, they didn't want you in Neiman Marcus. So you went to Wolf's. Your cafe was there, your cafeteria was there, your mechanic was there, your gas was there, everything was in that black community. . . . [The old clubs] are just lots.

The greatest transformation in Lightnin' Hopkins' career began in the late 1950s, when he and other blues masters started to attract the attention of white folklorists and record producers. This took place within the context of the urban folk revival of the time, wherein a young, white, urban audience focused its interest on the folk roots of American musical culture, including both country and urban blues. White blues fans and musicians began showing up at the blues clubs, along with record producers and concert promoters, as younger urban blacks began to drift away from blues toward other forms of African-American music. In Houston, Lightnin' began working with folklorists John Lomax, Jr., and Mack McCormick, who helped promote his concert and recording career beyond the black music market into the mainstream. Hopkins took his highly personal blues style into such local venues as the Alley Theatre, the Jewish Community Center, and Rice University, as well as to festivals and clubs in Berkeley (California) and other college towns around the nation. Lomax and McCormick also helped to connect Lightnin' with folk record producers Moe Asch, the founder of Folkways Records, and Chris Strachwitz, who launched his Arhoolie label initially to record Lightnin' Hopkins. For the next twenty years, Hopkins pursued what amounted to a second career, playing increasingly for white audiences from coast to coast and around the globe as a celebrated blues master.

Yet, Lightnin' found himself playing in an atmosphere that lacked the give and take characteristic of his black audiences. Playing for the Houston Folklore Society at the Alley Theatre in 1959, Lightnin' is said to have commented, "This preacher ain't gettin' no amens." Lightnin' certainly enjoyed the adulation, the opportunities, and the income afforded by this new white interest in his music. But he never felt they understood it, or could distinguish a blues master [i.e. himself] from a mediocre blues singer. David Benson comments:

> There were a lot of people who were seen as blues musicians who were not [blues] musicians because white kids couldn't tell the difference. . . . If I got up on the stage right now and got a guitar and went and started singing some songs, I wouldn't be

held by the same standard because they'd say "He's an old blues musician, he traveled with Lightnin' Hopkins" and it might not even be the true standard of what would be required to be a quality musician. [Lightnin'] thought there was a saturation of this impostor market. People would fall for it, and he would say, "Aw, he wasn't around, and they think he's a blues musician. He's fooling them white kids, and the white kids like that." . . . [In his later years,] 99 per cent of the time Lightnin' played for white audiences who were romanticizing blues music and saw him as being bigger than life. He couldn't quite believe . . . all of a sudden everybody thinks you're God. . . . I think that's what really went down.

According to Benson, in all his dealings with white society Lightnin' never completely overcame what Benson calls the "Emmett Till complex," a worry engendered by the case of a Mississippi black man who was lynched for whistling at a white woman. This worry is shared to varying degrees by many southern black men.

Although young white guys may be enamored of the blues and in love with the image of Lightnin' Hopkins, he couldn't quite believe that. . . . He came from that era of lynchings . . . from a world where there were no known good white people. . . . [This was] not a paranoia, but a certified feeling that he never was able to transcend.

Despite Lightnin' Hopkins' skeptical view about whites understanding his music, the best portrayal of his life and music within his African-American community is a documentary made by a white filmmaker from California. Les Blank shot the material for *The Blues According to Lightnin' Hopkins* in Houston and Centerville in 1967. Instead of using interpretive narration, the film allows Lightnin's words and music to speak for themselves and touches on many of the themes that made up his life. Lightnin' jams with friends in his apartment, hangs out on the streets of the Third Ward, tells a story about a run-in with southern cops, sings a gospel song and plays the piano, and plays his old Stratocaster guitar at a barbeque with friends and relations in Centerville. The final scene of the film is must viewing for anyone who would understand Lightnin' Hopkins and the blues. Lightnin' is sitting slumped on his couch with a sad and weary look, his hair in disarray. It is three o'clock in the morning, and Lightnin' has the blues. He has had a spat with his wife who has stormed off to Louisiana to visit relatives. As he improvises a slow, spare lament about "that woman named Mary," Lightnin' delivers a master class in the blues. Even though he is sitting in bright lights with a camera in his face, his delivery is heartfelt, intimate, and without artifice. The scene transcends mere performance, it captures a moment of true vulnerability that penetrates to the heart of a blues master.

Ah-hah!

Notes

1. Title of Les Blank documentary film, "The Blues According to Lightnin' Hopkins" (Flower Films, 1968).
2. David Benson is currrently active in Harris County politics and government as an assistant to County Commissioner De Franco Lee.
3. The focus of this paper is the blues <u>man</u>, Lightnin' Hopkins; however, this should not obscure the fact that there were many outstanding women blues singers as well.
4. For a good background discussion of this development, see: Charles Keil, *Urban Blues* (Chicago: University of Chicago Press, 1967), and James H. Cone, *The Spirituals and the Blues: an Interpretation* (Maryknoll, NY: Orbis Books, 1991).
5. Author's interview with David Benson, Houston, Texas, May 9, 1995, available at the Center for American History, University of Texas at Austin (hereafter cited as CAH, UT-Austin). All Benson quotations which follow are from the same interview.
6. Lightnin' Hopkins quoted in Paul Oliver, *Conversation with the Blues* (London: Cassell, 1965), pp. 55–56.
7. Jeff Todd Titon, *Downhome Blues Lyrics: An Anthology from the Post-World War II Era* (Chicago: University of Illinois Press, 1990), p. 2.

8. The Aladdin producer, upon meeting "Thunder" Smith, turned to Hopkins and said, "Then you must be 'Lightnin'.'" Hopkins, whose nickname had always been "Black Snake," was known as "Lightnin'" from then on.

9. See introduction by black scholar Richard Wright, in Paul Oliver, *Blues Fell This Morning: Meaning in the Blues* 2. ed. (New York: Cambridge University Press, 1990), pp. xiii–xvii.

10. Mance Lipscomb, the country bluesman and songster from Grimes County, relates his version of this ballad and of the Moores' legacy in Glen Alyn, *I Say Me for a Parable: The Oral Autobiography of Mance Lipscomb* (New York: Norton, 1993), pp. 307–14.

11. Author's interview with Robert Murphy, Houston, Texas, May 9, 1995. (CAH, UT-Austin).

12. Oliver, *Conversation with the Blues*, pp. 74–75.

13. Card game where players match pairs.

Suggested Listening

Lightnin' Hopkins' early recordings for the Aladdin and Gold Star labels have been reissued on compact disc:

Lightnin' Hopkins. *The Complete Aladdin Recordings* [1946–1948]. EMI, CDP-7-96843-2, 1991.

Lightnin' Hopkins. *The Complete Gold Star Sessions, Volume 1*. Arhoolie CD 330, 1990.

Lightnin' Hopkins. *The Complete Gold Star Sessions, Volume 2*. Arhoolie CD 377, 1990.

Lightnin' on the Internet

Lightnin' Hopkins is one of many American musical greats profiled in the All-Music Guide, compiled by Matrix Software; Big Rapids, Michigan, 49307. Entries include a biographical profile, discographies, and critical reviews. Access the All-Music Guide at: AMG@ALLMUSIC.FERRIS.EDU.

Bongo Joe at the Texas Folklife Festival. (Courtesy, F. E. Abernethy)

"Bongo Joe": A Traditional Street Performer

by Pat Mullen

In 1967, I recorded black street performer "Bongo Joe" in Galveston, Texas, and in 1970 I published an article about him entitled "A Negro Street Performer: Tradition and Innovation." Looking back from the perspective of the 1990s, I see that the essay is dated in more ways than the obvious use of "Negro" in the title, and I thought it might be useful to revise that paper in light of changing concepts about folklore and African-American culture. (This article is used with permission of the original publisher, The California Folklore Society.)

Bongo Joe performed for many years on Seawall Boulevard in Galveston and later at the Alamo Plaza and at the Texas Folklife Festival in San Antonio. In Galveston, no one called him by his real name, George Coleman; his white audience called him "Bongo Joe," and the blacks in the community knew him as "Calypso." Joe was born in Florida in 1923, and he learned to play the drums at the age of twelve. As with some economically marginal males in American society, he has been highly mobile. He started traveling as a teenager when he left Florida to see the rest of the United States. He wandered extensively in Texas, usually working as a street entertainer but also appearing in nightclubs such as "The Purple Onion" in Houston and "The Cellar" in Fort Worth. Joe performed in Galveston from 1954 to 1968 when he moved to San Antonio where he continued to perform until the late 1980s. Arhoolie Records recorded him and released an LP of his performances in 1968 (Coleman). He is currently retired and residing at the Extended Care Center of the Veteran's Administration Hospital in San Antonio.

It was there, on October 16, 1995, I had the opportunity to interview George Coleman. He has diabetes and some other health problems, but is taking medication and undergoing therapy in order to return to his normal life outside the hospital. I spent the afternoon talking to him on the porch of the hospital, and he was pleased that an article about him would be published by the Texas Folklore Society. There had been a story in the Austin paper about his death, and he wanted all his fans and friends to know that he is very much alive and eager to have visitors. He still has his steel drums although he does not get to play them very much; he does play the piano at the Veterans Hospital on occasion. As we sat talking, one of the patients started to roll his wheelchair away through the parking lot. When an attendant ran out to bring him back, George yelled out in that falsetto voice familiar to all who saw him perform on Seawall Boulevard or at the Alamo, "Hit him in the ass with a frying pan!" I said, "Now I know that you're the real Bongo Joe." He seemed pleased.

Galveston was a lucrative place for a street performer in the 1960s because of the growth of tourism. It is a Gulf coast resort town situated on an island just off the mainland. The main tourist section is along Seawall Boulevard which runs next to the beach. Joe performed on the sidewalk in front of a souvenir shop on "the Boulevard" in the middle of the most active area.

On a Saturday afternoon in the spring at the beginning of the tourist season, Joe could be found dressed in a gaudy costume of high pants with suspenders, a baseball cap, and brightly sequined shirt which is in sharp contrast with the deep blackness of his skin. When he begins to play, only a small crowd gathers since the big tourist season has not yet begun. But the tourists that are there cannot miss seeing and hearing "Bongo Joe." His two steel drums are painted orange and green in a crazy, wavy pattern. He whistles and sings through a microphone rigged around his neck and amplified through radio speakers.

The size of his audience on this particular slow day is about twenty-five. Some of the audience sit on the steps of the shop, but most stand in front or on the sides of Joe; a few people sit in parked cars. The crowd is constantly shifting, sometimes dwindling to only two or three people. They are a mixture of both young and old, with many family groups. Most are white tourists who are in Galveston for the day; there are only a few blacks. Most of the people laugh, tap their feet, and generally seem to enjoy the performance. A few teenagers even dance to the rhythm of the drums. Most who stay are attentive; others just stop for a second as they walk by. One man who came to Galveston specifically to hear Joe says of him, "He is a real clown." Only a few throw money into his orange and green washtub, and few dollar bills are offered. The young tend to stay longer, but they also offer less money.

The performance itself is made up of much clowning, making faces, and distorting the voice with falsetto tones. Joe beats on the drums with two hammer handles with rubber foam wrapped around the end; he also shakes two maracas for additional rhythm. Joe keeps time with his hands and his feet so that at times he is almost dancing. He usually sits on a folding chair on top of "coke" cases. As he performs, a look of delight appears on his face; he closes his eyes and seems to go off into another world while he is playing a drum solo. His voice is high-pitched and becomes shrill when he laughs. He does not sing much, but he does talk while he plays. He calls his talking routines "clowning," emphasizing that he does not want to be thought of as a singer but as a drummer. He uses his musical clowning routines only occasionally; mainly he plays instrumental numbers although he does a lot of informal talking with the audience between numbers. When there is a larger crowd, he is likely to do more talking and go into his set routines.

The performances of "Bongo Joe" are in the African-American tradition which has always included received community styles combined with individual innovations. "Bongo Joe" is a combination of many different entertainment influences and traditions, some of them based on his observations of small group performances by singers and talkers as he grew up and traveled around the country, and some on exposure to electronic media. He learns many of the tunes he whistles from radio, television, juke boxes, and records. He had a jazz record collection at one time, and he listens to jazz on the radio. Joe is highly informed about certain types of music: jazz, blues, calypso, and popular. Jazz seems to be his favorite type of music, and he knows the big band jazz of the 1930s and 1940s best. He plays such jazz standards as "Flyin' Home" and "Night Train," and his favorite songs are Erskine Hawkins's "After Hours" and Woody Herman's "Blue Flame." He knows the music of Duke Ellington and Lionel Hampton and some of the 1960s jazz performers such as Herbie Mann. Most of his material is either jazz or popular music. He whistles popular songs learned through mass media, but like a jazz performer he uses the framework and melody of a well-known tune as a basis for improvisation. Some of the familiar tunes he uses are "Mammy's Little Baby Loves Shortenin' Bread" and "Pop Goes the Weasel."

The music of "Bongo Joe" is typical of African-American music in that many forms have merged creating a complex interchange of new strains. As Charles Keil points out, "The Afro-American tradition represents not only a variety of mixtures between European and African elements but a series of blendings within itself" (33). Jazz, blues, calypso, and Cuban influences can be heard in his musical performances. His steel drum style is a combination of these types, but it is most influenced by the big band drummers of the 1930s and 1940s. He received his Afro-Cuban sound from jazz recordings and not from hearing it live, although he might have heard Cuban rhythms while in Florida. Joe says that he was playing steel drums long before he heard any records of it or even knew it was being done in the West Indies, but he plays the steel drums strictly as a rhythm instrument and not for melody as is the case in the West Indies. It is hard to categorize "Bongo Joe's" music, but it can be said that it is a secular music based on blues and jazz; like most twentieth-century folk music it is a mixture of oral face-to-face influences and electronic media.

"Bongo Joe" is closely aligned to a folk tradition in the structure he works within and in the content of his performance. The tradition of the black street entertainer is an old one in the United States going back to the nineteenth century. Unfortunately not much scholarly investigation has been made of this tradition, and the little that has been done has concentrated on the singer rather than the comedian or "man of words" (the exception is the work of Roger Abrahams). Also in the study of the tradition most of the emphasis has been on the content, the lyrics and music, and not on the context, the social setting of a street performance. One of the few scholars to offer even a brief description of the setting is Harold Courlander: "Ballads and other entertainment songs were, as they are today, sung on the streets and in establishments such as barrel houses or saloons, wherever people gathered together. . . . They stood or sat in groups along the sidewalks, or in front of the general store, talking, exchanging news and gossip. . . . In this natural, ready-made setting, the Negro minstrel exploited his talents" (186). In most cities with a black population, a performer could be found playing for coins on a street corner. Every shoeshine boy in the South used to do sidewalk parodies and dances. Many blues singers still wander the streets of large cities in America picking up change. "Lightnin'" Sam Hopkins played and sang on the streets of Houston. "Most of his 47 years he's wandered a few blocks of Dowling Street, a cocky, loping figure with a guitar slung across his back pausing now and then to gather a crowd and coax their coins into his hat" (McCormick). San Francisco had its black street minstrel in Jesse "Lone Cat" Fuller, and Beale Street in Memphis is still the territory for a few sidewalk blues singers. Entire street bands have not been uncommon in the history of Afro-American music. In the North, in such cities as Philadelphia, the amateur storyteller and rhymester regales black audiences on the streets.

"Bongo Joe" is working within a traditional framework, but he has expanded traditional conventions by adding steel drums. Even in this change he is still traditional because it is characteristic of the black musician in the United States to adapt whatever materials were available to fit his own sound. Harold Courlander points this out:

A typical itinerant Negro street band, as seen almost anywhere in the South and in large urban communities of the North, might be equipped with such devices as frying pans, lard tins, a wash-board, a washtub bass, a harmonica, a kazoo, a guitar, and clack-ing sticks or bones. As makeshift as these instruments may seem, they are anything but haphazard. Certain specific sound quali-ties are demanded of each piece of "hardware." There is a stan-dard of what is good sound and what is a bad one which can only be explained by the existence of tradition. (206)

"Bongo Joe" spends several minutes periodically adjusting the tone of his steel drums by beating on them with a hammer in order to get the sound quality which is good to him. There is a long tradition of metal percussion instruments going back to West African origins and still extant in Haiti, Cuba, other West Indian islands, Brazil, and Venezuela. Metal percussion also exists within the United States in the form of the frying pan, cymbal, and triangle. Drums are still widely used in the small group contexts of African-American blues performance, and they have always been an important part of African-American folk music (Courlander 208–10). In "Bongo Joe's" role as a street entertainer, in his sound, and in his instrumentation he is a traditional performer, and in his jazz and mass media influences, he is like other black folk perform-ers in the twentieth century.

Within the traditional framework of the street performer there is considerable room for innovation, and Joe takes advantage of this by improvising in playing his instrument and in spontaneously compos-ing his spoken routines. Joe has had no formal musical training; he cannot read music, and he is self-taught on the drums and piano. He developed his technique through the experience of playing on the streets and first used steel drums as a matter of expediency.

Well, I's at this Carl's Drive-In, and I wanted to show him that I had an act that I had practiced doin' with one drum and a pi-ano. He wouldn't buy me one so I went out and got a can, and used the can to take my little breaks on; songs like "In the Mood," songs like that I'd take a little drum break, use my hands instead of sticks. I bent it up so that I'd get a different sound, it wouldn't sound quite like a can and that's how I got started doin' that.

Here again is the importance of the right sound. Another innovation Joe has developed is the use of a steel rod stuck inside a hole in the drum which he strikes with his mallets. This device came about accidently after he was using the rod for a flagpole to attract attention. Besides improvising on the drums, Joe also composes many of his own tunes to whistle, and he is extremely proud of this ability. He says that certain tunes have been stolen from him by big name musicians. Herbie Mann is supposed to have recorded one of Joe's songs although Mann himself has never heard Joe play. According to Joe, people hide tape recorders in their cars and steal tunes that way; he has heard his compositions on radio and television.

Perhaps even more innovation is found in the improvisation of Joe's spoken clowning routines. Improvisation is traditional in African-American expressive culture as a key element in other forms—blues, calypso, and narrative toasts. Joe makes up humorous lines as he goes along by what he calls "rapid concentration." He is aware of the improvisational nature of what he is doing, and he is quite articulate at expressing his technique. The drums are used as an interlude device to help him think and perform. In fact, he even preferred to be interviewed while he was performing because he could think better. As he talked to me during the interview, he played the drums softly and kept this up throughout the questioning period. During his clowning routines, he uses drum interludes to think of the next line, as an aid in improvising. He plays longer interludes while thinking up entirely new sketches. He has certain set subjects or themes to improvise with, but he also uses things he sees on the street to suggest new topics: car bumper stickers, people riding or walking by, sweat shirt lettering, beautiful girls, and children. As a performer he uses the context of his surroundings as a part of his act. Joe does not have a set formulaic pattern as a basis for his improvising; rather it is flexible and almost conversational. This places him closer in style to improvisatory stand-up comics than to any epic tradition.

He is also like many modern comedians in that he uses topical events as a basis for his routines, but in this he is also tied to African-American tradition. Street singers have long used current happenings as subject matter. Courlander points out that "various natural disasters, tragedies, and other events—including fires, floods, and crop failures—have been the inspiration of songs sung by religious street singers" (75). An example of this type of song is "God Moves on the Water," which tells the story of the sinking of the *Titanic*. Courlander also reports a gospel street song from New Orleans which has as its subject matter a Russian rocket shot at the moon (78). The "natural disasters and tragedies" which "Bongo Joe" sang about in 1967 were up-to-the-minute and included LSD, racial problems, the United States Congress, Jim Garrison's investigation of the John Kennedy assassination, Adam Clayton Powell, and President Lyndon Johnson.

In one topical routine he uses a setting of the jungle as a framework for his remarks.

What I like about the jungle [drums]—all them wild animals, forests, trees, marsh, Everglades, woods [drums]—well, jungles—that covers all that, don't it? Wild animals and beasts and things. Get in the middle of the jungle, and you don't have to worry about protection. Texas Rangers won't mess with ya out there [drums]. You don't have to worry about our present-day situation [drums]. Out there in the jungle you ain't got nothin' but peace [drums]. You don't have to hang no sign on your door talkin' about "Please don't Disturb" [pause]. Might have to hang one on a tree [drums]. What I like about the jungle is, all them barks, and roots, and herbs [pause], and berries. I could drink or eat as much as I want to. Didn't have to worry about no federal control and prescription and all that stuff. They served their purpose for two, ah, twenty thousand years. Two hundred years did a good job of keepin' one of 'em a secret, 'til the Americans come over, bombarded, confiscated, brought it over here, slapped a label on it, and called it LSD [loud drums].

What I really like about the jungle [pause] is [pause] I ain't there [laugh, drums].

The jungle is a traditional setting in African-American folklore (Abrahams 1964), and in this instance the jungle seems to be a metaphor for Africa which gives added political meaning to Joe's routine. Here the jungle is pictured as a paradise in contrast to the corrupt civilized world of America, and Joe uses the contrast to satirize restrictions on American freedoms, significantly citing the Texas Rangers who were notorious in the black community in the 1960s for their oppression of blacks. The image of Africa as a paradise almost seems to echo the desire of many blacks to find a cultural identity in Africa, but Joe's final words tell us that with all the advantages of the jungle, he prefers not to be there. He seems to recognize that although Africa is a good dream, ultimately black people must make their place in America. Meanings are fluid, though, and there may be more subtle meanings here given the fact of his white audience, including a white folklorist. Bongo Joe might have been playing with white expectations and stereotypes: instead of the jungle being an African-American ideal, it could have been a means of signifying (Abrahams 1985, Gates) on the white stereotype of the African-American as primitive. When he says, "What I really like about the jungle is I ain't there," it could be a literal statement, a rejection of the white stereotype of him as primitive. Bongo Joe might have been manipulating his audience and the folklorist who was recording him; certainly, there is an African-American tradition of this kind of manipulation. Only George Coleman knows for sure.

Another of his topical routines focuses on the New Orleans district attorney who became famous in the investigation of the John F. Kennedy assasination.

Read all about it. Want volunteers to enlist [drums]. To protect Jim Garrison. He know too damn much [laugh, drums]. Read all about it. Jim Garrison got a lead [drums]. Men wanted to enlist to protect Jim Garrison. He's in hot water. Read all about it [drums]. Read all about it. Christ made an attempt to come back to earth. Saw what was goin' on and changed His mind [drums].

Although ostensibly about the Garrison case, this routine also reflects Joe's satiric attitude toward society. If Christ cannot handle the mess that the world is in, then there seems to be no hope. Besides being satiric, Joe's routines are also pessimistic. He attacks society, but he offers no solutions for the problems. Oppressed black people may not have solutions to the problems of racism, but they can still protest against it through traditional expressive forms.

The first two topical routines were taped when fairly large crowds were present, and they came about spontaneously. The third routine was artificially induced by a request from me when there was only a very small crowd.

Once there was a man named Sam [drums]. He had a nephew named [drums] C-O-N-G-R-E-S-S, Congress [drums]. Man named Sam, he had a nephew named Congress [laugh, drums]. You know somethin' [drums]. Congress took sick. Yeah, damned near died with the piles [laugh]. Sam had an operation; he got rid of the piles [drums]. Now he's recuperatin'. Keep pushin', Sam. You'll be well [drums]. Johnson got to get a operation himself. It ain't gall bladder this time [drums]. He's gotta get Powell off his back, Clayton Powell [laugh, drums, whistle]. The moral of this story was, history does repeat herself [drums]. Yeah, she really do. I been here before and I'm here again and be here another 'gain. As in the future. Everything that is, has been, and everything that is, is, and will be. Right? Right [drums].

Joe uses conceits and personifications to make his satiric point; the common personification of the government as Uncle Sam is carried a step further with Congress becoming his nephew. The operation image is used as a transition to remarks about Lyndon Johnson and Adam Clayton Powell with Powell becoming the black trickster harassing and embarrassing the more powerful white figure, Johnson. The remarks about history repeating itself are illustrative of the importance of the control of words as power devices in African-American culture (Abrahams 1964, 45). This display of verbal dexterity is both a parody of serious philosophy and a philosophical statement about the human condition. Either way, it gives Joe control of the language and, symbolically, control of the situation.

The power of words becomes even more important in a sexual context, and many of Joe's routines are on sexual subjects. One long number is composed of two sketches linked together by the sexual subject matter.

[Drum introduction] I was playin' this same thing for my gal last night. Yeah, I really was. I was playin' the same thing on the same drums. The same sticks. She looked at me with that glare in her eyes as if I didn't think she appreciated what I was puttin' down [drums]. I hit a riff somethin' like this [drums]. Then I looked at her, and I'm gettin' mad. I think she don't like the way I'm playin' the drums. I'm goin' to tell her what she should think about the way I'm [pause] playin' the drums; so I tries it again [drums]. I looked at her again. She looked at me, and I looked at her deeper. She looked at me even more deeper. She say [in a falsetto and panting], "You don't have to tell me; I know it's good" [laugh, scream, drums]. If I didn't know no better, I'd swear I'd been around [drums]. What're you laughin' at? This is my fun [drums, whistle].

This routine is typical of all Joe's material on sex in that it is suggestive rather than explicit. He uses conceits and metaphors for humor since he is performing before a family audience. He compares playing the drums to having sexual intercourse, with a shift to looking into the girl's eyes having the same meaning. The other part of this routine also uses metaphorical suggestion.

Walkin' down the boulevard last night, after I left her house [drums]. Saw that cute thing leanin' against the wall. I slid up, and I admired her. Tall and skinny [drums]. I felt her hand touch me on the backside. Said, "Hey fella." I say, "What?" "You like that?" I say, "Why, why not?" "Well, get with it." I grabs it away from the wall; I runs down on the beach with it. I throws it down in the sand [drums]. And I looked back up on the sidewalk. I was standin' down on the sand. [falsetto] "Go ahead go on, top it." I said, "Don't worry, by God, I am." I shook it out in the water. I crawled up there. Just couldn't stay on it. I crawled up again. I couldn't stay up there. [falsetto] "Why?" "Surfboard" [laugh, drums, whistle].

Joe waits until the last line to reveal the real nature of his metaphor thus giving it the humorous impact of a punch line. Both of these routines are expressive of the sexual attitudes of some urban African-Americans. In them the words, through the use of clever conceits and suggestive metaphor, take on a sexual power; language becomes a male control device in any contest of the sexes. Roger Abrahams makes note of this phenomenon among south Philadelphia blacks in the 1960s, "the man of words, the 'good talker' has an important place in the social structure of the group . . . throughout most of his life." He adds: "Words are power to him in a very real way. And they function powerfully . . . as elements in the sexual battle . . . " (1964, 46). Language has no such direct function for Joe in the context of his performance, but his verbal dexterity does seem to be a display of his personal prowess as a lover, just as any performer who uses sexual material, black or white, can use public performance to project personal sexuality.

In at least one instance Joe used his clowning as a more direct sexual device. He sees a white girl in a sweat shirt and shorts acting as though she is cold. This scene suggests an entirely improvised routine which he appends to the previous sexual sketches.

What you got on a sweat shirt for? So bad as all that, why don't you put your clothes on [drums]? Don't feel bad [drums]. All this stuff you hear about people wearin' clothes and people bein' naked and all that, it's just a bunch of propaganda, anyway you wanna look at it. We're all naked; we's born naked [drums]. What all do clothes do but just hide our nakedness, that's all. We're still naked. The clothes is on top of it [laugh, drums, scream]. What do clothes do? All they do is hide our nakedness. It's still there [laugh, drums].

For a black man to be talking in public about a southern white girl was unheard of in the South at this time, but it was permissible in the context of play and performance. His disguised approach to the girl becomes a display for his manipulation of words as he philosophizes on the nature of human nakedness.

This is not the only case where Joe's white-oriented frustrations have an outlet in his performing. He uses the performance situation as an outlet for his aggressions against whites because it is socially acceptable. As Abrahams says, the aggression of the individual "is usually allowable in a play (or contest) situation" (1964, 41). Joe's performance as a play situation hides some serious remarks beneath a clowning facade. He can express himself on current events, even racial problems, and he can satirize people walking down the street, be they black or white. He could never do this under normal circumstances. This has already been shown in his routines, but it can be seen even better in his interactions with the audience. Most of the interchange is in a humorous vein as he makes fun of people or their situations. At one point he picks up a little white girl and says, "Boy, the Grand Dragon oughta see this, oughten he?" Making a direct statement about white bigotry in a joke context is acceptable.

At another point Joe has an exchange with an adolescent white boy which also shows him venting some aggressions.

Boy: How about a little "Wipe Out"?
Joe: I wish I had my baseball bat, I'd wipe you out.
Boy: I been wiped out all my life, daddy.
Joe: If you wanna rub it in, I was born wiped out. I got you.
Boy: That's your fault, not mine.
Joe: Say man, hey. When I don't talk back at you, that's when

you should worry about it. When I talk back at you, you know
you're safe.
Boy: I'm always safe. Did you ever see a roadrunner, daddy?
Joe: All right, he stole the show. You got your problems and I
got mine.
Boy: Oh, I got a gang of 'em.

This verbal contest is very similar to other expressive forms in black
culture, especially "playing the dozens" or "sounding" (Abrahams 1964,
49). The verbal contest is probably the most popular manifestation of
the power of words, and in it the man of words can achieve his greatest
heights. The oral "cutting session" calls for aggressiveness on the part
of the antagonists, but in this particular case Joe shifts his projected
image from the aggressive, bragging, bad, black man to something closer
to the accomodationist so that instead of continuing the session, Joe
gives up early. Both of these images, among a myriad of other roles some
blacks play, are often used by black people in front of whites. Joe seems
to favor the aggressive role, and he played it through most of his performance.

The underdog role only comes through occasionally in his performance, but during the interview his insecurity as a black man in a
white man's world became more apparent. Joe was especially aware of
his low economic position, and he made many references to money and
material acquisitions. He says a record promoter recorded him once but
never gave him a dime, but Joe could not refuse to let the man record
him. "You see when you're broke you can't be independent." He added,
"I don't give a damn how much you make it or how hard you make it,
whichever way you want to term it, you still ain't gonna get it unless
you got it first. You gotta have it to get it; I don't care how much you
done made it." He believes that never having any money has relegated
him to a low social position from which he can never rise. Because of
this, he wants material things more than ever, and this is true for certain socio-economic segments of African-American and Anglo-American society. There are constant references to money in Joe's routines:
"You don't see me carryin' no placards either. If you do, it'll read 'In

God We Trust'; it'll be about this long, green." He knows he will probably never have any money; he has been "wiped out" since he was born. "A short happy life is better than a long miserable life. You can bet on that. I done lived 'em both."

"Bongo Joe" is not simply a victim, though; like many black men and women throughout American history, he used his role as a public entertainer as a basis for his personal dignity and as a means of achieving personal and cultural success. He is proud of his role as an entertainer. It is his primary source of income, but more than that it is a way of establishing his own identity. He continually draws attention to himself as an entertainer, not just while he is performing but also during his everyday activities. He wears his brightly colored clothes and rides his bicycle all over town with radios and loud speakers attached to it blaring out music constantly. He is a familiar character in Galveston; all of the blacks seem to know him, and the whites know of him. He goes by a "stage name" even among black people, and he has "Bongo Joe" written prominently on his bicycle. His personality has become the personality of a performer; his very identity depends on it. His ability to entertain raises him above the mass of black society, and this has helped him to resist the image of inferiority which white society has placed on blacks in the United States.

"Bongo Joe" has used his own individual innovations on the style and content of traditional expressive forms of African-American culture to create an art which attracted and entertained an audience wherever he went. He moved from Seawall Boulevard in Galveston to the Alamo Plaza in San Antonio, but wherever he performed, the tourist audience was there ready to laugh and dance and be entertained by the wit and musical ability of a man who made a successful career out of street performance. He never broke into big time entertainment, but he delighted thousands of people in the more intimate setting of folk performance.

Bibliography

Abrahams, Roger D., ed. *Afro-American Folktales: Stories from Black Traditions in the New World*. New York: Pantheon, 1985.

___. *Deep Down in the Jungle: Negro Narrative Folklore from the Streets of Philadelphia*. Hatboro, Pa.: Folklore Associates, 1964.

Coleman, George. *Bongo Joe*. Arhoolie 1040, 1968.

Courlander, Harold. *Negro Folk Music, U.S.A.* New York: Columbia University Press, 1963.

Gates, Henry Louis, Jr. *The Signifying Monkey: A Theory of African-American Literary Criticism*. New York: Oxford University Press, 1988.

Keil, Charles. *Urban Blues*. Chicago: University of Chicago Press, 1966.

McCormick, Mack. Liner Notes to Lightnin' Hopkins, *Country Blues*. Tradition TLP 1035, 1959.

Mullen, Patrick B. "A Negro Street Performer: Tradition and Innovation." *Western Folklore* 29 (1970), 91–103.

Bongo Joe and close friend, Helen Glau at Audie Murphy Memorial Hospital, San Antonio.

Fiddler playing a home-made, three-stringed fiddle, from *Harper's New Monthly Magazine*, 1878.

West African
Fiddles in Deep
East Texas[1]

by John Minton

"The fiddles we had then made music," boasted Bert Strong, born July 1864 near the Louisiana line in Harrison County, Texas, the slave of Dave Cavin. Entering life over a year after the Emancipation Proclamation (January 1, 1863), and only a year before Juneteenth (June 19, 1865, the day Federal troops finally arrived in Galveston to enforce that directive in Texas), Bert, like many of Cavin's thirty-odd slaves, remained with his "old Master" for ten years after freedom, maintaining Cavin's plantation in conditions for the most part unchanged by Lincoln's Proclamation, the Federal Occupation, or the 13th Amendment. Over a half century later, Strong dictated his memoirs to an interviewer for the Depression-era WPA ex-slave narratives project. Of the weekly entertainments on Cavin's 400-acre farm, he recalled, "My old Master give the chil'ren a candy pulling every Saturday night and had them wrestling and knocking each other about. The big fo'ks had dances and parties. They had fiddles but they warn't like these things they have now. The fiddles we had then made music."[2]

While Bert Strong may have been a bit hard on twentieth-century fiddling, his disdain is understandable nevertheless. Although black

▼

fiddle music didn't disappear entirely after 1900, it indisputably diminished, especially relative to earlier years, when black violinists dominated music-making within their own communities—and held considerable sway among whites as well. Fiddling slaves were remarked in the American colonies as early as the 1600s; from then until the end of the nineteenth century, the violin proved the most popular of all instruments among black musicians, surpassing even the banjo, an instrument of known African origin.

By the turn of this century, however, all that had changed, a shift conveniently illustrated by the contrast between Texas's great "songster" Mance Lipscomb (1895–1976) and his father, Charles. Born a slave in Alabama, Charles Lipscomb was "sold away" from his parents as a child and brought to the Brazos bottoms. Here he fashioned his first fiddle from a cigar box and, following Emancipation, advanced to the status of full-time professional—still something of a rarity in that time and place—playing dances for blacks and whites alike. It was at such functions that Charles' son Bowdie Glenn—or "Mance" as he came to be known—gained his first experience as a performer, seconding his father not on the violin or even the banjo but on the guitar, the instrument that in the twentieth-century would eclipse all others among southern blacks, assuming the first place once held by the fiddle. And although throughout his life Mance continued to perform many of the genres characterizing his father's generation—dance tunes and ballads, love lyrics and spirituals, even Tin Pan Alley compositions filtered through oral tradition—he also excelled in a newer idiom inextricably linked to the guitar: the blues.[3]

But if black fiddlers were in this century largely drowned out by guitar-playing bluesmen, their influence is audible to this day in the playing of their white counterparts, reflecting the lasting though largely neglected African-American contribution to American fiddling generally. Ironically, while this tradition is popularly viewed as a quintessential expression of America's Anglo-Saxon-cum-Celtic heritage, its truly distinctive character arguably derives from its African-American roots. As Roger Abrahams has written, the fiddle music of nineteenth-century blacks "was not African, though the tunes were made uniquely

Afro-American as they were rendered by slaves." Even if "the fiddler played a European instrument," he usually succeeded in "bending it to his own aesthetic purpose, . . . working within the constraints of [both] the intensely melodic [European] as well as metrically layered [African] tradition."[4] Moreover, just as blacks adopted the European violin, whites quickly assimilated the Africanized idioms that resulted. Accordingly, by the end of the nineteenth-century, American fiddling—whether performed by blacks or whites—was distinguished from its British and Irish antecedents largely by its "blackness," apparent, for instance, in the syncopated rhythms blending African-American metrical concepts and European-American melodic forms such as the reel, jig, and horn-pipe, or in the minor tonalities or "blue notes" similarly reflecting the influence of black tradition.

Curiously, few figures in American music are at once as renowned and recondite as the black fiddler. Notwithstanding the fiddle's longstanding preeminence in American black music, the most conspicuous evidence for that long tenure is its mere passing mention. Such is the case, for example, with the notorious notices for fugitive slaves, often described for would-be pursuers as "fond of playing upon the fiddle," having "played well on the violin," and so forth.[5] More detailed accounts do exist, of course, scattered throughout printed ephemera from the colonial period to the present. It is only recently, however, as more benign detectives have tracked these fugitive sources, that a fuller, more humanistic portrait of the African-American fiddler has began to emerge, exemplified by Abrahams's *Singing the Master*.

Actually, Abrahams's interest in fiddling is incidental to its role in the cornshucking as a cultural institution in the plantation South simultaneously revealing the perpetuation or reinterpretation of African, the assimilation or adaptation of European, and the creation and dissemination of distinctively African-*American* traditions. More fundamentally, Abrahams and I also share as a primary resource the astounding body of narratives gathered from ex-slaves during the 1930s by the Federal Writers' Project of the Works Progress Administration, truly one of the more promising vistas in black music research. Not that previous scholars have neglected these data. In the half century between the appearance of Benjamin Botkin's *Lay My Burden Down* (1945)—the first major publication drawn from the WPA's collection—and *Singing the Master* (1992)—only one of the more recent—there have appeared literally dozens of books and articles drawn wholly or in part from the WPA corpus.[6] Still, there remain many unexplored byways, testimony to the breadth and richness of the ex-slave narratives. In Texas alone, the Project's fieldworkers interviewed over six hundred former slaves, whose reminiscences fill nearly six thousand pages of typescript. Moreover, it is only relatively recently that the full range of this material has become generally available. Long relegated to the Rare Book Room of the Library of Congress, or lying fallow in regional archives, the WPA oeuvre has over the past two decades been published almost in its entirety, an inestimable boon to researchers of black music and song.[7]

It is primarily from these narratives, then, and primarily from the Texas materials, that I have attempted to sketch one underappreciated facet of American black fiddling. It is, in fact, from one of these narrators that I have taken my cue. While some might dismiss Bert Strong's reminiscences as mere nostalgic bluster or off-hand hyperbole—perhaps that's even what he intended, we'll never know for sure—there's nonetheless more than a bit of truth behind his boasting. In one sense, of course, black fiddling and fiddlers indisputably were more prevalent in Strong's younger years—that much is certain. But maybe Bert Strong wasn't just stating the obvious. Because in reality, many of the fiddles that transported Africans played *really weren't* like these things we have now: they *really were* literally, physically, *objectively* different from the instruments we now know as fiddles. And these very real, *objective* differences, and their very real and lasting influence on the *subjective* responses of black musicians and their communities, may well explain why the music these fiddles made seemed so much more *real*, so much more like real *music*, to an East Texan only a generation or two removed from West Africa. I think we should take Bert Strong at his word, then, especially given the other overwhelming evidence that many of the fiddles that enslaved Africans played really weren't like these things they have now; rather, the things they had then still drew directly on American fiddling's West African background.

There can be little doubt that the facility with which enslaved Africans in the New World adopted, and adapted to, the European violin is attributable in large part to the prevalence of fiddles of various types throughout sub-Saharan Africa. And, in fact, many of the fiddles played by American blacks weren't European at all. Reports of homemade instruments like Charles Lipscomb's "cigarbox fiddle" are commonplace, and, while descriptions are often scanty, it only makes sense that these ostensibly unorthodox items at least partly perpetuated African traditions rather than merely imitating their European counterparts. Take the case of Jack Maddox. Born in Georgia in 1849 but brought to Mount Enterprise, Texas, about 1853, he recalled that "Judge Maddox [his owner] bought a nigger man who had a three string fiddle. I used to hear him play and sing." Clearly, at least, this wasn't a four-string European violin; more likely, it derived from West Africa, where one commonly finds fiddles of from one to five strings, including numerous three-string varieties.

Other evidence for West African fiddles in East Texas is still more conclusive. For instance, ninety-six-year-old Harre Quarls of Madisonville testified "Massa tells us we's free June 'teenth. I leaves. I made a fiddle out of a gourd 'fore freedom and larns to play it. I played for dances after I's free." Born March 12, 1844, in Rusk County, Anderson Edwards also recalled fiddles fashioned from gourds: "On Saturday nights we'd sing and dance," he declared. "We made our own instruments, which was gourd fiddles and quill flutes." So did Litt Young, born in 1850 in Vicksburg, Mississippi, but since 1865 a resident of Harrison County. "We had small dances on Saturday night and play ring plays, and have banjo and fiddle playing and knock bones together," he affirmed. "There was all kinds of fiddles made from gourds and things."

Young, Edwards, and Quarls are describing the gourd fiddle found throughout much of West Africa—and most of the American South. The Englishman Hugh Clapperton observed such an instrument in Dahomey (now the West African state of Benin) in the 1820s, constructed of "three strings of horse hair, not in single hairs but a number for each string untwisted, the bow the same; the body of the violin was formed of half a long gourd; the bridge, two cross sticks; the top, the skin of a guana [iguana] stretched tightly over the edges; the neck was about two feet long, ornamented with plates of brass, having a hollow brass knob at the end."[8] A year or two later, another British traveler, John Finch, encountered the same artifact in the United States, where, he reported, "A black boy will make an excellent fiddle out of a gourd and some string."[9] Actually, as in Africa, the American article was usually strung with horsehair—in the South the gourd fiddle was even called the "gourd-and-horsehair"—and covered with hide. Tellingly, although it was bowed instead of strummed or plucked, the gourd fiddle was of a kind with the banjo, which in its earliest stages also consisted of a gourd resonator fitted with a hide membrane and strung with horse hair. (In fact, the cast-off materials employed in other homemade fiddles—besides cigar boxes, sardine cans, tobacco tins, and the like were also commonly used—may simply have been ready substitutes for the traditional calabash.)

Despite occasional, casual commentaries from observers like Finch, the best evidence for the gourd fiddle's currency in North America comes from the ex-slave narratives, establishing that, at the very least, this instrument was known among slaves and their descendants in Georgia, Alabama, Mississippi, Louisiana, Tennessee, and Texas, with the most examples by far coming from the last.[10] Whatever the limitations of our documentation, then, the gourd fiddle's American currency seems impressive indeed, spanning seven contiguous southern states from the Atlantic to the Brazos bottoms and hinting at an even wider provenience, assuming, that is, that these confirmed cases are but a fraction of the actual total. This is just supposition, of course. Moreover, as with other African traits and traditions, the gourd fiddle clearly underwent various modifications in the New World, obscuring its precise lineage, even in those rare instances where we have reasonably concrete descriptions. However, its most likely ancestor is the one-string West African fiddle usually known as the *goge*. Typically consisting of a calabash resonator covered with the skin of a reptile (lizard, alligator, or snake) and strung with horsehair, the *goge* is played throughout the Sudan or savannah belt region, an area accounting for most New World slaves. Admittedly, many African-American fiddles are described as having two or more strings, but then so do many West African instruments, even within the *goge's* provenience. And one-string fiddles, whether made from gourds or otherwise, were until fairly recently common among American blacks. (In one striking example, Ruben Laird, born in 1850 in Panola County, Mississippi, remembered that on the plantation where he was raised "music was provided principally by a 'fiddle,' an improvised instrument made by bending a stick in the shape of a bow, holding it in shape with a string and sawing on it with a crude violin bow made of the hair of a horse's mane and tail."[11]) Anyway, we're probably safe in assuming that many if not most of the homemade fiddles played by black southerners are at least distant relatives of the West African *goge*.[12]

Sometimes, moreover, even the most casual mention of such homemade instruments is sufficient to implicate, if not precisely to demarcate, the profound cultural continuities within the African diaspora. Consider the recollections of another Harrison County native, Simp Campbell, or the corroborative testimony of Georgian Chaney Mack. Born in 1860, the slave of W. L. Sloan, Campbell exclaimed, "On Saturday night you'd hear them fiddles, banjoes and guitars playing and the darkies singing. All the music gadgets was home-made. The banjoes was made of round pieces of wood, civered (covered) with sheepskin and strung with catgut strings. One of the oldest fiddlers of slavery time taught my brother Flint to play the fiddle." Chaney Mack was also born around 1860, but in Georgia, where his father had been transported directly from Africa at the age of eighteen. "He made himself a fiddle outa pine bark and usta play fer us to dance," Mack related of his father.

> He taught me to dance when I wuz little like dey did in Africa. Dey dance by derselves or swing each other 'round. Dey didn't know nothing 'bout dese "huggin'" dances.
>
> I'd be settin' on my daddy's lap and he'd tell me all 'bout when he lived in Africa. He usta play de fiddle and sing 'bout

"Africa—dat Good Ole Land"—and den he would cry, when he thought of his mother back dere.[13]

Unfortunately for us, Campbell doesn't elaborate on the construction of all the "music gadgets" he mentions, nor does Chaney Mack explain exactly how a fiddle might be made of pine bark; nonetheless these narrators quite pointedly intimate how African fiddles and fiddling style might have endured for generations past the Middle Passage.

This isn't to say that these traditions retained their original form or existed in a vacuum, especially given the constant interactions of black and white musicians. On the one hand, white youngsters were also tutored by black musicians. W. S. Needham, Jr. (one of eight elderly whites interviewed as part of the Texas ex-slave narratives project) was born in Alabama but raised in Mississippi and Texas, where he learned to fiddle from one of his father's slaves, "a nigger by the name of Mance."

Mance was a good fiddler. He loved to teach me to play, and I picked it up right away. By rights, a nigger by the name of "Friday" gave me my first lesson, when I wasn't but three years old, but dad gave him to my oldest sister when she married. When I was six, Mance taught me to jig and play such pieces as "Turkey in the Straw," "Molly Put de Kittle On," "Run Nigger Run," "Old Dan Tucker," and such pieces, and taught me to go on like they did. I just picked it right up now, and made a many a dollar by playing for dances and such after I got grown.

It's no wonder, then, that white fiddling bears the imprint of black tradition. Of course, influences also flowed in the other direction. Born in 1850 in Louisiana but brought to Texas around 1860, Guy Stewart was just one of dozens of former slaves remarking that circumstance. "De Marster am a good fiddler," he recollected. "He larns some ob de niggers hows to play de fiddle and some de banjo. Lots ob times us all gets tugather, weuns den plays de music, sing and dance."

Granted, too, most black fiddlers eventually forsook homemade instruments for the European violin. As early as the 1830s, John Finch qualified his observation that "a black boy will make an excellent fiddle out of a gourd and some string" by adding that "the supreme ambition of every negro is to procure a real violin."[14] Finch is actually describing a common progression, since many black fiddlers learned to play on homemade instruments, only later securing the "fotched-on" variety. As an anonymous ex-slave from Tennessee told Ophelia Settle Egypt, "I used to be a great fiddler. I fust learned how to play on a long gourd with horsehair strings on it. 'Course I couldn't go very high on it, but it done pretty well. That was the fust of my learning to play. After a while I bought me a fiddle for $1.80, and after so long a time I bought me a fiddle sure enough."[15] Born in the 1830s near Buckhead, Georgia, Henry Wright offered a similar account. "I made a fiddle out of a large sized gourd," he related. "A long wooden handle was used as the neck, and the hair from a horse's tail was used for the bow. The strings were made of cat-gut. After I learned to play this I bought a better violin."[16] Aside from its cultural consequence or practical advantages (for obvious reasons, the acquisition of such a valuable object as a violin could prove a bit problematic for persons themselves regarded as chattel), the pattern obviously also encouraged the transposition of tunes and techniques from the gourd fiddle to the "store-boughten" article.

Intriguingly, Henry Wright's reference to cat-gut strings also suggests that, just as black and white fiddle styles merged, African and European instruments were sometimes literally combined, and other descriptions of gourd fiddles confirm that some of these incorporated features of the European violin. (The most dramatic illustration of this hybridization that I've encountered is an instrument fashioned by an anonymous Southern black around 1900, in which a gourd resonator is fitted with the neck, head, and tailpiece of a European-style violin.[17]) Again, the evidence is clear on one point: even as African-Americans selectively assimilated instruments, tunes, or techniques from their white neighbors, they re-tooled these according to indigenous templates.

Such tendencies were further reinforced by other instrumental traditions. True, the fiddle was not only the most popular instrument among nineteenth-century blacks; it was often the only instrument, as confirmed by innumerable ex-slaves. (Harry Johnson, for instance, insisted "I never seen no kind of music but a fiddle till I was grown," while Willie [Uncle Bill] Blackwell averred "We had lots of dances dem days [he was one hundred and three at the time of the interview] and with jus' one fiddle.") Just as often, however, black fiddlers performed with ensembles, sometimes composed entirely of homemade instruments based on African prototypes. The banjo is the best-known of these, of course (Emma Weeks of Austin even remembered a banjo picker called "Joe Slick" who'd been brought directly from Africa). However, the "quills" recollected by Anderson Edwards were also routinely paired with the fiddle. Actually, this term was applied both to pan pipes and, less frequently, to homemade fifes, both easily fashioned from East Texas's abundant cane or reeds, though green willow was sometimes used for the latter. Like Edwards, Bill Homer (born 1850) recalled the typical dance band as "de fiddle an' de quill."

> W'at am de quill? I's splain, dey am made f'om de willow
> stick w'en de sap am up. Yous takes de stick an' poun's on de
> bahk 'til it am loose, den slips de bahk off. Aftah dat, slit de
> wood in one end, an' down one side. Put holes in de bahk, an'
> den put de bahk back on de stick. De quill am den ready to
> play lak de flute. Some ob de niggers larn to be good quill
> players.

Ophelia Porter, by contrast, remembered that "quills [were] made out of joints of canes 'bout de size of you finger; dey would plait dese togedder with twine an' blow through dem like dey was a French harp [i.e., a harmonica]."[18]

Admittedly, pan pipes and cane fifes aren't unique to Africa, but they do figure prominently in African traditions, dispelling any doubt about the immediate antecedents of African-American quills. The same can be said of the bones remembered by Litt Young and others—take, for example, Louisiana native Charley Williams, who also recalled how the slaves would "go back to de quarter and git de gourd fiddles and de clapping bones made out'n beef ribs, and bring em back so we could have some music"[19]—merely one of many percussion instruments with African pedigrees, most of them teamed with the fiddle at one time or another. As with the gourd fiddle, these African archetypes were in the New World adapted to the ready-made or readily available. Thus the principle behind the bones was eventually transferred to the spoons. The African scraper or rasp also assumed a number of new forms in the New World, for example, the jawbone (the mandible of a draft animal played by raking its teeth with a key or the like), itself gradually replaced by the washboard or even an ordinary garden hoe. Joe Oliver was born in 1847 in Hill County. Describing white dances around Waco in the 1870s and 1880s, he noted that "If de w'ite folks fiddler did not come den dey has de ole black fiddler whose name wuz Caleb, he plays de fiddle, 'nother plays de jews harp, an' still 'nother one plays de hoe by scrapin' on hit wid a case knife." Sometimes a handsaw was put to the same use, an arrangement still closer to the jawbone. With a saw, though, one could even second the fiddle's melody line. George Strickland, a slave in Mississippi, Alabama, and Georgia, recounted how "De wimmen folks had a big time at quiltings and somebody would play old gourds with horse-hair strings, called 'old gourd and horse-hair dance.' Cornshucking was de greatest thing er tall, master took a jug er licker 'roun' and got dem tight and when dey got full, dey would histe master up and toat him 'roun' and holler, then the fun started and dey would play de old gourd and horse-hair dance, the hand-saw and case knife, dey could run dey hand up and down de saw to change de tune."[20]

So while circumstance often determined the stuff of such performances, style and function still depended largely on African precedents, discernible in even the most seemingly pedestrian instruments. For example, cowbells, skillets, and kettles were also beaten to keep time for fiddles, recalling the bell-shaped West African *agogo*, while the jugs lending their names to "jug bands" (which frequently included fiddlers) are relatives of the "hollow vessels that, in African music, are blown to represent the voices of ancestral spirits."[21] Cymbals or gongs too were improvised from common household items, as revealed by

Josephine Tippit Compton. Born near Waco in 1862, she remembered: "When we had de crowds to come to our house for dances we had a fiddle fur music an' kept time wid skillet lids hit together." Tambourines were sometimes specially fashioned from hides stretched over small wooden frames or bisected gourds—the similarity to the construction of banjos and African fiddles is hardly coincidental—but tin pans could also be used in a pinch. Indeed, the compound "banjo picking and tin pan beating" occurs so frequently in the ex-slave narratives as to suggest a distinct musical genre (almost predictably, tin pans were themselves sometimes used as resonators in homemade banjos), but tambourines (and tin pans) just as often kept time for the fiddle. Sarah Wilson, for instance, confided that "Dey [her owners] didn't 'low me to 'tend de nigger parties, but I 'member 'bout de fiddles an' de tamborenes dey had an' played."

Even lacking instruments, dancers and bystanders contributed, or contributed to, the fiddle's accompaniment by clapping and patting, shuffling and stamping, snapping their fingers, and so forth. Finally, the fiddle itself sometimes doubled as a percussion instrument, most notably, through the practice called "beating straws." Freestone County's Sam Forge (born c. 1850) described the technique in a wonderful early account of that venerable Texas institution, the fiddlers' contest. "W'en de contest start each man plays his best," he explained. "An' most of de time he has somebody to accompany him, sometimes wid a straw lookin' piece he put across de strings of de fiddle, den he bounce hit up an' down on de strings an' beat out his accompanyin' de fiddler, de faster de fiddler plays de faster de boy jig his 'companying for him." Actually, the second musician was more often equipped with a *pair* of straws (sticks, bones, or knitting needles were all popular alternatives), though the fiddler alone could achieve this same effect simply by striking the bow against the strings or the fingerboard. The practice of beating straws is also widespread among southern whites (in fact, it's unclear from Forge's description whether the fiddlers in question are white or black or, probably, both). It has even been attributed to European tradition, though the evidence for that claim is unconvincing. More likely, the custom originated in North America, where it is entirely more consis-

tent with black traditions, which routinely exploit the percussive possibilities of melodic instruments (or the melodic possibilities of percussion instruments), often in contrast to white approaches to the same
items.[22]

Ranking among the most consistent and striking components of
American black fiddling, these percussive traditions accordingly offer
still another direct link to Africa, where most of the same percussion
instruments—or, for that matter, gourd lutes prefiguring the banjo or
cane flutes not unlike the quills—are traditionally played with the fiddle.
Tellingly, too, a gourd fiddle figures in one of the most comprehensive
accounts of such practices on American soil, the narrative of ex-slave
Wash Wilson. Born in 1842 in Louisiana, Wash was eighteen or so when
he and his family were brought to Texas; the music he heard both in
Ouachita Parish and later in the Brazos bottoms was, however, barely
distinguishable from that of his African forebears. "Dar wuzn't no money
ter buy er muzic insterment," he remembered.

> Us 'ud take pieces of sheep's rib, er a cow's jaw, er a piece
> ob iron wid an old kettle er a piece ob wood, a hollow gourd an'
> er few horse hairs an' make er drum er things ter make muzic
> wid. Some times dey 'ud git a piece ob de trunk ob a tree, hol-
> lowed out an' stretch er sheep er a goat's skin ober um. Dese 'ud
> be from one to four feet high an' six to er leetle more dan er foot
> ercross. . . . Dar wuz in general two togedder ter play wid dar
> fingers er two sticks on dis drum. Nebber seed meny in Texas.
> Dey had 'em in Louisiana an' on our place in Texas. Dey 'ud
> take er bufferlo horn an' scrape hit out an' make er flute. Dat
> 'ud shore be heard er long ways off. Den dey 'ud take er mule's
> jawbone an' rattle a stick ercross its teef'. Dey 'ud sometimes
> take er barrel an' stretch er ox's hide ercross one end an' er man
> 'ud set astride de barrel an' beat upon de hide wid he hands, he
> feet, an' effen he git ter feelin' de muzic in he bones, he'd beat
> on de barrel wid he haid. Anodder man 'ud beat on de wooden
> side wid sticks.

Actually, Wilson doesn't specify whether the "hollow gourd an' er few horse hairs" was bowed as a fiddle or plucked like a banjo, though circumstantial evidence indicates the former. In any case, the instrument is intrinsically suited to an ensemble as typical of West Africa as East Texas or Western Louisiana.[23]

Obviously the gourd fiddle never attained the banjo's popularity. Even so, it was widely adopted by southern whites. In the southern Appalachians especially, gourd fiddles (as well as gourd banjos) were at one time quite common among white musicians.[24] However, the most striking example I've found is an isolated instance from far West Texas, the case of Alexander Campbell "Eck" Robertson, undisputed patriarch of modern "Texas style" fiddling. Actually, Robertson was born November 20, 1887 in northeastern Arkansas. When he was three, however, his family moved from the Ozarks to Amarillo, where Eck was soon experimenting with the fiddle, eventually taking up the guitar and banjo as well. By the early 1920s, he had already established a reputation as one of West Texas's best old-time fiddlers, playing at dances and contests, in medicine shows, for silent movies, even traveling regularly to the Southeast to perform at the Annual Old Confederate Soldiers' Reunions. It was during one such event, held at Richmond in 1922, that Eck and Oklahoma fiddler Henry C. Gilliland detoured to New York and persuaded the Victor Company to record a few of their tunes. The results were some of the first commercial recordings of white country music, including Robertson's now-legendary "Sally Goodin," which, with its dozen-odd variations on a single melodic strain, remains to this day an article of faith among acolytes of Texas-style fiddling.[25]

In his later years, Robertson reckoned as his all-time favorite instrument a Jacob Stainer violin he inherited from his brother—"one of the best fiddles I ever pulled a bow on," as he characterized it.[26] Many a classically trained musician might have agreed. Jacob Stainer (1621–1683) was the greatest of all German violin makers, judged the rival of Stradivarius. A Stainer was a high-toned instrument indeed for a West Texas fiddler. It was also of a quite different order from Eck Robertson's first fiddle, which he fashioned himself at the age of five from a long necked gourd topped with a tanned cat hide.[27]

Considering the short shrift sometimes accorded black fiddlers, at least relative to their white counterparts, it's rather revealing, not to mention more than a little ironic, that such a seminal figure in "Anglo-American" fiddling as A. C. Robertson learned to play on an African instrument. It's ironic, too, that we may still hear a distant echo of West African fiddling in the playing of white Texans.

Not that black fiddling ever disappeared altogether. To the contrary, literally dozens of black fiddlers appeared on "race records" during the 1920s and 1930s; many others have been recorded by folklorists in the field. Some of these performances recall nineteenth-century traditions, others reflect black tradition's inherent resilience. In fact, while the guitar has always been the blues instrument par excellence, there is an established tradition of blues fiddling that persists to the present, for instance, in the playing of Texas blues great Clarence "Gatemouth" Brown. Individually, Brown embodies the generational shift represented by Charles and Mance Lipscomb, while taking that transition a step further still. Although he is among the last living exponents of the African-American fiddling tradition, he first made a name for himself as one of a school of Texas recording artists who in the post-War years adapted the rural blues to the electric guitar and the urban swing band.[28]

Even though the blues thus signaled a definite shift in African-American music, the break with nineteenth-century traditions was hardly absolute. To the contrary, during the early twentieth century especially, much of what went before was still being performed under the rubric of blues. Clearly that characterization applies to Big Joe Williams's "Baby Please Don't Go," one of the most influential blues records of the pre-World War II era, one of the most popular blues compositions of all time, in fact. First issued by the Bluebird label in 1935, Williams's original version features the Mississippi-born singer/composer on his own creation, the nine-string guitar, accompanied by a washboard—and a one-string fiddle.[29]

Recorded a century after the end of the African slave trade, an ocean and half a continent away from the African "slave coast," "Baby Please Don't Go" points us both back to West Africa and a half century ahead, both replicating and anticipating the work of contemporary Malian guitarist Ali Farka Touré. Often likened to such American bluesmen as John Lee Hooker or Lightnin' Hopkins, Touré's own bluesy performances bear comparison to the work of Joe Williams as well: alternating between acoustic and electric guitar, Touré, Mali's premier recording artist, is typically accompanied only by a calabash rattle, an instrument sounding distinctly like a washboard, and the *njarka*, the local version of West Africa's single-string gourd fiddle.[30]

Gatemouth Brown and Mance Lipscomb, Ali Farka Touré and Joe Williams, Bert Strong—and Eck Robertson. These are but a few links in a recursive chain of continual change and startling continuities stretching from the Western Sudan to East and even West Texas. Admittedly, the black fiddler's day appears to have passed, on this side of the Atlantic anyway. But folk traditions seldom really disappear, nor does their creative energy simply dissipate. So it is that today, the ingenuity and inspiration once spent on the fiddle are merely re-channeled into other pursuits.

There's no denying that Bert Strong and the many ex-slaves who voiced the same sentiments were at least partly right: black fiddles don't make music like they used to. Certainly, too, we share in that loss. But how lucky we are for those few that remain—and for these things we have now.

Critical References With Bibliography

1. The need for a study such as this was first suggested to me many years ago by Charles Gardner, fiddler and friend extraordinaire. I wish also to thank the editors, and especially Ab, my first folklore teacher, for seeing to it that I finally followed through on that suggestion.

2. Unless indicated otherwise, all quotations are verbatim, with only occasional emendations for obvious typographical errors or to standardize punctuation, from George P. Rawick's facsimile editions of the Texas ex-slave narrative manuscripts, *The American Slave: A Composite Autobiography*. Series 1, vols. 4 and 5, *Texas Narratives, Parts 1–4* (Westport, Connecticut: Greenwood Publishing Company, 1972), and *The American Slave: A Composite Autobiography*. Supplement, Series 2, vols. 2–10, *Texas Narratives, Parts 1–9* (Westport, Connecticut: Greenwood Press, 1979); the former volumes reproduce the typescripts deposited in the Rare Book Room of the Library of Congress, the latter the more extensive versions retained in state archives. In many cases, these separate series duplicate individual interviews, sometimes with significant variations. So, for example, Bert Strong's narrative appears both in Series 1, vol. 5, *Texas Narratives, Part 4*, pp. 70–72, and in the Supplement, Series 2, vol. 9, *Texas Narrative, Part 8*, pp. 3755–60, though the passage I've quoted appears only in the latter (p. 3758). However, to avoid a welter of superscripts and citations, I've omitted specific references in the case of the Texas materials, which are, like Rawick's editions as a whole, arranged alphabetically by informants' last names. (See also the "Slave Identification File" in Donald M. Jacobs, *Index to The American Slave* [Westport, Connecticut: Greenwood Press, 1981], pp. 3–76, as well as n. 6 below.)

3. For an overview of Lipscomb's life, see Mack McCormick's notes for *Mance Lipscomb: Texas Songster* (Arhoolie CD 306, 1989), which also contains an excellent cross-section of the singer's repertoire, and Glen Alyn's *I SAY ME FOR A PARABLE: The Oral Autobiography of Mance Lipscomb, Texas Bluesman* (New York: W. W. Norton and Co., 1993).

4. Roger D. Abrahams, *Singing the Master: The Emergence of African-American Culture in the Plantation South* (New York: Pantheon, 1992), p. 130.

5. The references are, respectively, to Gabriel, who fled New Orleans in 1814, and Abraham, who escaped from that city around the same time. Henry A. Kmen, *Music in New Orleans: The Formative Years, 1791–1841* (Baton Rouge: Louisiana State University Press, 1966), p. 232. Not surprisingly, most of the fugitive slaves identified by their musical abilities were in fact fiddlers. Surveying "a random dozen" notices for escaped slaves from New Orleans papers for the years 1810–20, Kmen finds that of those whose musical abilities are described, "most played the violin, but the tambourine, fife, and drums are also mentioned" (p. 231). That conclusion is borne out elsewhere; see, for example, the

similar items reprinted in Dena J. Epstein, *Sinful Tunes and Spirituals: Black Folk Music to the Civil War* (Urbana: University of Illinois Press, 1977), pp. 112–14; Eileen Southern, *The Music of Black Americans: A History*, 2nd ed. (New York: W. W. Norton & Company, 1983), pp. 27–29; and idem, *Readings in Black American Music* (New York: W. W. Norton & Company, 1971), pp. 31–35.

6. B. A. Botkin, *Lay My Burden Down: A Folk History of Slavery* (Chicago: University of Chicago Press, 1945). Among the many works that have followed Botkin's groundbreaking compilation, Ronnie C. Tyler and Lawrence R. Murphy, *The Slave Narratives of Texas* (Austin: The Encino Press, 1974) is obviously of special relevance here.

Two solid preliminary surveys of instrumental traditions in the WPA collection are Bruce A. MacLeod, "The Musical Instruments of North American Slaves," *Mississippi Folklore Register* 11 (1977): 34–49, and Robert B. Winans, "Black Instrumental Music Traditions in the Ex-Slave Narratives," *Black Music Research Journal* 10 (1990): 43–53. For an annotated index of music and song generally in the ex-slave narratives, see Eileen Southern and Josephine Wright, *African-American Traditions in Song, Sermon, Tale, and Dance, 1600s–1920: An Annotated Bibliography of Literature, Collections, and Artworks* (New York: Greenwood Press, 1990), pp. 208–26. This source should be used with some caution, however, as it omits many examples, also a factor in Jacobs's, *Index to the American Slave*, which features headings for "Slave Dancing," "Slave Music and Songs," "Spirituals," and so forth. A more complete listing just for fiddling in the Texas narratives alone would include the following: Rawick, *The American Slave*, Series 1, vol. 4, *Texas Narratives, Part 1*, pp. 10, 27, 38, 73, 79, 110, 121–22, 131, 155, 160, 166, 186, 192, 200, 206, 221–22, 252, 286; and *Part 2*, 7, 31, 51, 58, 76, 86, 137, 151, 183, 234–35, 238, 286; Series 1, vol. 5, *Texas Narratives, Part 3*, pp. 2, 15, 65–66, 223, 234, 240, 254; and *Part 4*, pp. 49, 59, 62, 68, 74, 86, 96, 129, 150, 181, 198, 206, 228, 237; Supplement, Series 2, vol. 2, *Texas Narratives, Part 1*, pp. 138, 261–64, 304, 311–12, 342, 371–72, 393, 443, 461; Supplement, Series 2, vol. 3, *Texas Narratives, Part 2*, pp. 479, 498–99, 614, 634–35, 645, 693, 708, 728, 909–10, 933; Supplement, Series 2, vol. 4, *Texas Narratives, Part 3*, pp. 975–76, 1050, 1064–65, 1083, 1188–90, 1262–63, 1310, 132. 1373–75; Supplement, Series 2, vol. 5, *Texas Narratives, Part 4*, pp. 1524, 1624–25, 1720, 1779, 1788, 1804, 1815–17, 1897; Supplement, Series 2, vol. 6, *Texas Narratives, Part 5*, pp. 2001, 2024, 2062, 2098, 2104–2106, 2111, 2204–2205, 2297, 2324, 2328, 2364, 2366–67, 2414–15; Supplement, Series 2, vol. 7, *Texas Narratives, Part 6*, pp. 2531–33, 2546, 2606, 2647–48, 2905; Supplement, Series 2, vol. 8, *Texas Narratives, Part 7*, pp. 2949, 2980–81, 3139, 3273–74, 3289, 3354–55; Supplement, Series 2, vol. 9, *Texas Narratives, Part 8*, pp. 3547, 3612, 3692–93, 3701, 3724, 3733, 3752, 3758, 3764, 3789, 3838, 3851; Supplement, Series 2, vol. 10, *Texas Narratives, Part 9*, pp. 3917–19, 3955, 4018–19, 4048–49, 4164, 4181, 4216, 4257, 4302, 4319–20, 4364–65.

7. The majority of the extent narratives are included in George P. Rawick's incredible *The American Slave: A Composite Autobiography*, Series 1 and 2; and Supplement, Series 1 and 2, 41 vols. (Westport, Connecticut: Greenwood Press, 1972–1979). The Virginia and Louisiana narratives have been published separately as *Weevils in the Wheat: Interviews with Virginia Ex-Slaves*, ed. Charles L. Perdue, Jr., Thomas E. Barden, and Robert K. Phillips (Charlottesville: University Press of Virginia, 1976) and *Mother Wit: The Ex-Slave Narratives of the Louisiana Writers' Project*, ed. Ronnie W. Clayton, University of Kansas Humanistic Studies, vol. 57 (New York: Peter Lang, 1990).

8. Hugh Clapperton, *Journal of a Second Expedition into the Interior of Africa from the Bight of Benin to Soccatoo* (1826); quoted in Southern, *The Music of Black Americans*, p. 13.

9. John Finch, *Travels in the United States and Canada* . . . (1833); quoted in Epstein, *Sinful Tunes and Spirituals*, p. 149.

10. All of the relevant examples that I've found in the ex-slave materials are included in the text of this essay; the predominance of items from Texas may simply reflect the fact that so much more material was gathered here than in any other state.

11. Rawick, *The American Slave*, Supplement, Series 1, vol. 8, *Mississippi Narratives, Part 3*, p. 1299. Except for the playing technique, which obviously suggests a monochord fiddle, this instrument closely resembles a musical bow (cf. n. 22 below), which in both Africa and the Americas often employs a gourd or a can as its resonating cavity. Although Laird doesn't indicate as much, a resonator of this sort would also seem virtually indispensable to the "fiddle" that he describes.

12. The definitive work on the *goge* is Jacqueline Cogdell Dje Dje, *Distribution of the One String Fiddle in West Africa*, Monograph Series in Ethnomusicology, No. 2 (Los Angeles: Program in Ethnomusicology, Department of Music, University of California, 1980). For other accounts of the gourd fiddle in Africa, see Francis Bebey, *African Music: A People's Art*, trans. Josephine Bennett (London: Harrap, 1975), pp. 41–44; Paul Oliver, *Savannah Syncopators: African Retentions in the Blues* (New York: Stein and Day, 1970), esp. pp. 50–51, 87–88; and Eileen Southern, ed., *Readings in Black American Music* (New York: W. W. Norton & Company, 1971), p. 114. Accounts of gourd or single-string fiddles in the New World include Harold Courlander *Negro Folk Music, U.S.A.* (1963; rpt. New York: Dover, 1991), pp. 205, 213–14; Epstein, *Sinful Tunes and Spirituals*, pp. 13, 159; and Southern, *The Music of Black Americans*, pp. 149, 182.

13. Rawick, *The American Slave*, Supplement, Series 1, vol. 9, *Mississippi Narratives, Part 4*, pp. 1417–18.

14. Finch, *Travels in the United States*; quoted in Epstein, *Sinful Tunes and Spirituals*, p. 149.

15. Rawick, *The American Slave*, Series 2, vol. 18, *Unwritten History of Slavery* (Fisk University), p. 131.

16. Rawick, *The American Slave*, Series 2, vol. 13, *Georgia Narratives, Part 4*, p. 200.

17. John Michael Vlach, *The Afro-American Tradition in Decorative Arts* (Cleveland: Cleveland Museum of Art, 1978), p. 25, plate 22, "Gourd-Bodied Fiddle." This item is credited to the collection of Roderick and Betsy Moore of Ferrum, Virginia (p. 161), though its provenience is otherwise unspecified.

18. Although both varieties of quills had virtually disappeared from Texas by the mid-twentieth century, the pan pipes were prominently featured in the work of black songster Henry "Ragtime Texas" Thomas. Born in 1874 in Upshur County, Thomas cut twenty-five sides for Vocalion in the 1920s, twenty-three of which have been reissued on Henry Thomas, *Texas Worried Blues: Complete Recorded Works 1927–1929* (Yazoo CD 1080/1, 1989), an invaluable aural portrait of the Texas quill tradition.

19. Rawick, *The American Slave*, Series 1, vol. 7, *Oklahoma Narratives*, p. 337. Although Williams was living in Oklahoma at the time he was interviewed, these recollections concern his rearing near Monroe, Louisiana.

20. Rawick, *The American Slave*, Supplement, Series 1, vol. 1, *Alabama Narratives*, p. 398; also Series 1, vol. 6, *Alabama and Indiana Narratives*, pp. 360–61. In fact, the "handsaw-and-case knife" scraper, an obvious affine of the musical saw, was apparently also regarded as a fiddle of sorts. Born a slave in Stewart County, Georgia, Rhodus Walton reported that during his youth "many 'frolics' were given in large numbers and everyone fiddled and danced where banjoes were available; also these resourceful people secured much of their music from an improvised fiddle fashioned from a hand saw." Rawick, *The American Slave*, Supplement, Series 1, vol. 4, *Georgia Narratives, Part 2*, p. 630.

21. David Evans, Booklet for *Good Time Blues: Harmonicas, Kazoos, Washboards & Cow-Bells* (Columbia/Legacy CD CK-46780, 1991). Evans's essay and the CD it accompanies provide an excellent introduction to the percussive traditions under discussion.

22. On "beating straws" in African-American tradition, see Abrahams, *Singing the Master*, pp. 103, 186, n. 40, 257, 286. The Europeanist argument is presented in Linda C. Burman-Hal, "American Traditional Fiddling: Performance Contexts and Techniques," and *Performance Practice: Ethnomusicological Perspectives*, ed. Gerard Béhague, (Westport, Connecticut: Greenwood Press, 1984), pp. 170–71. Notably, blacks in both the New World and the Old employ a similar technique with the musical bow, which is played either by plucking or striking its string with a stick.

23. Shortly before providing this account, Wilson had remarked "Us had music by de *banjo* an' odder things" (my emphasis). Since he chose not to apply this term to the "gourd an' er few horse hairs," instead employing a descriptive usually

reserved for the gourd fiddle, it appears fairly certain that this is the instrument he had in mind. For a detailed account of African ensembles including the *goge*, usually consisting mainly of percussion instruments but sometimes including two-string gourd lutes or various flutes, see Dje Dje, *Distribution of the One String Fiddle in West Africa*, pp. 17–19.

24. See, for example, Allen H. Eaton, *Handicrafts of the Southern Highlands* (New York: Russell Sage Foundation, 1937), pp. 198, 204–206; also Joyce H. Cauthen, *With Fiddle and Well-Rosined Bow: Old-Time Fiddling in Alabama* (Tuscaloosa: University of Alabama Press, 1989), pp. 50–51, 127. A photograph of one such instrument, reportedly made by Frank Couch of Hancock County, Tennessee, around 1840, appears in John Rice Irwin, *Musical Instruments of the Southern Appalachian Mountains*, 2nd ed. (Exton, Pennsylvania: Schiffer Publishing, 1983), p. 17.

25. Eck Robertson, "Sally Goodin" (Victor 18956, 1923; reissued on *Old-Time Southern Dance Music: The String Bands, vol. 2*, Old-Timey LP 101, 1965).

26. Earl V. Spielman, "An Interview with Eck Robertson," *JEMF Quarterly* 8 (1972): 184.

27. Norm Cohen, "Early Pioneers." In *The Stars of Country Music: Uncle Dave Macon to Johnny Rodriguez*, ed. Bill C. Malone and Judith McCulloh (Urbana: University of Illinois Press, 1975), p. 11; Linda C. Burman-Hall, "American Traditional Fiddling: Performance Contexts and Techniques," p. 161.

28. A good sampling of Brown's most important early work, recorded in Houston between 1952 and 1959 and featuring Brown on both guitar and fiddle, appears on *Clarence Gatemouth Brown: The Original Peacock Recordings* (Rounder CD 2039).

29. Joe Williams' Washboard Blues Singers, "Baby Please Don't Go" (Bluebird B6200, 1935; reissued on *Big Joe Williams: Complete Recorded Works in Chronological Order, vol. 1 [1935–1941]*. Blues Document CD BDCD-6003, 1991). The other musicians on this recording are probably Chasey Collins, one-string fiddle, and "Kokomo," washboard, though it's also been suggested that Colllins was actually the washboard player, and that the fiddler was one "Dad" Tracy.

Williams developed his unique "nine-string guitar," which doubles the high "e," "b," and "d" on the standard six-string instrument, during the 1920s. However, as a child he also played a traditional African-American monochord sometimes known as a "jitterbug" or "diddley bow." His own instrument was representative of the type, consisting of a single strand of cotton-baling wire stapled to a wall and suspended over two spools. The pitch was varied by sliding a bottle along the wire. Other instruments Williams recalled from his childhood were a two-string cigar-box guitar, a cane fife, a set of quills (pan pipes), and a bucket used as a drum. See David Evans, "Afro-American One Stringed Instruments," *Western Folklore* 34 (1970): 231.

30. Steeped in the musical traditions of the Songhai and Tuareg cultures of the region between Timbuktu and Gao, Touré is himself a master of the *njarka*, which he combines with his guitar work through multi-track recording. In fact, although he now favors the six-string European guitar, his first instruments were the monochord gourd fiddle and the *njurkel*, a single-string guitar. Among Touré's many fine recordings, *The Source* (Hannibal/World Circuit CD HNCD 1375, 1992) offers an especially good introduction to his music. Also of interest is his recent *Talking Timbuktu* (with Ry Cooder, Hannibal/World Circuit CD HNCD 1381, 1994). Recorded in Los Angeles in 1993, this album features appearances by several prominent American musicians, including Gatemouth Brown on electric guitar—and viola! For more on Touré, see also Andy Kershaw and Richard Trillo, "River Spirit Blues: The Songs of Mali's Ali Farka Touré." In *World Music: The Rough Guide*, ed. Simon Broughten, Mark Ellingham, David Muddyman, and Richard Trillo (London: Rough Guides, 1994), pp. 260–62. Generally speaking, a comparison of the playing of African fiddlers such as Touré with that of their American counterparts (e.g., Brown) appears to confirm that, to a great extent, the traditions of the West African gourd fiddle were in America transferred to the violin.

"The Yellow Rose of Texas": A Different Cultural View

by Trudier Harris

History, literature (poems, novels), folklore (songs, legends), and popular culture intertwine, intersect, and transform each other in a constantly influencing mixture of fact, truth, speculation, and downright lies. Appropriation of one cultural form by another may mean that a perceived historical truth outstrips fact to become legend. For example, did George Washington really cut down the cherry tree, or is that just a good story that epitomizes something Americans would like to believe about that historical figure? Was Abraham "Honest Abe" Lincoln really as honest as legend perceives him to be, or is that just a facet of his character that historians and regular folk like to emphasize? Where does fact, truth leave off and fiction begin? And why does fiction seem to reflect a truth larger than fact when it is applied to characters whose actions warrant our approval? In the crisscrossings of these perceptions of reality, claims to an absolute veracity give way to the human instinct and love for a good story, indeed perhaps to the preference for a good story over the starkness of reality. In the imaginative construction of various kinds of texts, whether they are grounded in history, biography, autobiography, folklore, literature, or whether they appear on television, in newspapers, or in other print media, a point can occur where

▼

those creations take on lives of their own, where the original intent becomes irrelevant in the face of the re-creation and re-structuring of events and incidents to the will and the realm of the imagination. There is a point where history is no more true than fiction, where a newspaper story, such as that focusing on Tawana Brawley, takes on such a life that it becomes impossible to sort out fact from fiction, legend from life, folklore from biography.

A good story. Connections made that are perhaps not as "truthful" as undisputed facts would make them. The preference for imagination over historical documentation. The preference for the sensational over the mundane. These patterns of cultural formation and creative interchange provide the context in which I would like to explore a story—and the novel about the story—that is sometimes perceived to be true, at other times discounted, but that continues to intrigue Americans more than one hundred and fifty years after the events around which the speculation occurred. Whether true or fictional, documentable or discountable, the events have seeped into the American cultural imagination sufficiently to warrant their treatment as seriously as one would presumably treat a "factual" account of the battle of Bull Run.

I would venture to say that most Americans are familiar with the folksong, "The Yellow Rose of Texas." If they cannot recall all of the lyrics, there is still a resonant quality about the song. I would also venture to say that few of those Americans—Texans notwithstanding—have reflected overly long on the implications of the fact that the song is not just about a woman, but about a black woman, or that a black man probably composed it. Scholars such as Martha Anne Turner have linked the song to its contextual origins—that of the Texas war for independence from Mexico in the 1830s and a specific incident in 1836—and others have argued its irrelevance to that event. It was only in 1989, however, when Anita Richmond Bunkley published *Emily, The Yellow Rose*, a novel based on the presumed incidents that spawned the fame of the yellow rose, that the fictionalized expansion of the facts encouraged a larger and perhaps different audience to become aware of the historical significance of Emily D. West, the hypothetical "Yellow Rose of Texas."[1] This publishing event certainly re-centered the song and the incident in African-American culture, for over many years and numerous versions, the song had been deracialized. Bunkley, herself an African-American woman, researched the complex history of another African-American woman and imaginatively recreated and reclaimed it.

The presumed historical facts are simple and limited. Emily D. West, a teenage orphaned free Negro woman in the northeastern United States, journeyed by boat to the wilderness of Texas in 1835.[2] Colonel James Morgan, on whose plantation she worked as an indentured servant, established the little settlement of New Washington (later Morgan's Point). When Santa Anna and his troops arrived in the area, he claimed West to take the place of his stay-at-home wife in Mexico City and the traveling wife he had acquired on his way to Texas. The traveling wife had to be sent back when swollen river waters prevented him from taking her across in the fancy carriage in which she was riding. Santa Anna was either partying with West or having sex with her when Sam Houston's troops arrived for The Battle of San Jacinto, thus forcing him to escape in only a linen shirt and "silk drawers," in which he was captured the next day. West's possible forced separation from her black lover and her placement in Santa Anna's camp, according to legend, inspired her lover to compose the song we know as "The Yellow Rose of Texas." Publicity surrounding the hotel in San Antonio that was named after Emily Morgan asserts that West was a spy for Texas. Other historians claim that there is absolutely no tie between West and the events of the Texas war for independence from Mexico. Still others claim that it was only West's heroic feat of keeping Santa Anna preoccupied that enabled the Texas victory.[3] Broadening perceptions of how texts are created and the purposes to which they are put provide the context, during the course of this paper, from which I want to explore West's story and take issue with the assigning of heroic motives to her adventure.

Bunkley's novelistic representation of the events provide motive, emotion, sentiment, and introspection to flesh out the bare bones of the presented history. According to Bunkley, a twenty-year-old orphaned Emily D. West journeyed to Texas in the hope that its status as Mexican territory would help her to realize more freedom than she had experienced in the so-called free environment of New York. Upon arriving in Texas, West discovered that her freedoms were minimal, that the land was much more harsh than she had anticipated, and that her circumstances were not appreciably different from those of enslaved African-Americans. She fell in love with a black man, a musician, thought to be a runaway from slavery. Bounty hunters and the pressures of the fast-approaching war for independence from Mexico interrupted their sustaining relationship. Her lover attempted to get away from his pursuers and the war, while West found herself in the midst of both; their separation led to his composing "The Yellow Rose of Texas."

Unfortunately for West, the plantation on which she worked lay directly in the path of the oncoming Mexican soldiers, led by Santa Anna. Upon arriving, burning most of the plantation, and killing several of its inhabitants, Santa Anna discovered West and ordered that she be taken captive. Forced to engage in sex with the repulsive, rapacious, and opium-eating Santa Anna, West unknowingly but greatly aided the Texan cause. After an opium, sex-satiated encounter with West, Santa Anna fell into a slumber from which he could not arouse himself sufficiently before Sam Houston's troops attacked his camp, killed many of his soldiers (who were quickly scattered without the commanding voice of their leader), and captured Santa Anna. During the battle of San Jacinto, West made a convenient escape.

The presented history and the novelistic depiction of it are certainly the stuff of which legends are made, and Bunkley appropriately subtitles her novel "A Texas Legend." As the events come to us today, therefore, West is considered to be "the yellow rose," the woman in the song, and the incident of its composition is equated to lovers being separated during the war for Texan independence, with West subsequently playing her alleged historical, legendary role with Santa Anna. The black woman, Santa Anna, the black male composer, 21 April 1836, The Battle of San Jacinto, the song—these are the people, the time, the place, the incident, and the creation surrounding it that have merged history, legend, biography, and musical composition. No matter who would desire otherwise, the links are now inseparable in viewing the story of the song and its presumed subject, Emily D. West.

What fascinates about the story beyond its legendary proportions is its centering of an African-American woman in a significant piece of American history. The forced separation of the lover from his loved one, with the events of the war as backdrop, led to the composition of the song. Following are the first verse and the chorus:

> There's a yellow rose in Texas
> That I am a going to see
> No other darky [sic] knows her
> No one only me
> She cryed [sic] so when I left her
> It like to broke my heart
> And if I ever find her
> We nevermore will part.

Chorus

> She's the sweetest rose of color
> This darky every knew
> Her eyes are bright as diamonds
> They sparkle like the dew
> You may talk about dearest May
> And sing of Rosa Lee
> But the yellow rose of Texas
> Beats the belles of Tennessee.[4]

The centering of the black woman in the song and its ensuing historical significance comprise an unprecedented circumstance matched only by the second fascination—a love story between black people that was powerful enough to be immortalized in song. The woman and the song serve Texas history well, but they serve African-American history, folklore, and culture even better.

Unlike Emily D. West, African-American women who have garnered places in African-American history and folklore have done so because of their money, moral strength, or sexual promiscuity, not because of their sexual victimization. Indeed, keepers of American history and culture have not generally recognized that black women could be victimized sexually. Cultural myths developing out of slavery made it imperative that black women be portrayed as almost bestial in their sexuality, as always the offenders in sexual contacts between white males and black females. If black women were not so promiscuous, so this skewed logic went, why would these good southern plantation owners want to sleep with them? And if they did not possess some ungodly sexual power over men, why would these men desert the beds of their wives for lowly shack mattresses where black women lay?

Black women who escaped such categorization, who were outside the purview of the sexual myths, fell into others. Mammies, obviously a contrast to the promiscuous types, had to be stripped of sexuality in order to be made keepers of the manners and morals of white children. Seldom did the creators of cultural myths pause to think that the mammary glands which often fed those white children had to have sexuality embedded in them somewhere. Nonetheless, this compartmentalization of the black woman's body and roles in slave society made it possible for the promiscuous and the virtuous to exist on the same plantation, but not in the same woman.

The black women who were not confined to slavery could carve out space for themselves in different directions, but these were not without stereotypical overtones. Mary Ellen ("Mammy") Pleasant (1814–1904), for example, who was a civil rights pioneer and who inherited a fortune from her first husband in Boston before moving to San Francisco in 1849, where she bolstered that fortune through cooking, running a boarding house, lending money, and operating a procuring service for wealthy white men, had to be excused from womanhood in order to account for her successes.[5] By making her an honorary (white) man, her evaluators could live with the fact that she made money, owned property, assisted (allegedly) in paying for John Brown's raid on Harper's Ferry, and generally transcended all efforts to relegate her to a category of violable black woman. In terms of how black woman are ultimately viewed in American society, however, Pleasant's very successes worked against her. Historians, popular culturalists, and folklorists remember her strength, her money-making know-how, the financial power she wielded, her almost witch-like power over white men. They do not remember her as a *beautiful* black woman, or an *attractive* black woman, or even a marriageable black woman (though she was twice married, note the use of the asexual "Mammy" in reference to her). And they have certainly composed no songs about her. Indeed, her reputation was significantly tainted by her work of bringing together rich, older white married men and single young women in San Francisco. She might have been able to fulfill the American Dream, but she did it by sacrificing her claims to femininity and perhaps even by sacrificing her position in the factual realm of black female sisterhood. She transcends flesh and blood by being more frequently considered a constructed entity, an exceptional woman, rather than reflecting the more mundane reality of black women's lives.

Pleasant's contemporaneous position with Emily West makes her a natural point of comparison. However, "The Yellow Rose of Texas" is an ongoing song, so later portraits of exceptional black women would also be relevant for averaging in to this equation of larger-than-life black female figures. Early twentieth-century examples are "Pig Foot Mary" and Madame C. J. Walker. Lillian Harris Dean (1870–1929), who became known as "Pig Foot Mary," migrated to New York from the Mississippi Delta. She amassed a fortune selling pigs' feet, chitterlings, hog maws, and other southern delicacies to nostalgic African-Americans on the city's streets. Her success mirrored the spirit of the expansive era commonly called the Harlem Renaissance. Though she was well-known in her day, she has not yet risen to the level of ongoing, contemporary, popular myth or song.

Sarah Breedlove McWilliams Walker, commonly known as Madame C. J. Walker, was born in Louisiana in 1867 and died in New York in 1919. She has been immortalized as the black woman who taught other black women how to care for their African hair in an America not geared toward their beauty interests. By inventing the straightening comb, along with the hair care products that would make its use effective, Madame Walker became a millionaire. Known in black communities throughout the United States, she was perhaps as much a phenomenon as Booker T. Washington. She freed black women from such problems as lice infecting their hair, but her intended helpful improvements inadvertently led to black women imitating the hair styles of white women. Straightening hair thus developed cultural in addition to grooming implications. Like Washington in his bid to get black people to learn trades and thus perhaps further enslave them to whites, Madame Walker's freeing of black women from hair problems created issues related to the lack of racial identification and racial pride.

Madame Walker's name was certainly a household name in black communities in the early part of the twentieth century. While there were many whites involved in her operations, they were not as consistently aware of her reputation as were African-Americans. In its personalized nature, however, her historical role, like Pig Foot Mary's, contrasts to those of West and Pleasant, both of whom are tied to events of major American historical consequence. It is noteworthy that, although Pleasant shares overtones of sexual transgression with West, hers is viewed negatively but West's is viewed positively; national interest elevates one, diminishes the other. While Madame Walker has references in any number of historical and literary texts, and while the daughter who spent her money spread her mother's name even farther, Walker has not earned a song or, to my knowledge, a poem in her honor. Her granddaughter recently published a biography of her, but such endeavors usually attract scholars rather than listeners to folksongs.[6]

Within the small and select group of African-American women with whom she shares a substantial historical reputation, therefore, Emily D. West is an anomaly. She is also an anomaly among black women depicted in various African-American folk sources. Usually, such women are objects to be won in courting contests, misguided church sisters, crude competitors in fornication rituals, or otherwise window-dressing to the exploits of men. While historical blues singers, such as Bessie Smith and Ma Rainey, along with women who appear in blues songs, may at times—with their smoking, drinking, cursing, and lovemaking—provide a striking contrast to the church women, the overall folk and historical patterns maintain black women in subordinated relationships to men (the primary theme of blues music, after all, is the lamentation of the loved one whose lover has deserted her). Rarely do black female characters appear sufficiently in folktales or other venues to warrant attention focusing on them overly long. Their claims to (brief) legendary status come primarily from their affiliation with legendary male figures. John Henry's lover, for example, who is variously named Julie Ann or Polly Ann, among others, might be a strong woman who finds her way to his death site and eventually "drives steel like a man," but she does not succeed in earning a ballad in her own right. She exists in John Henry's space, in the aftermath of his exploits. Because her three seconds of fame come on the trail of what he has already accomplished, she does not carve out new territory for herself, does nothing to shift the pattern of legend from him to her. What she does merely highlights his achievement and his legacy.[7]

At least Polly Ann has a name that transmitters of the folklore can remember. Most black female characters who appear in toasts or tales with legendary black male characters do not have even that measure of distinction. Stagolee might pause long enough after his infamous shooting of Billy to have sex with a woman, but she is never named. She is the vehicle through which toast tellers highlight his sexual prowess; her value does not extend beyond that exclamation point (Abrahams 137). Black women in fornication contests and "freaks balls" occasionally get named— frequently for the sake of making poetic lines rhyme— but the circumstances are not such that they or their creators would probably want to recall in an aboveboard, altruistic way. Church sisters in African-American folk tradition spend their time cooking for or sexually servicing preachers and deacons, arguing about which denomination is preferable, or carrying out the business of their churches. Even those who achieve what would otherwise be considered legendary feats, such as being temporarily placed in hell when heaven is somehow overfilled and managing to raise enough money to put air conditioning in that overheated place, do not get their names lit up in toast, ballad, or folktale tradition.

A rare exception is Aunt Nancy (or Aunt Dicy) in the sequence that African-American folklorist J. Mason Brewer collected in Texas. Aunt Nancy manages to perform a number of actions that win approval from the tellers of her tales. The singularity of her achievements becomes quickly compromised, however, when we know that her name is generally believed to be a corruption of "Anansi," as in the African—usually male—trickster. Aunt Nancy's exploits, then, are overshadowed by the masculine tradition that may have accidentally spawned her, emphasizing yet another way in which female potential in African-American folk tradition is subverted. For the tellers who were unaware of this problem in historical origins, however, perhaps Aunt Nancy was just as heroic as John Henry—or nearly so. Her name and her exploits make her one of the few named rarities in lore in which African-American women appear.

Too frequently taken to be undistinguished parts of the folkloristic landscape, black women (and females in the animal tales) have not been particularly valued in African-American folk tradition. The stereotypes about them within the lore (promiscuous, loud and demanding) have sometimes paralleled the stereotypes about them in society. Such stereotypes have not allowed for the elevation of black women to positions of reverence, and certainly tale-tellers have not put them on a pedestal. A search through African-American folklore reveals that few black women have been painted as desirable and sexually healthy persons. One little known strand of the lore has vestiges of viewing black women in the way that Emily D. West came to be viewed in "The Yellow Rose of Texas." I refer to nineteenth-century courtship rituals during slavery and Reconstruction. These rituals suggest the black women to whom they were addressed were viewed as special females indeed. Documented in sources such as the *Southern Workman*, a journal published at historically black Hampton Institute, these rituals are brief exchanges in which a man ascertained, through double entendre meanings, whether or not a woman was free for him to pursue and, later, whether or not she would consent to give him her hand in marriage.

Twentieth-century readers of African-American folklore perhaps know the pattern best from Robert Hemenway's study of the works of Zora Neale Hurston. Hurston depicts a scene in which a black man asks a woman, "Is you a flying lark or a setting dove?" Her answer, to indicate whether she is single or married, would signal to him that he could proceed with his courtship. If she turned out to be a "setting dove," then he would have to desist (Hemenway 154–56; Banks and Smiley 251–57). These short rituals, therefore, indicate a willingness to let the woman choose, not to force her into a liaison—a very important distinction during slavery. Similarly, if the relationship proceeded to the point of proposing marriage, the man could ask, "Kin I join my fence to your plantation?" Now, twentieth-century readers might balk at the poetry, but the question and its existence are perhaps more important than the language; they clearly record a strand in American history when black men pursued black women in dramatically different ways from those usually depicted in the lore or in popular representations.

I like to read "The Yellow Rose of Texas" as presaging that strand of African-American folklore. I like to think that the composer of the song so revered the woman he compared to a rose that his choice of expressing her beauty through nature elevated her to a position of value that has few comparative patterns. We cannot say, "the song about Emily's value is like . . . " because there is no immediately comparable "like." What we can say is that the separation, the pain this composer felt, led him to create a song about a beautiful woman, one who became the center of his existence as well as his creativity. The fact that she was "yellow" (mulatto) was less important to him than the human longings that are the essence of love.

How he viewed her as woman, lover, universal human partner, however, is obviously not how she or the legacy she left came to be used in American history or folklore studies. Her name has certainly served the tourist trade in San Antonio. Her presence or not at The Battle of San Jacinto has engaged many lively minds. But I want to focus on her body and how it has been used historically and popularly. I would argue that Emily D. West's body has been exploited in at least three different ways. Historians, folklorists, and people of general interest have used the "body" of the song about her to shape Texas and American history. They have also used her corporeal body to build a sense of unity and shared experience where there was previously animosity and distrust. And they have decentered a formerly centered body, transformed context, and created a legend about a legend—that Emily's primary concern was the welfare of Texas instead of her own. Ultimately, Emily D. West has become the mammy figure on which Texas has nurtured its image of conquering hero in the Mexican war; she has thereby, for all her legendary qualities, slipped back into the traditional role that black women in America have been expected to play—nurturing white folks into a healthy image of themselves.

It is no new revelation that poems are frequently viewed as having or being "bodies." This separate entity, these lyrics, this poem called "The Yellow Rose of Texas," contextualized less for its love story than its historical value, has blotted out, overwritten the body about which it was created. Singers of the song and commentators on it are less concerned about the reality of a black woman and the minutiae of the pain she experienced in being effectively "owned" and brutally raped than they are about the moment of triumph, the moment at which Santa Anna's attention was less focused on his warring campaign against Texas and what that enabled Sam Houston to accomplish. The poem allows readers and hearers to elide history, to ignore crucial parts of the story in a selective recall of the circumstances that led to the creation of the song. In this consideration, the part West played in a successful military campaign effectively erases her from the most significant parts of her own life. The irony is obvious: a black woman gains fame only because she is exploited, but the price of that fame disallows her exploitation.

In being transformed into a state icon, West loses the individuality of a personal life, but not the individuality of a symbol. Her name, the song, and the circumstances of Texan triumph become emblems of the best the American frontier had to offer. How could the heathens from south of the border possibly overcome righteous Americans, ones who, though initially defeated, came back in one of those great triumphs of the underdog over stronger adversaries? In this script, West is subsumed under the great American concept of Manifest Destiny—with a slight detour southward—that did not allow for fissures in the sometimes fragile pot of nationalism. The history and the song suggest that in the killing frontier, where trueblooded Americans were always subject to attack by some ungodly force, these Americans lived up to the best of their inheritance from back east; they fought, some of them died, but they ultimately triumphed over the forces of evil and repression. The body of the poem stands as a testament to these patterns, these issues, these triumphs.

West's physical body, subject to exploitation as readily as those black persons who were legally enslaved, serves in this legendary capacity to elide the brutality to which black female bodies were potentially victim. There is a clash between the ideal (romanticized Texas history) and the real (a black woman being raped during the process of history-making events). By elevating West's role in the capture of Santa Anna, by making her a seeming voluntary participant in the sequence of events, commentators and appreciators of the tale and the song could effectively deny slavery—or certainly deny black women's exploitation during slavery (since technically West was not an enslaved person). More specifically, they deny the brutal fact of rape, which West experienced not only from Santa Anna, but from a Texas soldier as well. Territorial and national unity implied in the events behind the song does not allow for the fact that black people were treated as badly, in this instance, by the Texans as they were by the Mexicans. The song becomes a pretty site, a pretty body, on which troubling issues about war, slavery, and sexual exploitation can be overlooked in the praise for a beautiful woman who evoked images of a yellow rose. The body of the poem does not encourage readers and listeners to contemplate the body of the woman, thus ensuring a version of the romanticized, universal history that informs most national tales of expansion and conquest.

By suggesting that West's primary concern was the acquisition of Texas from the Mexicans, commentators on the song have separated her body from itself. That this woman, a black indentured servant who knew little about politics and whose lover had recently been separated from her, should have been thinking about the fate of Texas immediately after Santa Anna had raped her is remarkably absurd. "Deny the pain and humiliation, Emily. Think freedom for Texas. Here comes the calvary in the form of Sam Houston's soldiers. You've done a wonderful job." Somehow this little scenario does not quite seem to work. Glossing over the pain of rape to focus on the so-called beauty of freedom—that is the gap over which West's body transformed Texan territorialists into American nationalists.

Arguably, the exploitation of West continues in yet another direction. The recently raped yet desexualized body, as the site for emphasizing nationalistic ideals, is plucked from being the yellow beauty and transformed into being the black mammy. In essence, the legendary West, at the moment captured in the incidents behind the song, nurtures Texas into a sense of its own potential as a free territory. She is thereby little different from the black women throughout their period of enslavement who sacrificed their bodies, their health, their creative potential to the needs, desires, wants of the whites who claimed to own them. The yellow rose is a giving figure; not only does she give up her lover, but she gives up her pain, her racial history, and her indenture to the nationalistic cause.

Clearly West assists in nurturing the image of Texas into being. More important, as implied in earlier statements, she assists in nurturing a collective, universal, nationalistic history. In this reading, she makes a sacrifice in a "war" as assuredly as any other "soldier" would. Whereas other soldiers may have given arms, legs, eyes, or lives, she gives up the significance of her identity as a black woman in the larger objective of salving the wounds of a society assaulted from without. It would be treasonous, therefore, for an Emily D. West to focus on self when the territory and national interests called for great sacrifices from everyone during the period of the Mexican war. It would be similarly "treasonous" for post Mexican war and twentieth-century commentators on the song to focus on the value of an individual black woman in the face of the greater call for emphasis upon issues that historically have been larger than single lives.

Prior to the appearance of the novel about "the yellow rose," at least one critic joined in the exploitation of West's body. In an article published in 1972, R. Henderson Shuffler is almost pornographic in the suggestive overtones he uses to trace West's role in the events with which she is now linked (121–30). He—humorously to his mind—draws upon stereotypes about black female sexuality as he paints West hotly waiting for the interlude with Santa Anna. He presumes that his audience shares the same conceptions of black women's bodies and places in history that he holds, and he is not hesitant in putting forth his ideas.

In his account, West begins with "questionable virtue." He describes her involvement with Santa Anna as "turning a trick" during which she went "into action in no other uniform than her satin-smooth beige birthday suit." He reports that her contemporaries considered her "beguiling and built like nobody's business," that "her deliberately provocative amble down the street on a hot afternoon was probably the most exciting event in town, for the male population, at least," and that "it is quite likely that Emily was both flattered and intrigued by her sudden rise to recumbent eminence." He further asserts that she was "a gal on the make" who took Santa Anna "for a ride" in the sexual blues sense of that phrase.

For Shuffler, West is a joke upon whom he can hang all the sexual baggage he carries about black female bodies—black women are promiscuous, always on the make, and can thus never be raped. Shuffler assigns responsibility to West for her own victimization, thus he joins others who have used her body to their own ends. He concludes his relation of the Santa Anna/Emily West story by asserting that a band of Texans was forming to honor West by planting "a small patch of pussy willow, encircling a garden of yellow roses. And in the center, a modest stone, on which will be engraved this legend: In Honor of Emily/ Who Gave Her All for Texas Piece by Piece." Shuffler's aggressive and dangerously playful phallicism and his reduction of West's body and sexuality to the colloquial "piece" illustrate the confidence with which he controls his presentation of the black female image. In Shuffler's rendition, the black woman becomes her sexualized body, exploitable not only by Santa Anna but now symbolically raped again in an account that Shuffler obviously intended would bring smiles if not uproarious laughter from all who read his article. The legendary black female body can thus be "screwed," kept in its "proper place," through the ongoing imaginations of this "hardy band" and all their allies.

Anita Bunkley's effort to resurrect the emotional essence of West's body in *Emily: The Yellow Rose of Texas*, her relationship to Joshua Kinney (the "J. K." of the song's original composition), works to accomplish that objective as it also simultaneously and inadvertently plays into the exploitation theme. Bunkley sacrifices West's body to multiple rapes before she redeems it for the historically unrealized romance of the lovers finally ending up together. Bunkley must romanticize history and legend in order to romanticize romance. She allows West to suffer in order to redeem the tale that should have occurred. Her graphic depictions of rain and mud in Texas, of black workers trying to elevate sleeping spaces to escape standing water, and of ragtag and ruffian soldiers who make unpleasant demands of West and others, serve as the moral imperative against which the tale should have a happy ending. So too does the rape of West by a Texas soldier, an attempted second rape by the same soldier, and the rape at the hands of Santa Anna. Weather, landscape, and physical abuses combine to paint a picture of a woman without protection beyond her wits (which can fail her) and whose lover, by law, custom, and circumstance, cannot consistently rescue her. When he does—by killing the white captain who rapes West on one occasion and tries to rape her again—it makes them both potential fugitives. Bunkley then uses the Santa Anna plot to effect an escape for Joshua and his reunion with Emily. The events as presented historically, therefore, give way to poetic license as a romantic, strikingly improbable ending becomes the vehicle to transform tragic events and a potentially tragic future into a heartwarming love story.

Ultimately, "The Yellow Rose of Texas" is a fascinating study in elision, erasure, and transformation. The song, its subject, its history, and its creator have all been used. Obviously there are good uses and bad uses to which any work of art, any historical event, can be put. Add to these usual patterns the fact of folklore and legend and the uses become even more expansive. Where all of this ends, however, is with the exploitation of the creator of the song. He who created the yellow rose is more lost to us than the subject about which he sang. Yet it is because of this black man's song that researchers have been able to uncover as much as they have about Emily D. West. We have all, collectively, "taken his song and gone"—far beyond the pleasure of appreciating it, far beyond the popular interest in transmitting it. Folklorists, historians, and scholars have made the song as much a legend as its subject, have made the events surrounding the composition of it as much an issue of erasure of composer as erasure of Emily D. West.

Notes

1. Martha Anne Turner has completed several works about the legend. See, for example," 'The Yellow Rose of Texas': The Story of a Song," *Southwestern Studies*, Monograph No. 31 (University of Texas at El Paso: Texas Western Press, 1971): 3–19; and *The Yellow Rose of Texas: Her Saga and Her Song* (Austin, Texas: Shoal Creek Publishers, 1976). Anita Bunkley, *Emily, The Yellow Rose* (Houston, Texas: Rinard Publishing, 1989).

2. Having traveled to Texas under her own name, Emily D. West, West's name was changed to Morgan to coincide with the southern practice of indentured and enslaved persons using the last name of the person on whose property they worked. Turner skirts this issue by declaring that West "adopted the name of her master and benefactor in conformity with nineteenth-century custom" (Turner, *Saga*, 6), an assertion that, if true, would have given West an unprecedented agency in the matter.

3. For a summary of varying historical views, see Bob Tutt, "The Yellow Rose: Was She Really a Heroine, or was it all Historical Humbug?" *Houston Chronicle* (21 April 1984): 1, 12.

4. Bunkley quotes the song in *Emily, The Yellow Rose*, p. iv. The version she uses is the one that Turner identifies as the original, manuscript version mailed to E. A. Jones in the months after The Battle of San Jacinto, probably between 1836 and 1838 (Turner, *Saga*, 46–47). Turner traces the transformation of the song and its lyrics from its composition into the 1950s. It was a marching song during the Civil War (music with different lyrics), a popular song in the early twentieth century, a slightly altered composition that earned well known composer David W. Guion praises from President Franklin D. Roosevelt (1936; deracialized lyrics), and served as a hit Mitch Miller rendition in the 1950s.

5. For an account of Mammy Pleasant's life and activities, see Helena Woodard, "Mary Ellen Pleasant," in *Notable Black American Women*, ed. Jessie Carney Smith (Detroit: Gale, 1992), pp. 858–62.

6. See A'Lelia Bundles, *Madam C. J. Walker* (Chelsea House Black Americans of Achievement Series, 1991). For a recent inclusion of Walker in a work that treats African-American women from all parts of culture and society, see Joan Curl Elliott, "Madame C. J. Walker," in *Notable Black American Women*, ed. Smith, pp. 1184–88.

7. For a representative discussion of the legend of John Henry, see Richard M. Dorson, "The Career of John Henry," in *Mother Wit from the Laughing Barrel: Readings in the Interpretation of Afro-American Folklore* (1973; rpt. University of Mississippi Press, 1990) pp. 568–77.

Bibliography

In the completion of this work, I am particularly grateful to Dr. Betty Taylor-Thompson of Texas Southern University for forwarding copies of sources to me that I could not readily obtain in Atlanta.

Abrahams, Roger D. *Deep Down in the Jungle . . . Negro Narrative Folklore from the Streets of Philadelphia.* Chicago: Aldine Publishing, 1970.

Banks, Frank D. and Portia Smiley. "Old-Time Courtship Conversation." *Mother Wit from the Laughing Barrel: Readings in the Interpretation of Afro-American Folklore.* Ed. Alan Dundes. University of Mississippi Press, 1990.

Brewer, J. Mason. *Aunt Dicy Tales.* Austin: Privately Published, 1956.

Hemenway, Robert. *Zora Neal Hurston: A Literary Biography.* Urbana: University of Illinois Press, 1977.

Shuffler, R. Henderson. "San Jacinto As She Was: Or, What Really Happened on the Plain of St. Hyacinth on a Hot April Afternoon in 1836." *Observations and Reflections in Texas Folklore.* Ed. Francis Edward Abernethy. Austin: Encino Press, 1972.

YELLOW ROSE OF TEXAS
here's a yel_low rose in Tex
that I am
other darkey knows her,
And if I e-ver

Norris Wright Cuney (1846–1898)

Matthew W. Gaines (1842–1900)

Joshua Houston (1822–1902)

Walter M. Burton (1840–1913)

The Texas Trailblazer Project

by Patricia Smith Prather

Growing up in Houston, Texas, in the 1950s, my knowledge of Texas history and tradition was essentially Sam Houston, Jim Bowie, Stephen F. Austin and other Anglo-American heroes.

It never really occurred to me or my peers that Texas had an African-American hero such as Norris Wright Cuney, who was chairman of the Republican Party beginning in 1884. Even though we knew about the Cuney Homes Housing Project in Houston, we did not know that Cuney was a black man.

In 1990, sociologist Bob Lee and I set out in search of facts about Norris Cuney and other African-American Texas pioneers. These people were all Texans' cultural ancestors, and they brought with them and handed down to us a rich supply of history and folklore, of customs and traditions and beliefs, of tales and songs and ways of life that we still follow. The ways we cook, talk, dance, and sing—the ways we dress and believe and see ourselves—our timeless connection to the culture and heritage of our past: these are gifts from our Trailblazing ancestors.

We started by identifying the heroes of the community where we grew up, known as the "Fifth Ward" and located in the inner city of

▼

Houston. We found a treasure trove of facts about the contributions of educators, clergy, business owners, and civic leaders who were responsible for Fifth Ward survival in the midst of a segregated society. Many of those leaders now have schools and other buildings named in their memory. We researched such trailblazers as E. O. Smith, the first principal of the high school in Fifth Ward; A. K. Kelley, who started Evergreen Negro Cemetery over one hundred years ago; and Nat Q. Henderson, who became known as the Mayor of Fifth Ward for his civic deeds. We located the oldest church in the Fifth Ward, which had humble beginnings on the banks of Buffalo Bayou just after the slaves were freed in Texas on June 19, 1865 (now known as "Juneteenth").

Then, we began exploring towns in East Texas. We studied the history of the oldest churches and schools, and there we found more trailblazers. We learned about William Goyens, a free black who came to Texas in the 1820s and acquired thousands of acres of land, owned a blacksmith shop, and helped General Sam Houston negotiate with the Cherokee Indian tribe.

Within two years, we had well over a hundred names and had researched and collected quite a few facts about the contributions of African-Americans and other Texans who received scant if any mention in Texas history books.

It was time to share our findings with others; thus the Texas Trailblazer Series was launched. Bob Lee and I decided upon a simple format—a one page summation of the contributions of each leader which also features his or her photograph. This decision was made because we wanted it to appeal to young people. Also, the decision was dictated by the fact that there was limited information about the trailblazers since most had not been written about before. And, we decided to feature one trailblazer each month and to distribute several thousand copies of each profile to schools, libraries, churches and other public places.

The first of the Texas Trailblazer Series was published in May, 1992. The leader featured was Joshua Houston, who had been a servant to General Sam Houston. We learned about Joshua Houston from his granddaughter, Constance Houston Thompson, who was ninety years old and had a portrait of him in her extensive family collection. She told us the story of her grandfather having offered General Houston's widow $2,000 in gold after the Civil War, when Mrs. Houston was left with a lot of worthless land and Confederate money. Constance Houston Thompson told us that after slavery ended, Joshua Houston became a very important man in Huntsville, Texas. We took this oral history and verified facts through research of such documents as land and other records. We found that Joshua was among the first ex-slaves to own land, that he was both an appointed and elected official, and that he was a trustee of a college for newly freed blacks. He died in 1902 at the age of eighty and is buried not far from the grave of General Sam Houston in Huntsville.

The next trailblazer we profiled was equally prominent. Bob Chatham was born a slave in 1859 and became a successful businessman in Hemstead, Texas. He bred and grew so many watermelons that he was known as the "Watermelon King." Each summer he delivered his watermelons via his private railroad spur track to Houston, and in 1916 one shipment of 169 rail cars was worth some $20,000.

After Chatham, we featured such trailblazers as Emmett J. Scott (1873–1958), who graduated from college, became the first editor of a newspaper that is now over a hundred years old, and then became the personal secretary of Booker T. Washington.

Some of our trailblazers were leaders of organizations formed when African-Americans were barred from joining Texas organizations. We featured L. C. Anderson, founder of the Colored Teachers State Association of Texas in 1884, and J. H. Wilkins, first president of the Lone Star State Medical, Dental and Pharmaceutical Association in 1886. We featured several women, including Mary Branch, who was one of the first women college presidents in Texas.

Word of the Texas Trailblazer Series began to spread and the media took an interest. The Texas Trailblazer story was told by television, radio, newspapers, and newsletters. This enhanced our ability to attract support, and now the Texas Trailblazer Preservation Association, a non-profit organization which we formed in 1990, has the support of several corporations and foundations, over 120 individuals as well as a united fund, and libraries and educational institutions. The organization's board of directors is chaired by trailblazer A. I. Thomas, Ph.D., President Emeritus of Prairie View A&M University.

To date, we have profiled over thirty-five individuals in our Texas Trailblazer Series, and we continue to publish one new profile each month. Many of our readers have asked that these articles be published in a book, and one will eventually be forthcoming. We have many more individuals who need to be researched and included in a finished volume.

But the major mission of the Texas Trailblazer Series is to educate the public, especially young people. We believe that as more people become educated about the deeds of Texans of all ethnic and economic backgrounds, there will be increased respect for one another's differences. We hope the series will help with that education. We want more people to be aware that the great state of Texas was built by Anglo Americans, African-Americans, Mexican Americans, Hispanic Americans and others. And we also hope all Texans will pay special tribute to Native Americans, who paved the way, long before any of us came.

▼ Appendices

The Texas African-American Photography Collection and Archive

by Alan Govenar

The Texas African-American Photography (TAAP) Collection and Archive consists of approximately 16,634 photographic items, including negatives and prints, spanning the period from the 1870s to the present and representing a variety of processes and makers.[1] The Collection is unique in its comprehensiveness.

The collection focuses on the growth and development of vernacular and community photography among African-Americans in Texas. The material in the collection elucidates the context of social gatherings, including weddings, funerals, Juneteenth parades, church services, high school and college graduations, neighborhood businesses, and day-to-day activities in African-American communities around the state. In addition, the images chronicle social protests and political demonstrations.

The collection includes work by identified photographers from around the state as well as photographs by unidentified picture makers. Within the historical context of the work, the collection includes undocumented tintypes and other early prints that were found in Texas African-American communities. The TAAP Collection provides a broad overview of African-American life in Texas over the last century and places the work of older artists alongside of that of their younger peers. The known photographers represented in the collection include Calvin Littlejohn (Fort Worth), A. B. Bell, Marion Butts, George Keaton, and Carl Sidle (Dallas), Curtis Humphrey (Tyler), Eugene Roquemore (Lubbock), A. C. Teal, Elnora Frazier, Juanita Williams, Rodney Evans, Earlie Hudnall, Jr., Herbert Provost, Benny Joseph, and Louise Martin (Houston), and Morris Crawford and Robert Whitby (Austin).[2]

The processing of the TAAP collection is directed by Alan Govenar, President of Documentary Arts in Dallas. The Project Archivist is John Slate. African-American student interns, selected by a liaison committee of the Texas Association of Developing Colleges, will assist in the conservation of the TAAP Collection by working with the staff of Documentary Arts. The institutions participating in the internship program include Texas College (Tyler), Jarvis Christian College (Hawkins), Wiley College (Marshall), Paul Quinn College (Dallas), and Huston-Tillotson College (Austin). The African-American Museum in Dallas is committed to helping to make the TAAP Collection accessible to the public through a series of independent exhibitions over the next decade, focusing on individual photographers represented in the archive.

The TAAP Archive is housed in a new, state-of-the-art archival facility, constructed over the last two years through a major private contribution. This facility is located in the 5501 Columbia Art Center complex, operated by Documentary Arts and Contemporary Culture, another non-profit organization, which also has made a commitment to assisting in the development of the TAAP Collection. The archive building itself has warehouse storage, a fireproof, climate-controlled vault with a temperature regulated alarm system, and secured and lighted parking. The TAAP Collection will be open to researchers and the general public.

The Texas African-American Photography Archive is supported in part by private contributions and by grants from the Meadows Foundation, the Summerlee Foundation, Texas Commission on the Arts, and the Texas Committee for the Humanities.

Notes

1. For more information on the Texas African-American Photography Collection and Archive and related touring exhibitions, contact Documentary Arts, P.O. Box 140244, Dallas, Texas 75214.

2. For more information on these photographers, see Alan Govenar, *Portraits of Community: African-American Photography in Texas* (Austin: Texas State Historical Association, 1996), and Alan Govenar, *The Early Years of Rhythm and Blues: The Photography of Benny Joseph* (Houston: Rice University Press, 1991).

The African-American Museum of Dallas

By Alan Govenar

The African-American Museum of Dallas is the largest institution of its kind in the southwestern United States devoted to the research, identification, acquisition, presentation, and preservation of visual art forms and historical documents that relate to African-American life and culture. Started in 1974 as part of Bishop College, the African-American Museum is now located in a permanent facility in Fair Park. The new building, opened in 1993, is funded through private donations and through a city bond issue approved by voters in 1985.

Since its beginning, the museum has built an impressive collection of African and African-American art. In 1986, the museum began developing an African-American Folk Art Collection and Resource Center. The permanent Folk Art Collection was established with a cash gift from a founding board member, Billy R. Allen. With the assistance of Dr. Regina Perry, Professor of African and African-American Art History at Virginia Commonwealth University, a collection of slides, articles, and other documents has been assembled as part of the Resource Center.

Now included in the collection are works by Clementine Hunter, David Butler, J. B. Murray, Sister Gertrude Morgan, Mose Tolliver, Henry Speller, George White, Willard "The Texas Kid" Watson, Reverend Johnnie Swearingen, Alma Gunter, Royal Robertson, Sultan Rogers, Herbert Singleton, Bessie Harvey, Jimmie Lee Sudduth, Georgia Speller, Mary T. Smith, Artist Chuckie (Chuckie Williams), Ralph Griffin, and James "Son" Thomas.

In addition to the collection and preservation of folk art, the African-American Museum presents exhibitions, lectures, conferences, seminars, children's activities, and film and video screenings. As part of its living history program, the African-American Museum sponsors the Texas Black Invitational Rodeo, now in its eleventh year, which features more than 200 black cowboys and cowgirls from around the country.

For more information on the African-American Museum, contact Harry Robinson, Jr., Director, African-American Museum, Box 150153, Dallas, Texas 75315-0153.

Selected Listing of Resources for Further Study of African-American Folklore

Carver Museum
1161 Angelina
Austin, TX 78702

Black Arts Alliance
1157 Navasota Street
Austin, TX 78702

Texas Folklife Resources
P.O. Box 49824
Austin, TX 78765

Austin Blues Family Tree Project
109 East 10th Street
Austin, TX 78701

The Center for American History
University of Texas at Austin
Austin, TX 78712

Carver Cultural Center
226 North Hackberry
San Antonio, TX 78202

Institute of Texan Cultures
801 South Bowie Street
San Antonio, TX 78205-3296

Kumba House
811 Westheimer
Houston, TX 77006

Community Artists Collective
1501 Elgin
Houston, TX 77004

Community Music Center
5613 Almeda
Houston, TX 77004

Documentary Arts
P.O. Box 140244
Dallas, TX 75214

African-American Museum
P.O. Box 150153
Dallas, TX 75315-0153

Texarkana Regional Arts &
Humanities Council
P.O. Box 1171
Texarkana, AR-TX 75504

▼ Contributors

Francis Edward Abernethy is a professor of English at Stephen F. Austin State University, the Executive Secretary and Editor of the Texas Folklore Society since 1971, and a member of the Texas Institute of Letters. He is the editor of *Tales From the Big Thicket, Built in Texas, Legendary Ladies of Texas, Folk Art in Texas, Texas Toys and Games*, and numerous other volumes for the Texas Folklore Society. He has published poetry, short stories, a folk music book entitled *Singin' Texas*, a book of legends entitled *Legends of Texas' Heroic Age*, and two volumes of a history of the Texas Folklore Society. He has lectured widely, both popularly and academically. He plays the bass fiddle in the East Texas String Ensemble of Nacogdoches.

Glen Alyn graduated from the University of Texas in 1973 and spent the following years living in and around Mance Lipscomb's Navasota while researching Mance's music and life story. Glen recorded hundreds of hours of interviews with Mance and his friends and kinfolk. A portion of these interviews became the book *I SAY ME FOR A PARABLE: The Oral Autobiography of Mance Lipscomb, Texas Bluesman.* The book won the ASCAP Deems Taylor Award, Austin Writers' League's Violet Crown Award, and was nominated by BMI, New York University, and *Rolling Stone Magazine* for the Ralph J. Gleason Award. In his compact disc recording, "Tellin Stories, Sangin bout Suppas," Alyn recites readings from this book and performs his arrangements of some of Mance Lipscomb's musical repertoire. Glen established the Lipscomb/Alyn Collection (1981) and the Archives for Vietnam Veterans & Their Significant Others (1990) at the Center for American History, The University of Texas.

T. Lindsay Baker, author of a dozen books on regional and American history, recently co-edited with his wife the 1930s WPA Oklahoma

Slave Narratives for publication in their entirety by the University of Oklahoma Press. For twenty years Baker has engaged in historic foodways interpretation for museums and historic sites throughout the country, and he has personal experience preparing most of the foods discussed in this paper. He and his wife reside in a historic tenant house on his great grandparents' cotton farm in Hill County, while Baker teaches at Baylor University and serves as the director of academic programs for its Department of Museum Studies.

Richard Allen Burns earned his Ph.D. in anthropology with a concentration in folklore in 1990 at the University of Texas at Austin. He has presented numerous papers at annual meetings of the American Folklore Society and has published material on African-American folklore and articles from his dissertation, "Texas Prison Folklore." Currently an assistant professor of English and Folklore at Arkansas State University, he is teaching folklore, English, and anthropology while conducting a folklife survey of the Arkansas Delta.

Clyde E. Daniels is a former instructor in the Arts-in-Education Program, where he taught creative writing with emphasis on poetry in independent school districts in both Arkansas and Texas. He is a life-long resident of Hooks, Texas, where he resides with his wife and their two children, and a graduate of East Texas State University at Texarkana, where he received a Liberal Arts degree, with graduate studies in psychology and counseling. He is an active member of Alpha Phi Alpha fraternity. Clyde is a three-year member of the Ebony Players Ensemble, a student of black folk-history, an amateur genealogist, and a student of the Civil War Era. Currently, he is compiling the final arrangement of a second volume of poetry and rewriting the rough draft of his first novel. He is employed by the Defense Logistics Agency, where he serves as an Equal Employment Opportunity Specialist and Site manager at the Red River Defense Complex.

Alan Govenar is a writer, folklorist, photographer and filmmaker. He is President of Documentary Arts, which he founded in 1985 as a non-profit organization to broaden public knowledge and appreciation of the arts of different cultures in all media. He has B.A. with distinction in American Folklore from Ohio State University, an M.A. in Folklore and Anthropology from the University of Texas at Austin, and a Ph.D. in Arts and Humanities from the University of Texas at Dallas. Dr. Govenar is the author of nine books, including *Stoney Knows How, Meeting the Blues: The Rise of the Texas Sound, The Life and Poems of Osceola Mays, The Early Years of Rhythm and Blues, Flash from the Past: Classic American Tattoo Designs, 1890-1965, Portraits of Community: African American Photography in Texas*, and two collections of poetry, *Paradise in the Smallest Thing* and *Casa de Dante*.

Trudier Harris is Augustus Baldwin Longstreet Professor of American Literature at Emory University. She earned her B.A. from Stillman College, Tuscaloosa, Alabama. She earned her M.A. and Ph.D. from The Ohio State University (Columbus), which presented her with its first annual Award of Distinction for the College of Humanities in 1994. She taught at the College of William and Mary in Virginia for six years before joining the faculty at the University of North Carolina at Chapel Hill, where she taught for fourteen years, the last five of which she served as J. Carlyle Sitterson Professor of English. She has lectured in her specialty areas of African American literature and folklore throughout the United States as well as in Jamaica, Canada, France, Germany, Poland, Spain, and Italy. Author of numerous articles, reviews, and books, her most recent works are *Fiction and Folklore: The Novels of Toni Morrison* (1991), and *The Power of the Porch: Narrative Strategies in Works by Zora Neale Hurston, Gloria Naylor, and Randall Kenan* (1996). She has edited many projects and is currently co-editing *The Oxford Companion to African American Literature* and *The Norton Anthology of Southern Literature*.

James Thomas Jackson was born in 1925, in Temple, Texas, the youngest of three children. The family later moved to Houston where James Thomas was educated. He lived and worked in Houston until he went to Los Angeles, arriving just as the Watts riots exploded. Soon after, James Thomas joined Budd Schulberg's Watts Writers Workshop. Some of his work was printed in the *Los Angeles Times*, *Writers Digest*, and *Southwest Review*, but many of James Thomas's most powerful pieces were published for the first time in *Waiting in Line at the Drugstore*, University of North Texas Press. His writing chronicles his childhood in the 1930s, his years in the U.S. Army in Europe in the 1940s and 1950s, his years in Los Angeles and Houston in the 1960s and 1970s. James Thomas Jackson died in Wadsworth V.A. Hospital Los Angeles, in early 1985.

John Minton is Associate Professor of folklore at Indiana University-Purdue University Fort Wayne, having earned his B.A. and M.A. in English at Stephen F. Austin State University in Nacogdoches and his Ph.D. in anthropology with a concentration in folklore at the University of Texas at Austin. His field research, conducted mainly in Deep East Texas and around the Gulf Coast, has covered topics ranging from the remnants of rural ballad traditions and black country blues to the zydeco music of Houston's Creole community. Besides his many articles on American folk music and song, he is the author of *"Big 'Fraid and Little 'Fraid": An Afro-American Folktale*. Folklore Fellows' Communications No. 253 (Helsinki: Academia Scientiarum Fennica, 1993).

Patrick B. Mullen is a professor in the Department of English and Director of the Center for Folklore Studies at Ohio State University where he teaches folklore and American literature. He is the author of *I Heard the Old Fishermen Say: Folklore of the Texas Gulf Coast*, *Listening to Old Voices: Folklore, Life Stories, and the Elderly*, and co-author of *Lake Erie Fishermen: Work, Identity, and Tradition*. He has also published numerous articles on folk belief, folk narrative, and the relationship of folklore and American literature. He is a member of the Executive Board of the American Folklore Society and a Fellow of the Society. He has conducted field research for the American Folklife Center of the Library of Congress, for the Smithsonian American Folklife Festival, and for the Ohio Arts Council. He has taught at the University of Rome on a Fulbright Fellowship and delivered papers at the International Folk Narrative

Congress meetings in Helsinki, Edinburgh, and Bergen. He is currently conducting research on cultural representations of African Americans in folklore scholarship.

Dave Oliphant was born in Fort Worth in 1939, attended high school and Lamar State College in Beaumont, and took an M.A. in English at the University of Texas at Austin. After completing a Ph.D. at Northern Illinois University in 1975 and teaching for a year at the University of the Americas in Mexico, he returned to Austin where, since 1976, he has served as the editor of *The Library Chronicle* at the Harry Ransom Humanities Research Center while also teaching part-time at the Universitiy and at Austin Community College. One of his principal areas of interest has been Latin American literature, which he has translated, in particular the work of Chilean poet Enrique Lihn. A selection of his translations of a new generation of Chilean poets will appear in the summer 1996 issue of *Manõa* from the University of Hawaii. Another area of longtime interest has been Texas poetry, which he has promoted through essays, reviews, and edited collections by such poets as William Barney, Joseph Colin Murphey, Rebecca Gonzales, and Charles Behlen. His own poetry has been published widely and his 1987 collection, *Maria's Poems,* won an Austin Book Award. His most recent book is *Texan Jazz,* published in 1996 by the University of Texas Press.

Patricia Smith Prather is a native Texan and graduate of Tuskegee University in Tuskegee, Alabama. She is co-founder and Executive Director of a non-profit organization dedicated to preserving the important legacy of the African American presence in Texas history. Since 1992, the organization has published its *Texas Trailblazer* series, monthly biographies of Texas pioneers. Prather is co-editor of this publication. She is also author of over fifty articles about African-American Texas leaders. These articles have been published in state and national publications including *Texas Highways* and *American Visions* magazines. Prather is co-author, with Jane Clements Monday, of *From Slave to Statesman: The Legacy of Joshua Houston, Servant to Sam Houston* (University of North Texas Press, 1993), which won the Violet Crown Award.

Jan Rosenberg directs Heritage Education Resources, based in Texarkana, Arkansas where she has been engaged in folk cultural research, programming, and consulting since 1990. Rosenberg received the B.A. in Folklore from Indiana University and the M.A. and Ph.D. from the Department of Folklore and Folklife at the University of Pennsylvania. She is currently at work on a book for the Folklife in the South Series tentatively titled: *Chicken, Trees, and Gospel Music: Folklife in the Red River Region*. A member of the National Faculty and the Executive Committee of the National Task Force on Folk Arts in Education, Rosenberg specializes in folklife in education. Her publications are accessible through ERIC, the Education Information Clearinghouse.

Donald R. Ross was born and reared in the Church Hill community of Rusk County, Texas. After receiving B.A. and M.A. degrees from Baylor University, he served two years as a Peace Corps Volunteer in Thailand. He then earned a Juris Doctor degree from Southern Methodist University School of Law and returned to his home county where he was elected District Attorney for three years and is now serving his fourteenth year as the elected judge of the Fourth District Court of Rusk County, Texas. He has been active in Sacred Harp singing since his teenage years and has served as President of both the Texas State Sacred Harp Singing Convention and the more historic East Texas Sacred Harp Singing Convention. He has lectured on the history and traditions of Sacred Harp music and taught a number of Sacred Harp singing schools. He has been designated a "Master Artist" by the Texas Folklife Resources for his work in the preservation of Sacred Harp Singing.

Lorenzo Thomas is Associate Professor of English at the University of Houston-Downtown where he teaches American Literature and Creative Writing. Mr. Thomas is a widely published poet and critic whose works have appeared in many journals including *African American Review, Arrowsmith, Blues Unlimited* (England), *Living Blues, Partisan Review, Ploughshares,* and *Popular Music and Society*. He has contributed articles to the *African American Encyclopedia, Oxford Companion to African American Literature,* and *AmericanLiterary Scholar-*

ship. His books include *Chances are Few* and *The Bathers*, collections of poetry. Mr. Thomas currently serves the University as Director of the Minority Enrichment Center and is also active with the Cultural Arts Council of Houston/Harris County which he serves as Vice President.

Jesse Garfield Truvillion, born in the first house built for an African-American in Wiergate, Texas, was ordained a Baptist preacher in 1956 and became his mother's pastor at age 19. He became a Presbyterian in 1963, and has served pastorates in New Jersey, New York City, California, Texas and Ohio. He has served in university campus ministries, and has been an adjunct professor in three theological seminaries, and a teaching pastor in two others. Dr. Truvillion has delivered several lecture series, and is a motivational speaker on matters of faith and reconciliation. He has traveled extensively and has written worship material, sacred music and essays for several newspapers. Rev. Truvillion is a member of the Presbytery of Saint Augustine (Northeast Florida), and is Organizing Pastor for a new multi-ethnic and multi-cultural congregation in Jacksonville, Florida.

Alvia Wardlaw is Assistant Professor of Art History at Texas Southern University. She also serves as Assistant Curator for Twentieth Century Painting and Sculpture at Houston's Museum of Fine Arts. She is the official biographer for John Biggers and curated the traveling exhibit, *The Art of John Biggers: View from the Upper Room*, which was first mounted at Houston's Museum of Fine Arts, April 2 to August 28, 1995. Ms. Wardlaw wrote the biographical article for the catalog of that exhibit.

John Wheat is Music Archivist at The Center for American History, The University of Texas at Austin, where he oversees the Center's many collections in the field of Texas music. He brings to this work a background as historian, librarian, archivist, teacher, and translator. Wheat is a frequent lecturer on various topics of Texas music, including cowboy lore, Mance Lipscomb, Janis Joplin, and the Texas-Mexican Nativity drama *Los Pastores*. He is also a professional musician performing with the Brazilian music group Sambaxé and the Latin folk ensemble Toqui Amaru in Austin, Texas. For the past eight years, Wheat has hosted the Latin American stage at the annual Texas Folklife Festival in San Antonio.

William H. Wiggins, Jr. is a professor of Afro-American Studies and Folklore at Indiana University. His numerous celebration publications include *O Freedom!: Afro-American Emancipation Celebrations*, University of Tennessee Press, 1987, and *Jubilation!: African American Celebrations in the Southeast*, University of South Carolina Press, 1993. His recently completed book, *Joe Louis: A Folk Biography*, will be published by the University of Illinois Press.

▼ Index

Breinigsville, PA USA
12 April 2010
235946BV00002B/1/P